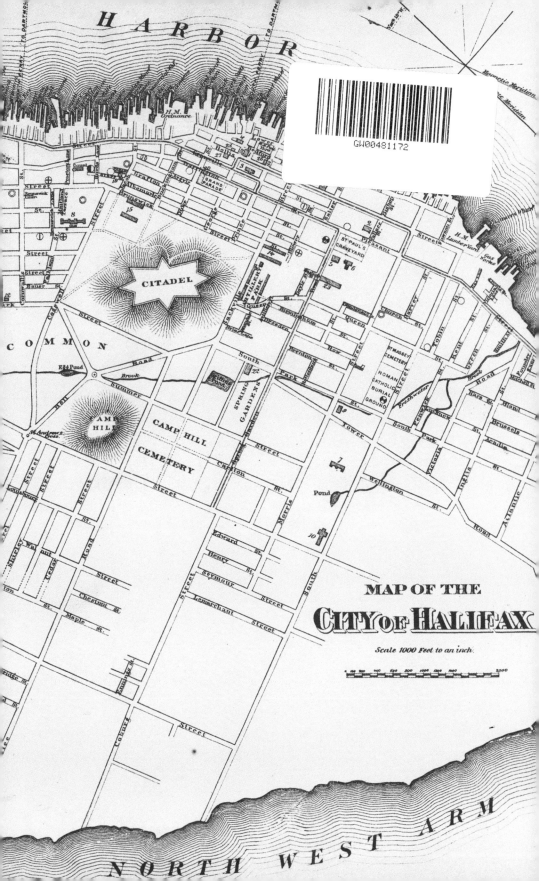

MAP OF THE
CITY OF HALIFAX

Scale 1000 Feet to an inch.

GW00481172

IN PURSUIT OF LOVE

By the same author:

Vera Brittain
Letters from a Lost Generation
Lives for Sale
Florence Nightingale
Because You Died
The Fateful Year
Vera Brittain and the First World War

IN PURSUIT
OF LOVE

The Search for Victor Hugo's Daughter

MARK BOSTRIDGE

BLOOMSBURY CONTINUUM
LONDON · OXFORD · NEW YORK · NEW DELHI · SYDNEY

BLOOMSBURY CONTINUUM
Bloomsbury Publishing Plc
50 Bedford Square, London, WC1B 3DP, UK
29 Earlsfort Terrace, Dublin 2, Ireland

BLOOMSBURY, BLOOMSBURY CONTINUUM and the Diana logo are trademarks
of Bloomsbury Publishing Plc

First published in Great Britain 2024

Copyright © Mark Bostridge, 2024

Mark Bostridge has asserted his right under the Copyright, Designs and Patents Act, 1988,
to be identified as Author of this work

For legal purposes the List of Illustrations on pp. 270–2 and the Acknowledgements on pp. 276–7
constitute an extension of this copyright page

All rights reserved. No part of this publication may be reproduced or transmitted in any form or
by any means, electronic or mechanical, including photocopying, recording, or any information
storage or retrieval system, without prior permission in writing from the publishers

Bloomsbury Publishing Plc does not have any control over, or responsibility for, any third-party
websites referred to or in this book. All internet addresses given in this book were correct at the
time of going to press. The author and publisher regret any inconvenience caused if addresses have
changed or sites have ceased to exist, but can accept no responsibility for any such changes

A catalogue record for this book is available from the British Library

Library of Congress Cataloguing-in-Publication data has been applied for

ISBN: HB: 978-1-3994-1602-3; eBook: 978-1-3994-1601-6; ePDF: 978-1-3994-1600-9

2 4 6 8 10 9 7 5 3 1

Typeset by Deanta Global Publishing Services, Chennai, India
Printed and bound in Great Britain by CPI Group (UK) Ltd, Croydon CR0 4YY

To find out more about our authors and books visit www.bloomsbury.com
and sign up for our newsletters

For R

Love is like a tree: it grows by itself, roots itself deeply in our being and continues to flourish over a heart in ruin. The inexplicable fact is that the blinder it is, the more tenacious it is. It is never stronger than when it is completely unreasonable.
Victor Hugo, *Notre-Dame de Paris*

My life is yours, your life is mine, you live what I see; our destiny is one. Take this mirror then and see yourself in it . . . When I speak to you of myself, I tell you about yourselves too.
Victor Hugo, *Les Contemplations*

Contents

I

Tides

My search for Victor Hugo's daughter – my pursuit, as it became – began on a spring day at the tail end of last century when I paid my first visit to Villequier. This picturesque former fishing village in the department of the Seine-Maritime has been a place of regular pilgrimage for me ever since. R and I generally enjoy a leisurely route to France in August. We drive from London to Dover and join the car ferry across to Calais. From there we make our way down to Normandy, skirting the battlefields and cemeteries of the First World War, before arriving at Caudebec-en-Caux, 3 miles south-west of Villequier. At Caudebec the fine stone church from the fifteenth and early sixteenth centuries, with its rose window of glowing reds and greens, and a single winding street of timbered houses are the only vestiges of the old town to have survived the fires of 1940. We book into the hotel La Marine and, after a brief skirmish over the respective merits – economic and nutritional – of the *menu touristique* versus its *gastronomique* rival, settle down to dinner in the hotel restaurant, overlooking the broad expanse of river.

Historically, the Seine in this region has possessed an unpredictable, sometimes violent character. It brings to mind T. S. Eliot's notion of a river, in his poem *The Dry Salvages*, as 'a strong brown god': untrustworthy, implacable and full of rage. Prior to the dredging of the Seine estuary, and the construction of the levees in the early 1960s, massive tidal disturbances, manifesting themselves in a deafening roar and a dramatic increase in the water level, were responsible for the capsizing of hundreds of vessels and the loss of many lives. During that era, if you arrived at the right moment – the day after a full moon, for instance – you might have seen the small harbour at Caudebec swept by the tumultuous inrush of a wave 300 yards long. This was the *mascaret*, the irresistible tidal wave, a clash between the current of the river flowing seaward and the pressure of the neighbouring sea as the tide flows up from Le Havre through the interior of Normandy. 'A high, rough and choppy liquid wall arrives as fast as a galloping horse,' wrote the astronomer Camille Flammarion in 1887, while half a century later another witness to the unstoppable force of the *mascaret*, the writer Maurice Leblanc, described 'jumping and whirling water mountains'.

CAUDEBEC-EN-CAUX.
Le Mascaret.

One morning we visit Caudebec's Muséo Seine and observe a small group of tourists and schoolchildren gasping in astonishment at the film being projected onto a large screen above their heads. Dating from the 1950s, these grainy images show hundreds of spectators, many of them holidaymakers, standing on the quay at Caudebec, their eyes fixed in the direction of Villequier, as a great influx of frothing water, full of mud, arrives much faster than anyone could have anticipated. It submerges the banks and quayside and lifts the waiting men, women and children off their feet, leaving them scrabbling to regain a foothold in the residues of murky brown liquid.

Today this part of the Seine is much less perilous. The phenomenal impact of the terrifying tidal surges has been confined by the ingenuity of human engineering to the extent that the *mascaret* has almost completely disappeared. Walking by the riverside along the shady road from Caudebec to Villequier, a pathway that rises and falls in gentle undulations at the base of wooded cliffs below the forest of Maulévrier, I find it difficult to believe in the river's once violent reputation. On the contrary, this tidal section of the Seine flowing out to the sea at Le Havre seems extraordinarily placid. Movement on the blackish-green water, thick and sluggish, is barely perceptible. You can watch a leaf floating on the surface, flaunting its indolence with its illusion of remaining steadfastly in one place, and forfeit all sense of time.

In the early morning, though, the fine white mist hanging dolefully over the water still seems redolent of a sinister power. The sudden appearance of the statue of a man gazing out across the river as one approaches Villequier is startling at first sight. The stone is so weather-beaten that the man appears to be naked. On closer inspection, this alarming figure turns out to be Victor Hugo, portrayed not in the guise of world-famous writer, author of *Notre-Dame de Paris* and *Les Misérables*, but as a heartbroken father. A concrete arrow helpfully points to the spot where Hugo's elder daughter, Léopoldine, together with her husband of seven months, Charles Vacquerie, and two other members of his family, his uncle Pierre, a former ship's captain, and Pierre's eleven-year-old son Arthur, were drowned in a boating accident on 4 September 1843. Léopoldine was barely a week past her nineteenth birthday.

In recent decades there's been debate about whether Léopoldine and the Vacqueries were actually victims of the *mascaret*. No sudden tidal surge is recorded for that day. Furthermore, Charles Vacquerie came from an ancient line of Seine fishermen and marine pilots who must have been familiar with this phenomenon, making the decision to set out in a light sailing vessel along the Seine estuary, where the winds and currents are known to be strong, something of a mystery. The likeliest explanation for the ill-fated voyage suggests that the *mascaret* was not a determining factor. The hull of the racing dinghy was too light for Seine sailing, but initially on that Monday morning there was not a trace of breeze, nor a ripple on the surface of the water. Léopoldine had decided not to accompany the party, but then changed her mind. On the return journey from Caudebec to Villequier, Charles and his uncle Pierre took advantage of a number of sandstone blocks lying on the quayside and brought them on board to add weight to the ballast of the dinghy. As they set off again, a brutal gust of wind a few minutes later caused the boat to keel over, with disastrous consequences. The sandstones, loaded to help the small craft, began to shift, bringing about a still worse state of imbalance.

A tiny nest of small alleyways and half-timbered houses in the Norman style, Villequier doesn't attract crowds of visitors. Even when I've been here at the height of summer I've never encountered more than two or three others exploring its little streets. Yet the village's name, together with its tragic associations, was immortalized by Victor Hugo in a long poem that occupies a standard place in anthologies of French poetry. Huge chunks of it were once committed to memory by generations of French schoolchildren. The poem forms part of *Les Contemplations*, Hugo's epic cycle of nostalgia, bereavement and spiritual discovery, in which Léopoldine's death – signalled like a series of mini-milestones by a row of dots across the page – marks the decisive break between youthful enthusiasm and adult despair, between joy and sheer terror.

Hugo was travelling with his mistress Juliette Drouet at the time of the disaster, and only learned of it five days later, when he accidentally discovered the drownings reported in a newspaper. In a café in Soubise in south-western France, Hugo ordered a bottle of beer, picked up a newspaper at random and suddenly exclaimed, 'This is horrible!' Drouet never forgot the expression on her lover's face at that moment: he seemed as if he'd been thunderstruck. 'His poor lips were white; his magnificent eyes were staring in front of him. His face and his hair were wet with tears. His poor hand was pressed to his heart as though to keep it from bursting from his breast.'

Hugo's grief was intense and prolonged. In time it would lead to a resurgence in his poetic voice. Soon after Léopoldine's death he began a series of anniversary pilgrimages to her grave in the cemetery of Villequier's sixteenth-century church of Saint-Martin. In the poem '*À Villequier*', written as he emerged, 'pale and victorious', from the grief he described as having darkened his soul, Hugo recalls one of these occasions. Addressing God, he bravely confronts the likelihood that, in the larger scheme of things, a dead child means nothing to its Creator, and that mankind's comprehension of a divine purpose in such matters must remain forever veiled from us and incomplete. But he also asks God to consider what it is to lose 'the child one loves', who is 'the sun of one's life and the fire of one's soul'.

Hugo's annual ritual of a day-long journey to Villequier to lay a spray of green holly and flowering heather on his beloved elder daughter's grave, commemorated in another of his best-known poems, '*Demain, dès l'aube . . .*' ('Tomorrow, as soon as day breaks . . .'), was soon to be interrupted by his own enforced 'burial' on islands far from home.

In the years following the 1848 revolution, Hugo became a leading voice in French politics. Elected to the legislative assembly in 1849, he was a focus of the opposition to the increasingly authoritarian Louis-Napoléon. Following Louis-Napoléon's *coup d'état* in December 1851, and his assumption of power as Napoleon III in the new Second Empire, Hugo was in flight for his life, with a police warrant out for his arrest. As a political exile for the best part of two decades, he would make his home with the rest of his family on the Channel Islands, initially in Jersey and then more permanently in St Peter Port, the capital of Guernsey. From here he would continue to excoriate Napoleon III in his writing, agitating for the Emperor's overthrow, sometimes satirically, sometimes with an explosive force of moral power.

Approached up a steep path from the centre of Villequier, with a commanding prospect of the river, Saint-Martin's small stone graveyard provides a final resting place for scores of sailors and Seine pilots. The Hugo and Vacquerie families occupy a group of 19 graves by the church wall. Victor Hugo himself is not among them. Following his death in 1885 he was interred – after a death rattle once described in an arresting simile as resembling 'the sound of pebbles dragged backwards by the sea' – with much ceremony in the Panthéon in Paris. But the Hugo women – though not Hugo's two sons – are buried here: wife and younger daughter, as well as Léopoldine, filling the same tightly enclosed space as her beloved husband Charles.

Like Hugo, who often portrays himself as the sole mourner at the graveside, I have never found any like-minded visitor in this Normandy churchyard, R, reasonably enough, not sharing my taste for the company of the dead. The flowering heather still sprouts on the Hugo and Vacquerie graves, along with a profusion of summer roses in shades of tepid pink, vulgar, vibrant orange and deep, intense crimson. In the stifling heat of an August day in 2016, when my concentration strayed to longings for a cool drink at the counter of the small billiard room down the hill, I noticed that the lettering on the arched headstones had been freshly gilded, and then reflected that it was just over a hundred years since a train from Great War Paris had brought the coffin of the last member of the Hugo family to be buried at Villequier: the woman on whose account I make my repeated visits to this quiet village.

André Maurois, a writer of tremendous industry, the extent of his literary output almost rivalling that of Victor Hugo, left behind an account of his visit to the Saint-Martin churchyard written while he was researching his biography of Hugo, not long after the Second World War. Then too it was summer, but black clouds were piling above the horizon as Maurois and his party looked down on the gloomy waters of the Seine and watched the ships, great and small, moving up the river. Suddenly a storm broke with unbelievable violence. Torrents of water swirled among the tombs, and for a moment Maurois imagined that Hugo, absent in the flesh from this place of family buryings, was there no less in spirit – 'and in the power and magnificence and dread magnificence of genius'.

Aside from the church, one of Villequier's few buildings of architectural note is the former Vacquerie home, a favoured holiday spot for Madame Hugo and her children from 1838. Purchased by the French government in 1951 and opened eight years later as a Victor Hugo Museum, it is a fine, red-brick, white-shuttered house, much altered since Hugo's day, with rose-filled gardens careering across to the riverbank. The interior, crammed with pictures, manuscripts, first editions and personal mementoes, but also with *salon* furniture evoking nineteenth-century bourgeois life, has an expensive, polished sheen. Auguste Vacquerie, Charles's younger brother, a brilliant writer and critic (and eventual owner of the house), became Hugo's most fervent disciple, and the drawing room is dedicated to his memory. A rococo-style room on the first floor, in the plushest of reds, celebrates Hugo's marriage in 1822 to Adèle Foucher; further along the corridor a small, windowed recess commemorates Hugo's long-term mistress Juliette Drouet. Hugo was notorious for his extramarital infidelities. In 1847 Charles Dickens called on the Hugos at their Paris apartment in the Place Royale (now the Place des Vosges) after a visit to the city morgue to gaze on the faces of the unidentified bodies of the drowned. He described 'a handsome' Madame Hugo, with her 'flashing black eyes', looking 'as if she might poison [her husband's] breakfast any morning when the humour seized her'. The personality and genius of Victor Hugo dominate everything here. One cartoon shows him, following his election to the Académie Française in 1841, bestriding the world of literature like a colossus, his gigantic dimensions matched only by Notre-Dame itself, on which Hugo leans a writing arm. Beneath the vast expanse of his forehead, his eyes stare down at his wide-open crotch.

I have retraced my steps through the house, examining its contents closely, many times. Should such pilgrimages to the shrines of famous writers be condemned as sentimental journeys, Virginia Woolf once asked in one of her earliest pieces of journalism. She then went on to argue that they were only permissible and not deserving of a ban if they added something to our understanding of a writer's books. Later, she backtracked very slightly and admitted that an hour spent, for example, in Thomas Carlyle's house in Chelsea could tell us more about Carlyle and his life than any biography. Lives, yes, but works, no? Or is the dividing line between a life and the literature it produces not as easy to draw as this statement encourages us to believe?

In Victor Hugo's case the welter of biographical information, if not exactly obscuring links between his life and writing, does make an attempt at any definitive statement about their complex inter-relationship particularly daunting and liable to error. An ongoing project created by the Hugo Group of Paris University, whose members include Jean-Marc Hovasse, author of a three-volume biography of Hugo, which, when complete, will run to several thousand pages, underlines this difficulty. The Group's collegial endeavours to establish a chronological database may one day make it possible to know Hugo's activity on any given date from his birth on 26 February 1802 to his death on 22 May 1885. At the other end of the life–writing spectrum, and a bit like a forerunner of a type of modern memoir, is Hugo's own *Contemplations*. Superficially at least the 'I' of the poems corresponds to our knowledge of the poet and his celebrated life as a writer, political refugee and visionary (though not, it should be noted, in stark departure from modern fashion, as inexhaustible lover). Indeed, the preface to the book specifically presents what is to follow as an autobiography. Yet it soon becomes apparent that a degree of falsification is at work. Dates and details have been shuffled – shaped and reorganized – with all the dexterity of a card shark dealing his pack. In part these distortions can be put down to Hugo's simple and understandable desire to conceal from the public some of the more intimate aspects of his private life. But they also serve an artistic purpose, both to make real life appear more plausible to his readers, and sometimes to heighten dramatic incidents from the poet's experience. At a fundamental level this is merely an elevated version of what we all do when we provide a receptive audience with an edited account of some part of our lives for their delectation.

Most of us enjoy a peek, at the very least, into someone else's world, especially when we get the satisfaction, a bit like a warm embrace, that comes from identifying with an experience or feeling that is no longer exclusively ours, but held in common with a figure from the past, even across the barrier of centuries. In a way this sensation is analogous to something else Victor Hugo is attempting in *Les Contemplations* when he offers his life as a mirror in which the reader can catch glimpses of him- or herself, and of such universal experiences as love and bereavement. 'When I speak to you of myself,' he declares, 'I tell you about yourselves too.'

One would be hard-hearted indeed not to be moved by the poignancy of glass cases containing the personal relics of the dead. The very survival of these relics in the house at Villequier is oddly compelling given that the natural fate, for example, of a piece of clothing belonging to a dead woman is to wear out or expire before the body that wore it and gave it feminine shape. A scrap of the muslin dress worn by Léopoldine on the day of her death, its chequered pattern of mauve and white still visible, inevitably retains a grim fascination. When Captain Derosan of the steamboat *Emma* led the operation to retrieve the four bodies from the ill-fated voyage, dragging a net through the water where the Vacqueries' boat had been found, he discovered Léopoldine, her small hands re-moulded into the tightly sculpted shape of a pair of iron clamps. So intense had been her grip on the underside of the boat, in her efforts to survive, that her fingernails were flecked with splinters of mottled wood. Charles Vacquerie, a strong swimmer, had circled round the upturned hull, desperately trying to save his wife. His efforts were in vain. Finally he gave up the struggle and let himself sink, disappearing under the water, never to re-emerge. Some call this suicide. Others prefer to describe Charles Vacquerie's final decision in a more positive frame. In those last few desperate moments, he was unable to conceive of a life without Léopoldine, and made the decision to die with her as a supreme assertion of the power of human love and devotion.

Over the years I've tried to write about this dramatic episode as fiction. However, the appropriate elements have never quite meshed together to make the scene believable. While it's true that a drowning person certainly isn't (*pace* Stevie Smith) capable of waving, or even of splashing around or calling for help – he or she instinctively extends their arms laterally and presses down on the surface of the water to lever their bodies out of the water in order to breathe – my depiction of Léopoldine's drowning on that September day on the Seine appears far too graceful and balletic in its act of perpetual slow motion. I may also have invented a significant detail purely for effect, when her hand sweeps down to her extended stomach 'in a vain gesture to protect her unborn child'. For I can now find no reliable authority or source for my supposition that Léopoldine was pregnant at the time of her death.

Something personal intervenes as well. The process of drowning fascinates me probably because I narrowly escaped being drowned at the age of three or four while on a seaside family holiday at Woolacombe in north Devon. Or at least the Kodachrome prints in the album, pinkish and yellowish in their Sixties tones, confirm the backdrop to the event. The low rocks, dark and knarred, the sloping sand dunes. My mother smiling with polite restraint for the camera, wearing a black bikini one-piece. My father, deeply bronzed from assiduous sun worship, prescribed to moderate his skin affliction, psoriasis, dictating the mood of the holiday as usual, and wearing the look of lower-lip-biting mild vexation that was his customary default expression.

One minute I had been floating peacefully, wrapped in a towel on the top of a lilo, a short distance from the shore; the next, I was underwater, struggling to free myself from the towel as I was swept helplessly to and fro by the motion of the waves. I believe I can recall the sick sensation produced by the involuntary swallowing of large amounts of salt water, and the feeling of the rough graze of the shingle on my cheeks during the buffeting backwards and forwards.

At some point I will interrupt my tour of the house to find R, who, bored by the familiarity of it all, has raced round to the exit, and is sitting sunning himself in the garden. I chide him for being concerned about little more than the prospect of his lunch, but then wonder if he is thinking of his own dead child, his 13-year-old son, killed in a car crash, along with R's wife, several years before I came to know him. For a moment, before re-entering the house, I chastise myself for my insensitivity in continuing to bring him back here.

In an alcove on the stairs there is a portrait of a dark-eyed, sombre beauty. Although the painting hangs in a shadowy recess, the woman in the picture instantly captures the attention of passers-by. This is Adèle Hugo (or Adèle II, as she is sometimes called to distinguish her from her mother), Victor Hugo's younger daughter, also known, in her various other incarnations and attempts to escape or lose her patriarchal moniker, as Mrs Pinson or Penson, Miss Lewly, or simply, and latterly most famously, in the film François Truffaut based on her life, as Adèle H. She alone is the reason for my being here. When Adèle was a 13-year-old, living in Paris in 1843, the novelist Honoré de Balzac wrote of her that she was the greatest beauty he had ever seen. And yet Adèle ended her days seemingly a pitiable figure in a dowager's bonnet, muttering a few unfriendly words to visitors in a dull metallic voice, and indulging in protracted, animated conversations with imaginary speakers from another world.

'Adèle who became mad because of an unfortunate love', runs the terse, stilted English of the museum guidebook. This is putting it mildly. While Léopoldine was drowned in the treacherous waters of the Seine, her younger sister, crossing the Atlantic Ocean 20 years later to be reunited with a feckless lover, is said to have been fatally overwhelmed by a destructive current of unrequited passion and obsessive love. In a letter commenting on Adèle's tragic plight, Victor Hugo compared his daughter's 'frightful peril' to a *quasi-naufrage*, a kind of shipwreck in which both her moral sense and her reason were submerged.

The collection in the Villequier house displays an assortment of items associated with Adèle's early life. There's a rather grotesque doll with thick ankles wearing an outsize hat decorated with an orange silk rosette, said to have been played with by both Hugo sisters as children; a charming pen and ink sketch of Adèle by 'Toto', François-Victor, the brother to whom she remained closest, showing her engaged in a domestic task, arranging flowers in a vase; and several photographs of Adèle from the early years of the family's exile in Jersey, taken by Auguste Vacquerie and Charles Hugo, enthusiastic adherents of the new-fangled craze, or technique '*de la mode*', as Madame Hugo liked to call it, the daguerreotype. In one of these, flower at her breast, she sits, eyes cast down, book in hand. The other, also from the mid-1850s, in which she holds an open parasol over her head, is more carefully posed. She continues to avoid the direct gaze of the camera, but wears a harsher, more abstracted expression. The effort of remaining stock-still for the necessary exposure lends a melancholy heaviness to the sitter and Adèle appears completely frozen in time.

These photographs date from the period of Adèle's journal. This was the diary she began in her early twenties as productive labour for all those unoccupied hours during which she shared her father's exile on the Channel Islands. Pinned to the wall beneath a sheet of Perspex in a corridor between two rooms is a facsimile of a single page. The journal was primarily an act of homage to Victor Hugo, a record of his table talk, of the pearls of wisdom that daily issued from his lips, and Hugo's overseeing of its entries – witness one or two corrections in his handwriting – has been seen as evidence that he planned one day to publish it.

However, interspersed among its pages, sometimes as marginalia, are stray entries from a more intimate record composed by Adèle in an elementary code. The picture they convey is a confused and incomplete one: of a young woman who yearns for love and romance, but not necessarily for marriage, and who writes about the anguish of involvement in a curiously erotic and impassioned way. This seems reminiscent in its intensity of her own father's prodigious love life, but it is also suggestive of the way her romantic feelings would eventually spin out of control.

The facsimile journal page on display points to muddle and disarray. It is a disjointed, barely decipherable, inky mess of second and third thoughts and haphazard interpolations connected to each other by a bewildering flurry of arrows. Some of this, undoubtedly, is due to the haste in which Adèle was forced to commit other people's conversations to paper, often hastily scribbling them down from memory. I wondered why, though, from the hundreds of pages of cogent reportage, this particular example has been chosen to represent her journal. It leaves behind it an impression of mental confusion, of madness even, as permanent and immovable as the rigid figure in the photographs.

I was the only visitor to the house on that hot August afternoon, trailed from room to room by a young female attendant in a black T-shirt as if I was a potential housebreaker stealing in on a family's most treasured secrets. On the way out I stopped to buy some postcards and a book from the museum's *directrice* at the till in the entrance hall. As I went to pay there was a problem with the connection on the chip-and-pin machine, resulting in what seemed like an interminable wait in the suffocating heat with no soft compensating breeze passing through the open door. To fill the silence I started a conversation, raising the point about the journal page. But the woman behind the till, in her curvy blonde bob and tight-fitting grey suit, was having none of it. Cutting across my faltering French with a rictus of a smile that brooked no opposition, she practically hissed as she enunciated in English the words '*This* is *Léopoldine's* museum'.

I was taken aback by the assertiveness of her response, but merely smiled in rueful recognition of how apposite her remark was. For, to a far greater extent than her two elder brothers, Adèle's existence was overshadowed and moulded, not simply by Léopoldine's early death, but even more lastingly and profoundly by Victor Hugo's idealization of his dead daughter. Adèle was called upon to replace the irreplaceable and, in biographer Jean-Marc Hovasse's words, 'to repair the irreparable', while living in daily proximity to her father's continuing deification of her sister, on whom death had bestowed all the lifeless perfection of a marble effigy.

The emotional climate created by these circumstances certainly contributed to what followed. In 1863, weeks away from her thirty-third birthday, Adèle Hugo made her decisive leap for independence and freedom. Without informing her family of her plans, she left her home in Guernsey and travelled to Southampton on her way to Halifax, Nova Scotia. She was in pursuit of Albert Andrew Pinson, stationed in Halifax as a lieutenant in the British army. Adèle had first met Pinson a decade earlier while the Hugo family were living in Jersey, and had been romantically involved with him for several years. At some point they may have planned to marry, though much about the course of the relationship and the motivation of its two protagonists is uncertain. Pinson himself has always been a shadowy figure. He barely seems to exist outside the sparse, coded references to him in Adèle's journal, leading at least one French writer, commenting on the story of Adèle's flight, to wonder whether he might not have been purely a creature of her imagination. In 1915, when Adele died at the age of 85, having outlived all the other members of her immediate family, the Symbolist writer Remy de Gourmont wrote that 'Everything touching on her is a mystery, from her birth to her death'. More than a century on there is still much truth in de Gourmont's observation. This is in spite of the publication of much of the surviving documentation concerning Adèle, and the lifting by the Hugo family of the veil of secrecy that had covered their ancestor for decades and kept her story hidden from the world.

The bare external details, however, of the sad trajectory of her life once she left the Channel Islands are more easily verifiable. In Halifax, living the life of a mysterious stranger under an assumed name, Adèle at first pretended to her family back home that she had married Pinson, and after this was exposed as a lie didn't cease in her attempts to win Pinson back and persuade him to marry her despite his rejection of her. In 1866, when Pinson transferred with his regiment to Barbados, Adèle followed him. When he returned to England three years later she stayed on, apparently unaware of his departure. She wandered the streets of the capital Bridgetown in rags, and was finally rescued by a local woman, Madame Baa, who discovered Victor Hugo's address in the reams of paper that Adèle carried with her, wrote to him, and then kindly escorted Adèle back to Paris, where, following Napoleon III's overthrow, Hugo had now returned. Adèle spent the remaining 43 years of her life in sanatoriums. The first was in a Paris suburb. Then, following her father's death, Adèle was transferred to a luxurious nursing home, also outside Paris.

At the end of 1863, just months after Adèle had deserted her family to join Pinson in Halifax, Victor Hugo put the finishing touches to his book *William Shakespeare*. It was published the following year to mark the tercentenary of Shakespeare's birth. As a conciliatory gesture, Hugo originally thought of dedicating it to his errant daughter overseas, but in the end the book's dedication read simply 'To England'. Hugo presumably ignored the irony that even as he completed his book about England's greatest playwright, his only surviving daughter was sacrificing her pride and dignity, her personal safety and, in the fullness of time, would lose her reason, in vain pursuit of an Englishman.

No matter that Hugo knew so little about Shakespeare or his plays – or indeed about the English language or Elizabethan literature or theatre. What mattered was that the book allowed him to discourse on his favourite themes, not least the subject of men of genius, among whom, naturally enough, he numbered himself (meanwhile, his younger son, François-Victor, the only member of the family with a command of English, was accomplishing the signal achievement of translating all of Shakespeare into French).

Anyone coming upon the book today with knowledge of the devastating tragedy on the Seine that went to the core of Victor Hugo's life and some of his greatest writing cannot help but be struck by Hugo's identification with King Lear, and Lear's howls of anguished grief on the death of Cordelia, his favourite daughter. However, over the years I've sometimes wondered whether Hugo ever mused on a further parallel, with the tragedy surrounding another of Shakespeare's heroines. For nineteenth-century Romantics, especially those in France, the character of Ophelia in *Hamlet*, who drowns in a fit of grief and insanity after her father forces her to reject Hamlet's love, represented a textbook case of a victim of erotomania or unrequited love. Ophelia doesn't simply drown: she drowns in a surfeit of feeling, literally because she loves too much.

'The English Lieutenant's Frenchwoman', R jested one day, half-mocking me in mild exasperation at being brought back time and again to Villequier. The joke inevitably becomes stale with repetition, but so too has my immersion in this story. I hoard information, fill notebooks with chronologies, quotations, unanswered questions and collect photographs, all in anticipation of that rainy day when I will finally commit my thoughts to paper. Only that day never seems to arrive, and I'm stuck like a record needle grinding away in the same groove.

The link, though, to John Fowles's famous novel has its own particular resonance, and sets me off on another mental trail. I remember reading somewhere that Fowles traced the moment of the conception of *The French Lieutenant's Woman* back to a single image that had fixed itself in his imagination. In his mind's eye he suddenly saw a woman standing at the end of a deserted quay, staring out to sea. All he knew for certain was that this woman belonged to the Victorian Age and that she had a mysterious, vaguely romantic quality about her. From this tiny kernel of inspiration sprouted Fowles's internationally bestselling, ambitiously metafictional-metahistorical-paratextual concoction of a novel.

I have an almost identical picture in my mind as I write now. It is of Adèle Hugo standing on a rock somewhere on the coastline near the Hugo home at St Peter Port in Guernsey, looking out to sea. 'The sea is the only place to which we can be faithful,' she wrote in her journal, a remark that initially perplexed me until I recognized it as an underlying expression of her desire to join Pinson, her English lieutenant, by embarking on a voyage overseas. In another decoded passage from her journal, written in 1862, the year before she departed for Canada, that desire is more transparent, as is the impress of her feminist ideas and her longing to escape from the prison that exile on the Channel Islands had come to represent: 'It would be an incredible thing for a young woman, enslaved to the point of not being able to go out alone for five minutes to buy some paper, to walk over the sea, to fly over the sea, to pass from the old world to the new world to rejoin her lover. This I will do.'

My dreams harbour other images: a bedraggled figure with matted hair in a Caribbean street being subjected to ridicule and taunts from local children. And disconcertingly these dreams have begun to be invaded by the dreams of others. One hot evening, a few summers ago, I booked into the familiar hotel at Caudebec. R was still in Paris and not due to arrive until the next day. After dinner, before turning in, I stood on the balcony outside my room and gazed at the twinkling red lights visible from the direction of Villequier, prettily situated and sheltered at a bend in the river. The temperature was warm and clammy as I closed and secured my bedroom windows – a necessary precaution, I'd discovered on previous visits, against the scourge of female mosquitoes whining in from the Seine.

In bed that night I sweltered, sweated, and endured a fiery heat. It left my throat parched and my head aching and jarringly disconnected from my body and unable to rest on the pillow. Soon after falling asleep I dreamed of a woman, skinny and pale. She didn't speak, but left behind her on a table a piece of paper covered with signatures. Later, reading Victor Hugo's notebooks, I discovered to my astonishment that Hugo had experienced an almost identical dream in March 1864, nine months after Adèle left for Halifax. Understandably, his absent daughter often appeared to him in dreams, on one occasion as a beautiful apparition dressed in black, carrying a light in her hand. Hugo's unconscious sometimes revealed the fears that overshadowed his daylight hours – he had a 'sacred horror' of such nightly visitations – the most disturbing being that Adèle might be pregnant, a state of affairs he worried would besmirch the honour of the family name and possibly even affect his own public standing. One night, awake and lying in bed, he was unnerved by the sound of his daughter's voice. *Je suis fiancée* – 'I am engaged' – were her words.

Another image of Adèle, this time in the form of a material object, a copy of one of the photographs of her taken by Auguste Vacquerie and her brother Charles, had – and this should be taken literally – once attached itself to me while I was in New York several years before the onset of my dreams. I had taken the opportunity of a trip there to visit the Morgan Library, a short journey on foot from Grand Central Station. Originally founded in the first years of the twentieth century to house the collection of books and manuscripts and prints and drawings amassed by the American financier J. P. Morgan, the Morgan preserves the bulk of the manuscript of Adèle Hugo's journal. Although much of this has been edited and published in several volumes, I longed to see the original and to turn its pages.

I had made careful preparations, contacting the library in advance of my trip and arranging the required letter of reference. Unfortunately a heavy cold prevented me from keeping the original appointment, and it wasn't until my final morning in New York, en route to the airport, that I arrived at the Morgan. Divested of my luggage, I was admitted to the library's darkened reading room leading off the richly decorated, polychrome rotunda, which resembles the interior of a Byzantine church. I hadn't left myself much time, and my lack of success in hurriedly attempting to decipher the handwriting didn't get me very far. The few stray pages I did look at closely appeared to be written on the back of an inventory, lists of china and glassware from Hauteville House, the Hugos' Guernsey address. Still, there was the satisfying sensory connection of my fingertips, beneath the white cotton gloves of obligatory library etiquette, making contact with the stiff and yellowing paper of the journal.

The staff went out of their way to be helpful. As I was preparing to leave, one of them, a young woman, approached me and asked if I would like to take a photograph of Adèle with me which they'd had printed from an original plate for inclusion in an exhibition that was now closed. I accepted the offer with alacrity. However, what I'd assumed to be a frameable snapshot was in fact a photo ten times that size, reproduced on a piece of white laminated hardboard, roughly 2 by 3 feet in dimension. With the picture wrapped in brown paper and tied with string under one arm, and a heavy bag gripped in my other hand, I emerged onto Madison Avenue. Feeling distinctly encumbered while at the same time keeping up an anxious search for a cab to take me to the airport, I stood in the street and attempted to reassemble myself into a more comfortable position for going on my way. Discarding the paper and making use of the pair of hooks on the reverse side of the picture, I constructed a cat's cradle of string to hang the board across my back before looping it over my arms. As I moved forward, several passers-by shot glances at this absurd spectacle to see what sort of product I might be advertising in my new guise as half-a-sandwich-board-man. Others in more of a pressing rush knocked their elbows against the edges of the picture as they blundered past, sending me momentarily stumbling and forcing me to halt and tighten the string as best I could.

'You don't seem to be able to shake her off, do you?' R remarked, laughing and rolling his eyes in disbelief, when I told him about the incident later. 'This really is getting to be a bit like a one-sided love affair.'

It's true, of course. Biography is after all sometimes defined in terms more often associated with a one-sided, obsessive and slightly deranged love affair. There are the false claims of intimacy made by the biographer in describing his relationship with the subject. There's the close stalking of the biographical prey, the invasive pursuit of every conceivable aspect of another person's life that the biographer can gain access to. Finally, and most weirdly, there is the presumption of ownership. I can understand you, says the biographer to himself in the lopsided monologue playing in his head. I can empathize with you, explain to the outside world your virtues and faults, your achievements as well as your failures. Who knows, perhaps there'll be a Day of Reckoning when biographers will be arraigned before the men and women they've written about to face a barrage of derision and scorn for all the dubious assertions and ill-founded speculation presented by them under the guise of unassailable truth.

Much less often explored, or even acknowledged, are questions about what it is that draws a biographer to a specific life story. Commercial motives aside (such as they are), what is it that compels him to exist for years in close proximity to a dead stranger – we are talking dead subjects here, not living ones – raking over the dry and dusty remains of a half-forgotten past? The inherent interest of a human drama, admiration for a life well lived or work well done, are obvious reasons; another is the chance to lose oneself in another world, as all writers do, but a world that possesses the clear advantage of having actually existed rather than being purely imaginary.

What, though, about the ways in which someone else's life might offer a prism through which to revisit or examine parts of one's own story?

When I ask myself what it is that keeps Adèle Hugo so vividly alive in my conscious and unconscious thoughts, the simple pathos of her existence comes instantly to mind. An accomplished young woman, full of potential, both as a writer and as a musician and composer, is caught in the web of a great man's life. Then there is the challenge of attempting to dispel something of the mystery surrounding her. At this distance in time is it possible to discover more about Albert Pinson, the man with whom she fell in love with such disastrous consequences, who precipitated the reckless act of daring that made her leave her family and contributed to her loss of sanity?

However, I'm aware too that my own experience of unrequited love is what I originally found compelling in Adèle's story, and that it's one primary reason, though far from the only one, for sustaining my interest in it now. Some might say that it's precisely this impulse of self-identification that should disqualify me from investigating her – except that any biographer, consciously or unconsciously, is making some sort of attempt at self-expression while ostensibly following another individual's path through life. All we can offer, in a sense, are versions of ourselves, and any pretence of detachment is just that – a pretence. To a greater or lesser extent, we all – readers as well as writers – view another person's life and character refracted through our own personalities and experiences. It should be obvious that we have no alternative.

It isn't fanciful to feel oneself pursued by a story. And sooner or later we may decide to ask ourselves why one particular story has rooted itself in the mind when so many others have blurred and disappeared and been forgotten. Returning to all the books and notes on the subject that I'd put to one side, I have resolved to ask this question for myself. As I pursue Adèle Hugo in the pages that follow, fragments of my story will shadow hers, rather as Adèle shadowed Albert Pinson in the streets of Halifax and Bridgetown 160 years ago.

2

Paper Trails

The woman standing on the rock, staring out to sea. She had always seemed more than just a product of my imagination, derived perhaps from my reading. But where had she materialized from? Settling down to work I soon realized the answer, and there was nothing in the least bit mysterious about it. Watching a DVD of François Truffaut's film *L'Histoire d'Adèle H.* ('The Story of Adèle H.'), I saw the woman on the rock again. Only this time I recognized her as the young actress Isabelle Adjani starring in the title role.

Truffaut's film, released in 1975, introduced Adèle Hugo to the wider world after her story had been kept deliberately hidden for decades, with any attempt at penetrating its mysteries frustrated for lack of information. Properly speaking, the film also represented my own introduction to the subject. Long before making that first visit to Villequier, and feeling the pull of the story, I'd seen the Truffaut film while I was a student at Oxford University.

Looking back I see that there were various reasons for my happiness at Oxford during the three years I spent there. Freedom from battling parents at home, the heady excitement of newfound independence, the enchantment provided by the seductive beauty of the city itself. I was also semi-intoxicated, not with any student's brew but by the discovery that every book I'd ever wanted to read was available to me on the shelves and in the stacks of the Bodleian and other university libraries. Oxford has often been described as a city built on books – quite literally so. Never tread on the patch of grass in Radcliffe Square, undergraduates were warned while being conducted on a tour of the Camera, the eighteenth-century neoclassical building that housed the open collections devoted to works of history, theology and English literature. A bare 9 inches of soil, it was said, separated our feet from the labyrinthine warren of library vaults and mechanical conveyor belts situated beneath.

Walking over Magdalen Bridge and into the Cowley Road, you left picture-postcard Oxford, with its grand, often austere buildings, quadrangles and manicured lawns, far behind. In its place you encountered a rougher-edged world of brash, outlandish colour splashed onto the walls of shops and houses, and unfamiliar but not unappetizing smells emanating from the many restaurants and cafes. Multicultural Oxford had put down roots here in the 1950s and 60s with waves of immigrants – Jamaican and Pakistani swiftly followed by Italians, Poles, Greeks, Turks and Russians – attracted by openings for unskilled labour and opportunities for cheap housing. Students from the university and the polytechnic had moved in in the 1970s, but the process of gentrification was still to come. There was a real scent of risk and danger about the area, quite unlike the traditional, almost staged, conflicts that flared up most boozy Saturday nights in the Cornmarket in central Oxford, between Town and Gown.

The Penultimate Picture Palace was among Britain's first purpose-built cinemas, opening just before the First World War and falling into disuse in the midst of it when the owner was conscripted into the army. Restored and resurrected in the mid-1970s, the PPP, to use its affectionate acronym, was in Jeune Street, an unobtrusive little side road off the main Cowley thoroughfare, There was nothing shy and retiring, though, about the way in which the cinema presented itself. A depiction of Al Jolson from *The Jazz Singer* was affixed to the top of the building's façade, a sculpture of his gigantic white-gloved hands reaching out as if to pull you in. Inside there were Salvador Dalí-style Mae

West lips on the pair of entrances to the auditorium; 'Pearl and Dean' weren't the adverts preceding the main feature but the labels on the doors of the ladies' and gents' loos, situated directly beneath the screen; and the two back rows contained double seats, designated 'love nests'.

Inspired by London art house cinemas like the Paris Pullman and the National Film Theatre, the PPP offered an enterprising mix of conventional and more controversial fare to self-consciously sophisticated student audiences. It was here that I received another education aside from my bookish one. Much of the foundation of my film knowledge was established at late-night showings at this dream palace. These programmes included early Woody Allen and the first two *Godfather* films; Jean Renoir's *La Grande Illusion*; Marcel Carné's interminable *Les Enfants du Paradis*, with its sumptuous evocation of the Paris of the July Monarchy of the 1830s and 40s, reconstructed in Nice during the Nazi occupation, making it the city that Victor Hugo himself might have recognized; and on a snowy January night in 1982, during one of the severest British winters of the twentieth century, François Truffaut's *L'Histoire d'Adèle H.*

The weather alone should have been sufficient to make that first viewing of *Adèle H.* stick in my mind, as I recollect now how we struggled along the Cowley Road in a fierce blizzard and entered the cinema shaking the snow from our boots. But what made the experience truly memorable for me was that I was accompanied on that trip to the cinema by the first person I'd ever seriously considered myself in love with. He was a male undergraduate from my year, at Magdalen, reading the combined Latin and French course and living in Oscar Wilde's old rooms in college, a fact he liked to make much of. I was 21, immature and gawky, and possibly a little long in the tooth for first love. However, as in the well-known John Clare poem of that name, I felt that I'd never been struck before 'With love so sudden and so sweet', even if, like the speaker in the poem, I wondered whether real love needed always to be so cold or seem so unattainable.

My love for Julien was not openly declared. Throughout the months of our often confusing, fairly tortuous friendship, I never explicitly revealed my feelings to him, and remained forever after in ignorance of what – if anything – he felt for me. All this must have appeared in stark contrast to the drama of a doomed but passionate declaration of love being enacted before us on the screen, though the film couldn't fail to be suggestive to me of the perils of opening one's heart to someone without first testing the likely strength of the love object's reaction.

So there were no love nests for Julien and me that night. Instead we sat near the front row. I leaned forward in my upright seat as if preparing to jump into the screen and enter the story, casting a glance at him now and again to register his reactions. My impressions of what struck me that first time of seeing the Truffaut film are inevitably overlaid by what I've carried away since from subsequent viewings. But without doubt the memory of Isabelle Adjani's defiantly expressive face, her pale, azure eyes, brimming perpetually with tears, and full, sensuous mouth, stayed with me. She was the 19-year-old theatre actress from the Comédie-Française chosen by Truffaut to play Adèle Hugo, despite the fact that at the start of the story the real Adèle would have been already in her early thirties. The director was in thrall to his young star. As he pulls the focus tighter and tighter on her face, you sense the emotional force of a powerful obsession.

What must have appealed to me too are the ways in which the film takes on at times the tone and texture of a novel by the Brontë sisters. I'd been besotted with the lives and works of the Brontës throughout my teens, visiting Haworth Parsonage, reading everything about the family I could lay my hands on, and publishing my first article in the Brontë Society's journal. Truffaut had dealt with Brontë themes earlier in his career in *Les Deux Anglaises et le Continent* ('Two English Girls and the Continent'), a film about a pair of turn-of-the-century sisters who fall in love with a Frenchman (according to Truffaut, a bit like the Brontë sisters falling in love with a young Proust). But *Adèle H.* was his Brontë film. It's not just the bonnets and shawls, but an array of other incidental details. There's a graveyard, where Adèle and Lieutenant Pinson meet; a Halifax bookseller who sells rolls of paper to Adèle for her letters and journals, like the Haworth stationer John Greenwood who provided paper for the sisters' novels; there's even a fierce dog who attacks Adèle as she tries to reach Pinson at his barracks, reminiscent of Emily Brontë's mastiff Keeper, who bared his savage-looking teeth to his mistress as well as to strangers.

Like a Brontë heroine Adèle shows a disregard for convention and makes passionate declarations of love. Only it isn't the fiery Jane Eyre that she suggests, but the altogether icier Lucy Snowe from Charlotte Brontë's final novel *Villette*: cold (hence the name), untrustworthy and, like Adèle H., withholding her full identity. The moments in which Adjani's Adèle, identifying with the dead Léopoldine, relives in nightmares the watery terror of her sister's drowning are strikingly similar to the imagery Lucy uses early on to describe her nightmare of a shipwreck: 'the rush and saltness of briny waves in my throat, and their icy pressure on my lungs'. This foreshadows the novel's famously ambiguous ending in which Lucy reveals the probable death by drowning of the man she loves, Paul Emanuel.

Filming on *L'Histoire d'Adèle H.* took place at the start of 1975, in an intensive two-month, location-based shoot. The film opened in Paris in the autumn of that year. The plot centres on Adèle's pursuit of Lieutenant Pinson, first to Halifax, Nova Scotia (played in the film, bizarrely enough, by Guernsey, the island of exile from which the historical Adèle had made her escape to Canada), and then to Bridgetown, capital of Barbados (for which Gorée, an island off the coast of Senegal in West Africa, provided an unconvincing stand-in). 'Even if you don't love me, let me love you,' Adjani's increasingly distraught Adèle tells Pinson before resorting to a series of desperate ruses that are increasingly delusional and which will finally overwhelm her.

Truffaut was in his early forties, one of the leaders of the new wave in French cinema. For reasons he couldn't quite fathom, he found the making of *Adèle H.*, his fourteenth full-length feature as director, an emotionally cauterizing experience. There was something 'strange and unbalanced' about it all, he admitted, that often reduced him to tears.

On 1 June 1885, 14 years after he'd returned to France from exile, Victor Hugo was given a funeral in Paris that was one of the most spectacular occasions ever witnessed by the city. It was as if France's Third Republic was paying tribute to the cult of Hugo himself, while at the same time burying with him part of its own recent history. His body lay in state under the Arc de Triomphe during a vigil on the night of 31 May. The coffin, mounted on a double pedestal of violet velvet in an enormous catafalque, was guarded by torch-bearing horsemen and dimly illuminated by electric light. Twelve young French poets formed a guard of honour. There was the monotonous sound of 'a multitudinous murmuring of verse', coming not only from the poets but also from the dense, jostling crowds forming in the surrounding avenues. An observer noted that Hugo's lying in state resembled

one of the great deifications of imperial Rome, though by the time darkness fell more of a carnival spirit predominated. There was drunken singing in the Champs-Élysées, and 'abominable outrages' were reported as having taken place behind the bushes in the Avenue Victor Hugo. The nation's 'sorrowful wake', Edmond de Goncourt cheekily recorded, 'was celebrated by a wholesale copulation', with the whores of Paris draping their pudenda in black crêpe as a mark of respect – 'c***s in mourning!'

The next day two million Frenchmen followed the hearse, and the 11 wagons laden with wreaths and flowers that preceded it, to the Panthéon. This was the former church of Sainte-Geneviève, secularized so that the remains of Victor Hugo could be buried there (on the principle presumably that there wasn't room for two gods in this particular temple). Hugo had made his wishes clear. Since all existing religions had failed 'in their duty to Humanity and to God', no priest would play any part in his funeral. After four hours of speeches the coffin was lowered into the crypt. Fourteen years later, a visitor to the Panthéon vaults discovered that Hugo's coffin still had no permanent resting place. It sat exactly where it had on the day of the funeral, surrounded by 'the spectres of roses' and the 'corpses' of decomposing flowers.

In the reams of newsprint published across the globe to mark Victor Hugo's death, reference naturally enough was made to his family life. It was initially assumed by some journalists that, at 83, Hugo had outlived his wife and all his children. Léopoldine, of course, had already been dead for more than 40 years. Madame Hugo had died in 1868. Charles and François-Victor had both predeceased their father, dying respectively in 1871 and 1873, Charles from an apoplectic stroke, François-Victor from tuberculosis of the kidneys.

There was what sounded like a collective gasp of astonishment, however, when word of the contents of Hugo's will revealed the survival of another, younger daughter, apparently long forgotten and now in her mid-fifties, residing in an institution outside Paris. Her father's final testament had left just 8,000 francs a year 'for the maintenance' of his closest surviving relative, Adèle Hugo.

The annual income of Charles Hugo's widow, Alice, who had remarried, to the journalist and politician Édouard Lockroy, was raised to 12,000 francs. An undisclosed sum had been put aside for Juliette Drouet, Hugo's mistress, though she had predeceased him by two years. The rest of Hugo's estimated fortune of seven million francs was bequeathed to his beloved grandchildren, the light of his declining years, Charles's son and daughter, Georges and Jeanne.

But Hugo had also left behind a vast accumulation of manuscripts, ten volumes of unpublished material, including letters, notes and other documents. These were to have gone to Juliette Drouet. With her death they passed by default to Adèle Hugo, who additionally became the principal copyright holder of her father's works and consequently, in a curious turn of fate, the inheritor of a great fortune. 'She is enormously rich,' someone calling themselves 'a Veteran Diplomat' wrote in the *New York Times* over a decade later, accounting for Adèle's luxurious accommodation in the nursing home at the Château de Suresnes, where she had a pavilion to herself and employed a personal companion. Her annual income at that stage was in the region of 50,000 francs. In 1907, a Parisian publishing firm would pay the sum of 250,000 francs to Adèle's trustees, a group headed by the writer Gustave Simon, for the right to publish a cheap edition of all her father's novels, poetry and plays.

Her wealth was hardly in dispute, but many of the salient details of the life story of this mysterious woman proved much more difficult to pin down. In reports at the time of Victor Hugo's death, at least three or four variants of Adèle's story were current. They would continue to be repeated – and embellished – for upwards of half a century. One version, in the form of a piece of newsprint that had been folded so many times that the paper was starting to wear away, fluttered out of a book I bought several years ago in a second-hand bookstore.

The book was undistinguished and commonplace, a kind of shilling *Life* of Victor Hugo by Frank T. Marzials, in a *Great Writers* series, published in Britain a few years after Hugo's death. Much more arresting was the cutting inside, extracted from the London *Daily Chronicle* of 11 March 1896:

> Most people have forgotten (says our Paris correspondent) that Victor Hugo had another daughter, who is still living in a lunatic asylum near Paris. A day or two ago a family gathering was held to appoint a guardian in place of M. Auguste Vacquerie, who held the office till his death. This sacred trust now falls upon Victor Hugo's next surviving friend M. Paul Meurice, to be succeeded in case of another vacancy by the poet's grandson, Georges Hugo. The story of Adèle Hugo is sad and romantic. She eloped with an English officer to India, and was married there without the French legal formalities. Her wedded life was unhappy and her mind gave way under the strain. The husband died some 15 years ago at [sic] Singapore.

Other accounts were more specific about Adèle's unremitting marital unhappiness. Her children were said to have died in infancy; her husband, described as a naval officer or an army lieutenant, had beaten her and had eventually committed suicide. In a variant on this, Adèle was said to have found her way to Singapore from India after her husband's death, and to have been rescued wandering the streets in rags. She was said to sit in her pavilion at Suresnes wearing expensive clothes that had been fashionable long ago, at the time of her wedding. This was a nice bit of descriptive detail, no doubt inspired by Dickens' Miss Havisham in *Great Expectations*, jilted at the altar and similarly caught in a time warp extending back to the period of her humiliation and heartbreak.

The *New York Times* obituary of Victor Hugo added a bit more dramatic colour to this tale of Adèle's past. It stated that as a girl Adèle had been kidnapped from the family home in Guernsey by an English officer.

> All Europe was searched for her by her parents, but they obtained no trace of her whereabouts. Several months later a girl

found wandering alone in the streets of New York, apparently demented, declared, 'I am the daughter of Victor Hugo.' This was the only statement she ever made.

This last version – of a kidnapping – was one I came across at Oxford while studying the history and culture of the early years of the French Third Republic. In an unwieldy, rigorously undefined syllabus, Zola and Proust competed for attention with everything from rural modernization to the socialism of Jean Jaurès and the *petit bleu* that had done for Dreyfus. It was with relief at times that I turned to one of the prescribed texts, the wonderfully gossipy journal of the Goncourt brothers, Jules and Edmond. At (practically) every word, to ape Alexander Pope, a literary reputation dies. The Goncourts chronicle the Parisian world of letters from the period of Napoleon III's *coup d'état* in 1851 to Edmond's death in 1896 (Jules died before his brother, in 1871, leaving Edmond to continue their work alone). The brothers are obsessed by literary celebrity, their own as well as that of other, and, to their considerable irritation, far greater names. Haunted by the inevitability of death – most often, in the case of writers, from drink or venereal disease – they keep a close watch on the transience of fame and the shifting of the hierarchy. When Victor Hugo died, Edmond noted that Émile Zola appeared relieved, for the thought had entered his mind 'that he was going to inherit the literary papacy'.

In a chilly, north-facing room in St John's College, under the cold, watchful eye of my Antipodean tutor, I turned over the pages of my edition, searching for the quotation about Flaubert we'd been discussing. My attention was captured by a pathetically sad account of the last days of Hugo's younger son, François-Victor. The dying man lay on a chaise-longue in a summer garden. His complexion was waxen. His eyes were 'at once vague and fixed'. And his arms were folded across his body as if he were feeling cold. However, Edmond continued, François-Victor's father, who was also present, was not feeling in any way diminished. On the contrary, he was 'full of gaiety, energy, and vitality', and apparently, in the full throttle of his egoism, unconscious of 'the death-agony' of his son.

For some of those present this was almost too painful a sight to bear. As they were leaving, a family friend turned to Edmond Goncourt to lament the fact that Victor Hugo evidently hadn't given a thought to his sick son for the entire evening. Instead Hugo's concentration had been taken up with an attractive woman in the party, yet another of his sexual conquests. Later, writing in his journal, Edmond reflected on Hugo 'the genius', but also on Hugo 'the monster'. The Hugos, he wrote, were certainly *Une Famille Tragique* – 'A Tragic Family' – adopting the title of a novel, published in 1861, by the elder son Charles. 'I started thinking,' Edmond went on, 'about that first daughter, who had been drowned, and that second daughter who had been carried off by an American and brought back to France raving mad.' Typically, halfway through his diary entry, Edmond Goncourt gives way to much more lurid and scandal-mongering inventions. Madame Hugo had committed adultery with her son-in-law, who in turn had 'practically' raped his sister-in-law. Hugo's mistress Juliette Drouet had continued to pursue his son François-Victor with her kisses right to the end. With a few strokes of Goncourt's venomous pen, the Hugos are suddenly less a tragic family and more a sex-ridden, sex-obsessed one, almost on a par with the Borgias.

Family secrets are perhaps the darkest kind. They go against the grain of what we sentimentally conceive a family to be: a unified, cohesive unit, inextricably bound by ties of love and confessional intimacy. Within the Hugo family, Adèle's fate was rarely alluded to and never publicly discussed. Sometimes, indeed, it was as if she had never even existed. Charles Hugo hid knowledge of the sister residing in the nursing home outside Paris from his wife Alice. Following their father Charles's death, Georges and Jeanne, Victor Hugo's grandchildren, while still quite young, occasionally accompanied their 'Papapa' on his visits to Adèle at Suresnes and gave their aunt a kiss, but afterwards never spoke of her to their own families. Georges's son Jean, subsequently a distinguished artist and associate of Cocteau and Picasso, remembered attending, at the age of eight, a performance of

Les Burgraves, Victor Hugo's play about the Emperor Barbarossa, to mark the centenary of his great-grandfather's birth in 1902. What he learned only much later was that his great-aunt Adèle was also present that evening, watching her father's play from the shadows of her theatre box.

In 1892, seven years after Victor Hugo's death, a document came to light in London that would bring the story of Adèle Hugo to public attention.

A brief article in the London review the *Athenaeum* announced that Samuel Davey, a well-known bibliophile and dealer, had acquired an intimate record, a *Journal de l'Exil* ('Journal of Exile'), of roughly 2,000 pages written by Victor Hugo during his years on the Channel Islands. The manuscript had been discarded with other waste paper from Hauteville House, the Hugo residence in Guernsey, and had ended up in the junk shops of St Peter Port. By some unknown route the journal had then found its way to London. Not the least bizarre of the mysteries surrounding the journal, as was eventually revealed, was the complicated route of its peregrinations.

This *Journal de l'Exil*, the article went on to explain, was a detailed, daily record of Victor Hugo's conversations from Jersey and Guernsey with his family, his friends and his distinguished visitors, many of them fellow *proscrits*, condemned to a life of exile through their opposition to Napoleon III's regime. No doubt was expressed at this stage that its authorship belonged to any individual other than Victor Hugo himself.

Further publicity was given to the journal in New York by *Scribner's Magazine* and in France by *Le Figaro*. Paul Meurice and Auguste Vacquerie, Hugo's executors, were both consulted and verified the authenticity of the content, though strangely neither of them was asked to confirm the author's identity. For questioning voices on this subject were already beginning to be heard. Alternative possibilities for the authorship were mooted. François-Victor Hugo, perhaps. Or, less plausibly, a suggestion that could only have been made by someone who hadn't examined the actual manuscript, was the journal a rough draft of Madame

Hugo's biography of her husband? The writing of this book – *Victor Hugo Raconté par un Temoin de sa Vie*, 'Victor Hugo: A Life Related by One Who Has Witnessed It' – had occupied many hours of Madame Hugo's island exile before its publication in 1863.

However, there was scarcely an opportunity to scrutinize the handwriting any more closely. Discussion was halted as the journal suddenly disappeared from public view for decades, its whereabouts unknown. When it resurfaced in the 1920s, the manuscript, just over 2,000 pages bound in two volumes of Moroccan blue, was in the possession of the Pierpont Morgan Library in New York. It had almost certainly been one of J. P. Morgan's earliest purchases for his magnificent collection, acquired from Davey, the London dealer, at some point between 1896 and 1905. In 1914, the academic and critic Fernand Baldensperger, one of the founders of the study of comparative literature in France, was shown the journal on a visit to New York. He considered it to be an important work, the publication of which would throw significant new light upon Victor Hugo's life and writings. Baldensperger didn't venture an opinion as to its authorship.

The possibility of publication seemed a lot closer by the mid-1920s. Frédéric Hoffherr was a professor of French at Columbia University in New York. In 1926 he began a long and arduous labour, attempting to decipher the manuscript. He believed the journal not to be by Hugo at all. Instead, at this stage he saw it as a work of dual authorship, shared between François-Victor and his sister Adèle. He also quickly recognized that the journal in the Pierpont Morgan was incomplete. For 30 years, until his death in 1956, Hoffherr devoted much of his spare time outside his teaching schedule to travelling to Paris, London, Jersey and Guernsey, researching background information about the Hugos and searching in vain for the missing sections of the manuscript. On several occasions he visited Paris for meetings with Gustave Simon, successor to Paul Meurice as Victor Hugo's literary executor, to seek his permission to publish the *Journal de l'Exil*. But Simon was adamant about withholding his authorization. The secrets of the Hugo family must remain exactly that, secret.

The gift came too late for Professor Hoffherr, but in 1950 another portion of the journal suddenly materialized in a box of family papers donated by Jean Hugo to the Musée Victor Hugo in the Place des Vosges in Paris. These too had originated at Hauteville House, discovered in the drawer of a chiffonier sold by Madame Hugo's sister Julie Foucher Chenay, who was responsible for the dispersal of the contents of the Guernsey house after Victor Hugo's death. This new cache of documents represented an even more significant haul than the volumes in the Pierpont Morgan. For here were a further 4,000 pages of the journal, written for the most part in ink, but also in faint pencil, on sheets of paper of varying size and quality.

Soon afterwards Adèle Hugo was publicly identified for the first time as the author of the journal. In 1952, the cultural attaché to the French embassy in New York, René de Messières, who had examined the volumes in the Pierpont Morgan, gave a lecture at Harvard entitled 'The Journal of Exile of Adèle Hugo'. And a decade later, yet more of Adèle's journal was uncovered. Another hundred sheets belonging to the diary had been found inserted among the pages of a sixteenth-century Geneva Bible. Purchased by the French diplomat Jean Delalande from a chair repairman in Guernsey whose father had been a clergyman in St Peter Port, this section of the manuscript was in turn acquired by the Pierpont Morgan in 1962.

The importance of what now amounted to more than 6,000 manuscript pages of Adèle Hugo's journal wasn't lost on a middle-aged professor of French from the city of Wooster in Wayne County, Ohio. In the late 1940s, Frances Vernor Guille had received her doctorate with a thesis on the life and work of François-Victor Hugo, published in book form in 1950. Alerted to the existence of the pair of volumes in the Pierpont Morgan, Guille gained the co-operation of Jean Hugo and began to study them, building on Hoffherr's transcriptions and gradually widening her sphere of study as more and more pieces of the puzzle represented by Adèle's manuscript revealed themselves.

Frances Guille was born in 1908 in Atlanta, Georgia, but her paternal ancestors came from Guernsey, where Guille is a common surname, a coincidence she came to think of as a lucky charm. The biographical information about her is sparse. She married late, and only briefly, in her mid-sixties, and from her subsequent dealings with François Truffaut has left behind the impression of a tough, though ultimately not uncompromising businesswoman. With her scholarship we are on surer ground. What Guille undoubtedly possessed were the cardinal virtues of the committed scholar: determination, patience and the ability to see the relationship of the tiniest detail to the larger picture.

Commitment and a driving dedication, it transpired, were also the hallmarks of Adèle Hugo's journal. For as Guille subjected the manuscript to closer examination, she came up with some surprising results. One was the extent to which Adèle had painstakingly drafted and re-drafted her daily entries. Her diary keeping was no hobby taken up in an idle moment and just as quickly cast aside, but an open-ended project, doggedly pursued. Sometimes Guille would find the same episode related three or four times, with only subtle or very small changes between the different versions. There was no straightforward demarcation either between the manuscript in New York and the tranche of documents in Paris. Entries covering the same dates were present in both collections, while occasionally the description of the events of a single day would commence on a page preserved in the Pierpont Morgan and conclude on one in the Place des Vosges.

The French have a wonderful word for a messy manuscript: *gribouillage*. This refers to a handwritten scrawl, though perhaps we might in this instance extend its meaning to cover the difficulty of comprehending a complex manuscript work as a whole. Adèle Hugo's handwriting, as I'd seen in the sample displayed in the museum at Villequier, is often hard to read, and occasionally indecipherable. This was at least partly a result of often having to throw down the reportage of her father's conversations in a great hurry, onto the nearest scrap of paper. But there was additionally for Frances Guille and her small team of research assistants the even greater problem, which might have proved insurmountable, of constructing a comprehensible whole from the scattered pieces.

And Guille remained ever vigilant to the possibility of finding yet more portions of the journal. She was tantalized by a statement that Adèle had made to a Halifax lawyer, Robert Motton, on her arrival in Nova Scotia in 1863. Motton, who years afterwards recalled somewhat fancifully Adèle's beautiful, almost copperplate script, maintained that one day she had shown him a 'large pile' of the manuscript she had written while in Halifax, offering it to him with the words, 'Publish it some day; you will startle the world and make a fortune'. According to Motton, he always regretted not having done so.

In pursuit of later continuations of Adèle's manuscript that might throw new light on her time in the city and the denouement of her relationship with Lieutenant Pinson, Guille arrived in Halifax in late 1964 (she appears never to have considered visiting Barbados, perhaps a likelier resting place for Adèle's manuscripts as her penultimate destination before being brought back to Paris). Accompanied by her young student Margaret Mark, a Princeton graduate also researching Adèle, Guille was photographed for the *Halifax Mail Star,* muffled against the harsh temperatures of a Nova Scotian winter and appealing to Haligonians for any information about Adèle. 'They are hoping that someone in the city still remembers Adèle Hugo,' ran the newspaper report a little optimistically, given that a century after Adèle's departure from Halifax findings were almost bound to be disappointingly limited.

Nonetheless, a descendant of Winthrop Bell, the Sheriff of Halifax during Adèle's time there, did come forward to tell Guille about a watch given to his ancestor by a mysterious French lady 'whom he had helped when she was in difficulties'. A Dr Martin recalled a Miss Torrie, a schoolteacher, who had boarded at 47 Cornwallis Street at the same time as Adèle. Miss Torrie had subsequently lived with the O'Connor family, and a Mrs O'Connor could have talked about Miss Torrie's memories of Adèle. There was only one problem: she'd died two years earlier. All that could be summoned up from the O'Connor family's folk memory after so long was the story of how the Hugos had sent bolts of cloth to Adèle in Halifax. She didn't bother to have them made into dresses.

Instead she wrapped them around her over her other clothes, using pins to keep the material in place. Sometimes the pins slipped and Adèle walked along the street with the cloth trailing behind her.

Halifax hadn't, then, yielded very much in the way of new information. If Adèle did leave a pile of paper behind her, it was conceivable that it had shared the fate of so much of the city's flammable material in the great firestorm that levelled a large proportion of Halifax to the ground during the First World War. In December 1917, two ships, one French, the other Norwegian, collided in Halifax's harbour, Canada's major sea port. The SS *Imo*, the Norwegian freighter, rammed what was effectively a floating bomb, for the French vessel, the SS *Mont-Blanc*, was carrying not only munitions bound for the war in Europe, but also barrels of the highly volatile aviation fuel benzole. The resulting explosion, often said to be the biggest man-made explosion of the pre-atomic age, killed 2,000 people, injured as many as 10,000 others and devastated much of the north end of the city.

Frances Guille sat in the Candlelight Lounge of Halifax's Cameo Inn one evening over a drink with the local historian Phyllis Blakeley, who had been assisting her with her researches. Any disappointment she felt at returning to Ohio with so little to show for her trip was for the moment forgotten in her glow of pleasure at the 'satisfactory arrangements' she was making with the Hugo family for the publication of Adèle's journal. Uncharacteristically for such a meticulous worker, used to keeping her scholarly eye narrowly focused on the evidence and allowing herself no deviation from the textual straight and narrow, Guille shared with Blakeley one of her theories concerning Adèle's eventual fate, for which there was as yet no written confirmation, only hearsay. It was as though the relaxed atmosphere of the dimly lit lounge released in her a rash desire to push the story to a definite, if unproven, conclusion. Guille believed that Adèle had been 'hustled' into an asylum when she was brought back to Paris from Barbados in 1872 and kept there because her family didn't want to face the social embarrassment of having her back at home when her marriage to Pinson had been formally announced a decade earlier, but evidently hadn't taken place. Furthermore, she questioned the extent of Adèle's supposed 'madness', citing the reminiscences of several people who had visited Adèle in her luxurious incarceration at the Château de Suresnes and remarked upon 'how well she played the piano and how interestingly she talked.'

After years of patient work, the first volume of Frances Guille's edition of *Le Journal d'Adèle Hugo* was published in Paris by Minard in 1968 (three more would eventually appear). It covered the entries for just one year, 1852, during which the Hugo family were reunited, following their flight from Paris, at Marine Terrace, their first house of exile, a quarter of a mile from St Helier, the capital of the island of Jersey. In the lengthy biographical essay about Adèle with which she prefaced the text, Guille commented on the historical significance of the diary and the constellation of famous figures who flit across its pages – George Sand, Liszt, Paganini, Gérard de Nerval, Heine, Delacroix, as well as its presiding anti-hero, Napoleon III.

However, other much smaller sections of the journal don't belong to this record of the daily events and conversations of the Hugo household. Instead they form part of Adèle's intimate journal, an expression of her innermost secrets, written in a basic code that even a child could crack, in which she makes simple inversions of words – *sans* becomes *snas*, for example, and *mais* is replaced by *siam* – or inverts the first and the last syllable of a word – so *chambre* becomes *brecham*.

Standing on the grille floor of the London Library's stacks one afternoon, I reached up to the metal shelves and pulled down a volume of Adèle's journal. Flicking through the pages, I found it fell open at the record of a memory of a dream: 'One night as I slept, in the dreams which precede one's deepest sleep the face of an Englishman appeared before me and told me that he would play the role of a lover in my life.'

François Truffaut first read about Adèle Hugo and Frances Guille's edition of her journal in an article by the historian Henri Guillemin, published in 1969 in the weekly news magazine, *Le*

Nouvel Observateur. Truffaut was always a voracious reader. He had used books almost as much as the films flickering on the screens of the darkened cinemas of post-war Paris as an imaginative escape from the emotional privations of his childhood and upbringing. Reading, he once claimed, was the best way of forgetting a mother who could only stand him if he was silent. Much later, as a leading *auteur* of French cinema, and one, moreover, who had made his first forays into film by means of his pen, as a critic, Truffaut was fond of saying that he didn't care to make films for a public that didn't read books. 'I like the word "story",' he declared. 'I am a hundred per cent in favour of the novelistic approach to film.'

At the time of chancing upon Guillemin's article Truffaut was immersed in pre-production for his next film, which, like his earliest, heavily autobiographical masterpiece, *Les Quatre Cent Coups* ('The 400 Blows'), was concerned with the wounds inflicted by childhood. 'A nightmare of no affection . . . a nightmare of solitude' was how he described his own childhood, unable to wrest himself free from the associations of his early life. *L'Enfant Sauvage* ('The Wild Child') was based on the story of the ten-year-old feral child discovered in 1797 living in woods in the Aveyron region of southern France. Under the supervision and instruction of a brilliant young doctor, Jean Itard, played in the film by Truffaut himself, the wild child – renamed 'Victor' – was 'normalized': taught to stand properly, eat at a table and, in the course of the five years that Itard worked with him, even speak a few words and comprehend simple speech.

Part of the initial tug of attraction for Truffaut of Adèle Hugo's story was that it seemed like a variation on the theme of *L'Enfant Sauvage*, but this time with the process operating in reverse. Concentrating on Adèle's all-consuming pursuit of an absolute form of love, by travelling first to Nova Scotia and then to Barbados, Truffaut would portray her gradual disintegration in terms of a virtual retreat from humanity. Indeed, one of the most disturbing aspects of his interpretation would be the sense one has in the finished film that Adèle only ever interacts with other members of society in order to feed her overwhelming obsession.

Jean Gruault, Truffaut's long-time collaborator, who had written the script for *L'Enfant Sauvage*, was commissioned to draft a screenplay based on Adèle's journal, and in particular on the biographical elements furnished by Guille's introduction. Jean Hugo, in his mid-seventies and by now Adèle's closest living descendant, was at first wary about giving his consent for a film based on the life of his great-aunt, and about breaking the silence that had surrounded this mysterious figure for so long. 'I wonder if this sad story, which was always a jealously guarded family secret, won't be shocking on the screen,' he wrote to Truffaut at the beginning of 1971 from his home at Lunel in the Camargue. 'Doesn't mental disease . . . give a pathological overtone to this love story and take away all its human value?' An early draft of the script went a long way towards placating him and gaining his support. His sole reservation, he told Truffaut in a letter in April, was the physical depiction of Victor Hugo by an actor in scenes in flashbacks that showed Adèle's life in Guernsey. This was easily resolved. The final screenplay would dispense with the flashbacks and Hugo would be represented by photographs and in voice-over. Truffaut had already told him 'how passionately involved Jean Gruault and I have become with Adèle'. Now he wrote to Jean Hugo saying that his letter had made him very happy, 'for this film matters a great deal to me'.

Nevertheless, a further four years would pass before the cameras started rolling on *L'Histoire d'Adèle H.* Meanwhile Truffaut juggled other projects, took an extended break from making films and faced the stumbling block experienced by filmmakers the world over, of trying to raise enough money to finance the project. His usual backers thought the idea 'too literary', forcing Truffaut to admit that 'the name of Hugo did not exactly fire producers with enthusiasm'.

Surprisingly, the greatest obstacle turned out to be Frances Guille – or more precisely the financial demands she had made for the rights to her material. She requested 30,000 francs for screen rights and a payment of 200,000 francs as co-scenarist, both hefty sums in the circumstances. Guille, as Truffaut wrote to Jean Hugo, had 'put an American spoke in our French wheel'. Negotiations to reach an agreement continued for two years, with Truffaut threatening at one stage to shelve the project as 'a fiasco'. The money she had demanded, Truffaut told Guille, in a letter full of bitter regret, was 'in defiance of all logic, convention and common sense'. To Jean Gruault he denounced Guille as 'grasping', but no doubt she would have defended herself by pointing out that she had already spent more than a decade of her life excavating Adèle's story. The editorial process inched forward slowly. In 1971 Guille published another volume of the journal, again for a single year, 1853. She may well have been hoping to shore up financial support to ensure the long-term future of the edition.

If Truffaut was playing a double game with Guille, pretending to be on the verge of giving up the film in order to put pressure on her to back down, he succeeded. For eventually she accepted a much-reduced sum. In the tense and at times heated atmosphere of the protracted discussions aimed at reaching an agreement, Truffaut had half-jokingly written to Jean Gruault that 'six months after the bitch's death' he'd be setting up the first shot of *Adèle H.*

The ruthlessness of fate enacted a savage variation on his prediction. A week after seeing the finished film in New York, towards the end of 1975, Guille, who had responded to it with great emotion, in tears from beginning to end, collapsed and died from a heart attack.

Truffaut's resolve to make his film version of Adèle Hugo's story may well have had roots in a turbulent emotional relationship of the director's own.

Several summers ago, after making a trip to Villequier, I met up with R at Paris's Gare Montparnasse. There we boarded a first-class compartment on the TGV to Saint-Malo, where we were to spend a few days. We were busy squeezing our luggage onto the racks above our seats when a young woman, birdlike and animated and clearly on a mission, pushed past us, glanced quickly at the seats in the open compartment adjoining ours as if to check them, and hurriedly retreated again.

Almost immediately, a woman who could have passed for a well-preserved late middle age, but was probably older, dressed in a couture black-and-white check ensemble, entered the carriage, pulling a small fox-like terrier on a lead behind her. 'Mutton dressed as lamb', muttered R unchivalrously as the woman strode past us, giving off a strong stench of nicotine. Following her was a two-man, two-woman entourage, including the woman who'd preceded them all onto the train.

As they took their seats, the woman with the dog sat facing us in an aisle seat, clearly visible from where we were sitting. I identified her immediately as Catherine Deneuve. R has a tendency to become unduly excited in the presence of celebrity – that is, on the rare occasions when he manages to identify one correctly. He hadn't recognized Deneuve yet and so, in as audible a whisper as was decently possible, while instructing him to maintain some semblance of calm and dignity, I pointed her out to him. I explained her fame as the *femme fatale* of Gallic cinema and as one of the facial models for Marianne, symbol of the French Republic. For the rest of the journey he sat upright as if mesmerized, staring at Deneuve's famous face. '*Assis, Jacques, assis,*' she kept commanding the little dog, apparently oblivious to the attention of anyone else in the vicinity – including that of a young man seated across the aisle from her, who was having some difficulty controlling his breathing. I checked subsequently and found that she must already have been over 70 at this time, but her hair still resembled thick ropes of spun gold, while her skin had a distinctly rosy glow about it. ('Do you think that's the result of a facial peel?', R asked later, revealing more knowledge of cosmetic procedures than I'd have given him credit for.) At Rennes, where the train divided, Deneuve disembarked to smoke a couple of cigarettes in record time, and was immediately surrounded by a motley group of men, behaving like a swarm of flies buzzing around the *confiture*.

'Indeed, Catherine Deneuve is so beautiful', Truffaut once wrote, 'that any film she stars in could almost dispense with telling a story. I am convinced that the spectator will find happiness in just looking at Catherine and that this contemplation is worth the price of admission!' Truffaut got to know Deneuve when he cast her opposite Jean-Paul Belmondo in his 1969 film *La Sirène du Mississippi* ('Mississippi Mermaid'), and immediately became enchanted with her. In this he was conforming to a pattern of behaviour he exhibited throughout his career of habitually falling in love with his leading ladies. However, his affair with Deneuve was a more involving 'amorous relationship', as he called it, and their break-up at the end of 1970, not long after he read about Adèle Hugo's journal and first conceived the idea of the film, plunged him into deep depression. For months he sank into 'a black nightmare', unable to sleep, dependent on sedatives and sleeping pills, meanwhile hoping in vain that Deneuve would reverse her decision to separate from him.

Deneuve was Truffaut's initial choice to play his Adèle. Given the relationship between director and star, this would have added a daunting layer of complexity to the film. (And there was a tragic subtext connecting Deneuve to Adèle: Deneuve's elder sister, the actress Françoise Dorléac, had been killed, like Adèle's, in an accident.) But when *L'Histoire d'Adèle H.* came to be made in the mid-1970s, the much younger Isabelle Adjani was cast in what would be her first film role.

For Truffaut, *Adèle H.* became the story of a face, as his camera moved in on extreme close-ups of the 19-year-old actress's expression, creating a mood of claustrophobia and at times of almost unbearable enclosure. In practical terms this stylistic decision was the result of restraints on the film's budget. Early drafts of the screenplay had envisaged a much more lavish, larger-scale film. Jean Gruault's original script showed Adèle arriving at the Halifax Hotel in 1863 to find it overflowing with Southern officers, planters and slave traffickers, all of them preoccupied in conversations about the ongoing American Civil War – like a scene from the Hollywood spectacle *Gone with the Wind*. 'We wanted to make *Autant en emporte Adèle* ('Gone with Adèle')', Gruault joked years later.

Being forced to pare down the screenplay to fit the demands of a reduced budget helped Truffaut to strengthen his main theme as well as give the finished film a greater narrative coherence. Dispensing with most of the historical atmosphere and detail allowed him to concentrate on Adèle's *idée fixe*. In this final version every scene is centred on her perpetual dogging of Pinson's footsteps.

However, as Truffaut pulled the focus tighter and tighter on Adjani's face, his own obsession with the actress was growing. His feelings for her were unreciprocated, but no less passionate for all that, and he found the strain of directing her at times almost too much to bear. 'I watch her act,' he told one newspaper reporter on the set. 'I help her as I can, uttering thirty words when she would like a hundred, or fifty when only one, but the right one, is needed . . . In the evening, my eyes are tired from having looked at her too hard and listened to her all day.' To the American writer Helen Scott, a long-time collaborator, he confessed, after one especially draining week in the middle of the shoot, that he'd drunk too much champagne in order to knock himself out and 'render myself senseless'.

Filming in Guernsey increased the crew's sense of isolation and contributed to the powerful intensity of Adjani's performance and its impact on those around her. The melancholy of the subject matter generated a tension behind the scenes. 'There are times when we find ourselves whispering all day long,' Truffaut wrote to Scott, 'and it's only in the evening that we get our normal voices back.' It wasn't uncommon to find the make-up girls weeping in the background while Adjani was performing. Truffaut sometimes referred to his 'exile' in Guernsey, but he promised Scott, tongue in cheek, that he wouldn't be staying on the island 'nearly as long' as Victor Hugo. ('Yes, but he took [his mistress] Juliette [Drouet] with him, I can hear you say with gritted teeth.')

In Truffaut's interpretation, Lieutenant Pinson is in a sense the real victim. As played by the young English actor Bruce Robinson – with cheekbones to die for and a plushy, debauchee's mouth – Pinson is a good-for-nothing individual, certainly not someone worth crossing the ocean for. He is callow, debt-ridden and mercenary. But Truffaut sees that there is a dark humour to be derived from his situation. Pinson knows that Adèle isn't really in love with him, and that all that matters to her is the purity of her own feelings. He knows too that the only reason she wishes to become Mrs Pinson is to gain an identity of her own and to escape from the crushing weight of her father's fame. Adjani's Adèle will stop at nothing to achieve this. In a string of blackly comic scenes Adèle tries to bribe him with money (what she offers him is never enough); she pretends to be pregnant by him, stuffing a cushion underneath her dress and then, suddenly, desperately, revealing the pretence; she sends him a whore and then experiences the voyeuristic pleasure of observing his lovemaking through a window. Most damagingly for Pinson, she wrecks his engagement to another woman by contacting his fiancée's father and pretending that the lieutenant already has a wife – none other than Adèle herself.

I'd yet to discover how much of this scenario had any basis in historical fact and how much was pure fiction. Yet watching the film again, decades on from that first viewing in Oxford, I found myself riveted by the way in which Adèle is set on her own destruction. We all know something about how falling in love can be self-destructive: of how, just for a start, it rips at the core of your being and leaves you fixated on one individual to the exclusion of anyone or anything else. But the fascination of Truffaut's Adèle, and what gives her a true singularity, lies in the way in which there appears to be no limit to how far she is prepared to go in her pursuit of love.

———

In the grip of an obsession, in moments of despair that admit the slightest glimmer of self-awareness, you begin to wonder if it'll ever end; if you'll ever again be able to wake in the morning without being consumed by a single thought: the prospect of seeing the loved one again. This feeling is only prolonged and intensified, the denouement endlessly postponed, if your love remains unspoken. This was how it was with Julien, my companion on that trip to see *Adèle H.* during our final months at Oxford. He knew of course that I was in love with him. He could hardly have mistaken for anything else my constant brooding over him, the spending of all my leisure hours in his company. Our friends noticed it as well. 'You two should get married,' one of them joked, a remark received with raucous laughter from everyone else in the room, enjoying to the full the (then) delightful absurdity of the notion. I remember inwardly welcoming it as wider recognition of the fact that we were destined to be together. Julien, meanwhile, permitted himself an enigmatic smile.

After all these years I still recollect the feeling, running through me like an electric current, the moment he laid his head on my shoulder while we were having dinner the evening we'd been to see Truffaut's *Adèle H.* That, though, was as far as physical contact between us ever went. For the rest it was a matter of secrets. The secret of what I was unable to come clean about to anyone else. The secret of whatever he really felt for me. As I approached my final exams that summer I was half barmy with exhaustion and unable to keep my mind on a vital programme of revision. Lying awake at night, marking the hours with the chimes of the church of Saints Phil and Jim in the Woodstock Road, I hatched a madcap scheme of running away from Oxford in exam week. Daylight showed up the plan for the obvious non-starter it was. I ended up failing to do myself justice in finals, having committed the 'cardinal sin', as I was told later in a lengthy post-mortem over the decomposing corpse of my academic career, of giving 'short weight' in my answers.

An Oxford ball at Magdalen College was the climax of those final university days. As the sun set that evening, the golden stones of Magdalen's New Buildings turned slowly to the colour of pale lavender. The white tents erected for dining and dancing on the wide lawn opposite were decorated with brightly coloured lights. The hard rock of Meat Loaf and his band was sending shock waves through the medieval cloisters. I'd slipped a copy of the Everyman edition of Charlotte Brontë's *Villette* into my pocket to read in the sitting-out room during the night's long pauses. The only element of diversion for me was my friend Donald's decision to bound up to Iris Murdoch and tell her in the middle of a seemingly innocuous conversation that none of the characters in the novels of hers that he'd read had ever convinced him. Murdoch looked startled, as well she might, but not without a trace of bemusement at his audacity. Shortly before seven the next morning, buttonholes wilting and feeling dead with exhaustion, we gathered for the traditional survivors' photo.

Julien had been distant for much of the evening. I saw nothing of him for two days after the ball, by which time thunderous rainstorms had swept across the placid blue skies. Finally I went to seek him out, and came across him emerging from the porter's lodge. As if conducting me to an interview, he guided me across the quad to his room. In what seemed too deliberate an attempt to inflict hurt, he enjoined me not to stand too close to him. He appealed to me not to try and see him again once the vacation started in a few days' time. The only fragment of speech that has stayed with me is of him saying that we were coming apart and that there was nothing I could do to push us back together again. The first and last time he made any direct reference to the relationship between us.

My world came crashing about my ears. Or rather it did, but then with surprising speed, and just as much suddenness, it repaired itself. By the time I saw Julien again in London the following summer I was beginning to wonder what all my fuss had been about. Clearly I didn't possess the necessary quality of unremitting (and hopeless) constancy to someone who had resolutely rejected it. Maybe, as is often the way with first loves, what motivated me more was a desire for desire, and Julien was simply a means to achieving this end. But occasional thoughts of him have pursued me throughout my life.

I think of him again when I watch the penultimate scene of Truffaut's film. Its inspiration possibly derives from Truffaut's love of Balzac, one of his favourite writers, and specifically from Balzac's short story 'Adieu'. This is the tale of a soldier who returns from the Napoleonic Wars to find that the woman he loves has gone mad in his absence and no longer recognizes him. All she can do is repeat the word she spoke to him as they parted: '*Adieu*'. The soldier's attempts to make her recognize him, by recreating the conditions of their last meeting, eventually succeed. The woman recognizes him, smiles, repeats the word '*Adieu*', and dies.

The film plays a variation on this. To the mournful strains of Maurice Jaubert's music, Adèle Hugo walks through the streets of Bridgetown. Her hair is a knotted, tangled mass, her clothes are torn and bedraggled. Her face is a mask of deathly pallor. Pinson sees her and follows her along the dusty route. But as he finally catches up with her and speaks her name, she walks on in a state of resolute abstraction, completely oblivious to him. She has arrived at her goal and realized herself in self-destruction. Pinson no longer exists for her. The obsession, and her unrequited love, have become her identity.

Now, half a lifetime after first seeing the film, I was setting out to see what more I could discover about Adèle's story.

3

Fathers and Daughters

In interviews about his film François Truffaut claimed not to understand the origins of his fixation with Adèle H. But he did admit to recognizing all too well the overwhelming effect an *idée fixe* can have on an individual, likening it to a bout of vertigo, which suddenly removes the ground from beneath one's feet and sends the world spinning uncontrollably around one's head.

Although he never articulated it, there was something more that drew Truffaut irresistibly to Adèle Hugo's story, and that was the unanswered questions they shared about their paternity. Truffaut was illegitimate, born of an unknown father. When he was not quite two years old his mother married Roland Truffaut, who adopted François and gave him his name. The adoption was kept secret from the child and only discovered accidentally by François as he was growing up. The identity of his biological father remained unresolved, despite Truffaut's attempts in adult life to search for him and his belief at one stage that a Jewish dentist by the name of Lévy, tracked down by a private detective who'd been set on the trail, must be his father.

And was Victor Hugo really Adèle's father? Rumours that she was not Hugo's daughter swirled around her name from her teenage years. As I turned back to the beginning of Adèle's story, I found that the uncertainty concerning her paternal origins has never been quite dispelled, though the degree to which she acknowledged or was even aware of it remains unknown. What gave these rumours a certain impetus, even an authenticity, was that they derived from someone who might have been supposed to have a decent-sized inkling of the truth: Adèle's godfather, the literary critic Charles Augustin Sainte-Beuve. Sainte-Beuve had insinuated himself at the Hugo family fireside before embarking on an affair with Madame Hugo. He subsequently claimed – admittedly more than a tad ambiguously – that Adèle was the product of their sexual union.

While her godfather would sow the seed of doubt that Adèle was Hugo's daughter, Hugo himself fabricated a false date of birth for her. This has fooled generations of writers, among them Frances Guille, editor of Adèle Hugo's journals. Hugo told friends that Adèle, his fifth and final child – his firstborn, Léopold, had died at three months in 1823 – was born on 28 July 1830 as gunshots were smashing the roof slates of his Paris home during the *Trois Glorieuses*. These were the three days of bloody protest and insurrection that saw the last Bourbon king, Charles X, swept away and replaced by a new, constitutional monarch, the popular Duke of Orléans, Louis-Philippe.

In fact, Adèle Hugo arrived almost a month after the July Revolution, on 24 August. This adjustment in chronology is another Hugolian sleight of hand, evidence of Hugo's growing tendency, as he moved into his thirties, of forcing his life to march to the rhythms of history, realigning the personal with significant public events in order to make the life and the times appear more coherent than they actually were.

With Adèle's birthplace we at last tread the terra firma of factual certainty. She was born at 9 rue Jean-Goujon, a single house, long gone, standing idly in an as yet undeveloped street surrounded by the deserted stretch of land, given over to market gardeners, known as the Champs-Élysées.

Her birth may not have coincided with the political tumult in Paris, but she could scarcely have arrived at a more critical moment in her father's career. Not yet 30, Victor Hugo was already being hailed as the guiding star of France's Romantic Movement. Six months earlier, the opening night of his play *Hernani* had become a battleground, as Romantics skirmished in the aisles with Classical supporters, pitting Shakespeare against Racine, liberty against convention and, as a prelude to that summer's violence, freedom against autocracy. Romanticism, Hugo declared, was as much a revolution as its political sister, and like wolves, 'revolutions don't eat one another'.

Already celebrated as a lyric poet, now a revolutionary as well as a notorious – some said barbarian – playwright, Hugo was seriously behind schedule with the historical novel set in fifteenth-century Paris that he'd been researching for the past couple of years. In late 1828 he had sold the rights to the book to the publisher Charles Gosselin. The first delivery date came and went. So did the second. Facing a fine for every week the manuscript failed to arrive after 1 December 1830, Hugo started writing on 25 July, three days before rioting broke out in the streets of Paris and stray bullets started flying across his garden. He begged for yet another reprieve. Revolutions were far from ideal times for the fulfilment of literary contracts, he advised Gosselin. As excuses for failed delivery go, this was a pretty good one, and Gosselin granted a final extension of a further two months.

Hugo bought a bottle of ink and wrapped himself in a huge grey knitted shawl. He locked away his formal clothes so he wouldn't be tempted to leave the house, 'and entered his novel', Madame Hugo later wrote, 'as if it were a prison': excellent advice for all errant authors.

Buried somewhere in the digressive depths of his fast-expanding novel, you get a sense of the presence of Hugo's months-old daughter in the 'tragic grimace' on the face of Pierre Gringoire, the struggling poet, described by Hugo as resembling that of a newborn baby with colic. For Adèle's christening at the church of Saint-Philippe-du-Roule in the last weeks of September, her father emerged fleetingly from his seclusion. Then it was back down to work.

His enforced self-imprisonment was successful. Hugo finished *Notre-Dame de Paris* in mid-January 1831 and the book was published with much fanfare, to mixed reviews and brisk business, that spring.

Until recently I hadn't read the novel since my schooldays. Finding what must have been an abridged English translation in the school library, I consumed it in a couple of sittings when I should have been studying for Physics O-Level. The version I read was called *The Hunchback of Notre Dame*. Inevitably this brings to mind the spectacle of an eye-rolling Charles Laughton as the grotesque bell-ringer Quasimodo in the famous 1930s film version, from whose pleading, imploring gaze I've always recoiled. Whereas the first English translation by William Hazlitt the younger stuck to the original French title, most of the many subsequent ones, beginning with Frederic Shoberl's in 1833, have called it by the Hunchback name. The change in title heralded a shift in the popular perception of the novel away from its true hero – the cathedral – and from Hugo's intention of reclaiming and redeeming the Gothic style of architecture, to an emphasis on the book's melodramatic and frequently far-fetched plot.

Going back to the novel, I felt overawed, and slightly oppressed, by the impressive tableaux that serve as the story's backdrop – or just as often as the foreground. Never for a moment do you forget Hugo's theatrical background, for the world of the novel is like a series of heavily detailed and constructed sets being rolled out across the stage. There's a lack of intimacy as a consequence, and, as the writer V. S. Pritchett so memorably put it, the characters are larger than life as individuals and only life-size when they are part of a crowd.

On this rereading, my attention is drawn to the relationship between Esmeralda, the beautiful gypsy dancer, and one of the secondary characters, Phoebus de Châteaupers, a captain of the King's Archers. Esmeralda is trapped in a marriage of convenience with Gringoire; she is lusted after by the wicked Archdeacon Frollo; and she is saved and protected for a time by Quasimodo, in an archetypal beauty-and-the-beast scenario. However, Esmeralda's own feelings of love are reserved for the dashing Captain Phoebus. 'I have long dreamt of an officer who would save my life,' she tells him. 'My dream had a beautiful uniform like you, and a noble bearing, and a sword.'

But hers is a blind love. Phoebus is vain, untrustworthy and a womanizer. He declares his love for Esmeralda, but all he wants from her is a night of passion before he marries another woman, the fashionable, wealthy Fleur-de-Lys. At a climactic moment Esmeralda gazes down from the roof of Notre-Dame and cries out for Phoebus to come to her: 'Her voice, her face, her gesture, her whole person bore the heartrending expression of a shipwrecked sailor making a distress signal to a ship sailing gaily past in a ray of light on the distant horizon.'

Here, in Esmeralda's doomed love for Phoebus, Victor Hugo seems to prefigure Adèle's later plight. It's as if he is laying an accidental curse on his baby daughter in the uncanny way in which fiction seems to be anticipating real life.

While Hugo was carefully totting up the daily word count that would enable him to meet the deadline on his novel, he received a letter from Sainte-Beuve, the critic who had contributed much to Hugo's reputation and growing mystique, and someone Hugo thought of as his closest friend. In the letter, Sainte-Beuve revealed that he was desperately in love with Hugo's wife. He did not say whether Madame Hugo returned his feelings.

At 27, Sainte-Beuve was nearly three years Hugo's junior. His praise of Hugo's *Odes et Ballades* in 1826 had introduced him to the poet's circle, and he had quickly become an intimate of both Hugo and his wife. Initially he lived – along with his mother – in the same street as the Hugos, and when they moved he continued to visit them, sometimes twice daily. He talked attentively and flatteringly to Hugo about his work, brought toys for the children, and found himself increasingly drawn to Madame, the angel of the hearth. In darker moments Sainte-Beuve spoke of the torment of never having been loved. With the Hugos he could enjoy the cosy domestic life he had always longed for. 'I no longer live except through you,' he told Hugo, 'I am inspired only beside you, and by what is around you.'

But now this situation had changed irreparably. Never again could he cross the Hugos' threshold, Sainte-Beuve wrote in his letter to Hugo. How could he sit at his fireside having betrayed his trust and with Madame Hugo unable to meet his gaze without first taking note of her husband's?

Every account of Sainte-Beuve harps on about his physical ugliness: the globular head too big for his body, his long, inquisitive nose, his scrubby red hair generally covered by a black skull cap. Biographers have sniggered behind their hands at his genital malformation. He suffered from hypospadias, a condition in which the urinary opening is not at the head of the penis, and the foreskin is often undeveloped. This can make it difficult to pee standing up and may affect the fertility of the sufferer.

Writers on Sainte-Beuve are no less agreed on the brilliancy of his talk. According to the Goncourts this was a kind of fluent chatter, made up of tiny touches, like a painter dabbing away at his palette. In full flow his unprepossessing appearance would be suddenly irradiated by a transforming intelligence. He was a natural confessor, with the concomitant disadvantage that what you told him generally did the rounds. To Madame Hugo, Sainte-Beuve offered himself as an empathetic listener. After nearly eight years of marriage she was exhausted by her sequence of pregnancies.

As a consequence, from the spring of 1830 she had felt forced to deny Hugo his conjugal rights. As Hugo burrowed deeper into his writing she felt neglected and undervalued, reinforced in her belief that she was of insufficient stature to be the wife of the man who was beginning to regard himself as a demi-god, an Olympio no less. Sainte-Beuve's motives in their relationship were a toxic mix. He was moved and inspired by Madame's goodness to him, but inclined to spite, jealousy, revenge even, whenever he felt excluded from the family circle, or shut out by other rivals for Hugo's attention. Like many others he was irritated by Hugo's growing egotism. Perhaps too he had reached a point of painful recognition that he was never going to break through as a poet or novelist. Sainte-Beuve would go on to consolidate his reputation as a great critic, but never begin to approach the creative genius of his estranged friend.

A definitive answer to the hotly debated question of whether or not – and, if so, when – Sainte-Beuve and Madame Hugo consummated their relationship is obscured by the destruction of the bulk of their correspondence. In the winter of 1885, with both long dead, an enormous bonfire of Madame's love letters took place in Paris. Each packet was read by a group of participants, including two of Madame Hugo's relations, before being cast onto a blazing fire in an auto-da-fé that in its mystery and intrigue has a place in French literary history, rather as the destruction of Lord Byron's memoirs in the grate of his publisher's London offices does in the English equivalent.

Some of those who read the letters that day testified for posterity that they offered irrefutable proof of adultery having taken place. All that can now be said with certainty is that in the autumn of 1831, nine months or so after his confession to Victor Hugo, Sainte-Beuve persuaded Madame to start meeting him in churches for half an hour of 'eternal and delicious memories' in the corner of a chapel, and then subsequently in rented rooms, and sometimes in the Hugos' apartments when Madame was alone. At this stage the affair begins to resemble a Feydeau farce. The concierge got used to seeing Sainte-Beuve climbing the stairs disguised as an old woman in a veil and a wig. At other times, the subterfuge involved anticipated by more than two decades a plotline from *Madame Bovary* as Sainte-Beuve and Madame trundled around the city in a closed carriage, like Flaubert's Emma and her lover, the law student Léon Dupuis.

Leaving aside the imponderable of whether Sainte-Beuve was actually impotent, this chronology appears to rule out the possibility that he could be little Adèle's father: the baby was conceived in late 1829 before, presumably, any physical relationship between Madame Hugo and Sainte-Beuve could have started in earnest. Yet a claim to Adèle's paternity is what Sainte-Beuve appears at first to be slyly suggesting in a poem dedicated to her at the age of two that was included in his collection *Livre d'Amour*. This was privately printed in 1843, but some copies leaked out – or were leaked. The final verse of '*À la Petite Ad . . .*' contains the lines, 'Oh you who came then, child, you whom I see /Pure, yet in some ways resembling myself!'

Was this a confession? Or, much more likely, merely an acknowledgement of the fact that Adèle was indeed Hugo's daughter, but conceived at a time (as the previous line of the poem implies) when Sainte-Beuve was 'swimming each night' in her mother's 'warm thoughts'?

In the review of *Odes et Ballades* that first brought him to Hugo's notice, Sainte-Beuve had praised the poems that spoke of the poet's love for his wife, and of 'the purity and chastity within the bonds of marriage'. It was these that he had subsequently set out deliberately to undermine and destabilize.

For Hugo the shock of the simultaneous loss of his greatest love and his most important friendship could not have been more profound. He realized 'with absolute certainty', as he told Sainte-Beuve in the concealed warfare that set the tone of the exchange of letters between them, that 'it is possible for one who had all my love to love me no longer'. Sometimes he signed these letters with the words 'your brother'. This idea of fraternity leaves behind the strong impression that he was reliving in his mind the distressing love triangle of a decade earlier between himself, Adèle Foucher (as Madame Hugo was before her marriage) and Hugo's brother

Eugène. Long in love with his younger brother's fiancée, Eugène's bitter jealousy had finally given way to madness on Victor's wedding day in October 1822. He was pronounced incurably insane and admitted to an asylum where he died 15 years later.

How often does a man who has been cheated on by his wife resist the compulsion to retaliate by having an affair of his own? A gorgeous apparition, dressed in pink and silver damask, pearls and feathers, swam before Victor Hugo's eyes on the first night of his play *Lucrèce Borgia*, early in 1833. Her name was Juliette Drouet, a second-rate actress in a minor role, with a pile of debts, a young daughter called Claire (by the sculptor James Pradier) and a murky sexual past. For the next half century she would be Hugo's mistress. Once tasted, though, the thrill of furtive romance needed to be experienced again and again. Over the years Hugo would indulge in numerous casual affairs, in addition to chancier encounters that risked exposure and dangerous scandal, as his sexual appetite, far from decreasing with age, seemed only to grow. 'It was very nice of me just now, and very trusting, to concede that a *blonde* hair could and did come from your brown mop,' Juliette wrote to Hugo in 1840, suspecting him of having strayed from her with a blue-eyed blonde.

Whether unfounded or not, Hugo retained his own suspicions about his baby daughter as he leaned over to look at her in her cradle. 'I know not, sleeping angel, if I am your father,' he wrote in a fragment of a poem not published until after his death, 'but I adopt you with my blessing.'

In the Eurostar departure lounge at St Pancras I drummed my fingers on the arm of my seat in a mixture of impatience and anxiety. The 8.31 service to Paris was delayed, passengers were informed over the tannoy, due to 'technical difficulties'. We checked our passports and tickets for the umpteenth time, charged our phones and bought newspapers, coffee and water. Eventually we were herded up the escalators onto the train and told that on current estimates we would be half an hour late arriving at the Gare du Nord. But then at our destination, the train having rolled in smoothly alongside the platform, the doors would not open, and the group of businessmen sharing my carriage stood on either side of the exit like caged runners itching to be set free.

I was in Paris to meet Jean-Marc Hovasse, Victor Hugo's biographer. Worried that I would keep him waiting, or miss him altogether, I hurried out to the front of the station, avoiding the canopied queue for cabs on the right side of the concourse, and hailed a taxi from the rank in the middle of the road. It's a twenty-minute drive to the Place des Vosges in the Marais and, as the cab entered this oldest and most desirable of Paris squares, surrounded on all sides by peachy-red brick house fronts with their blue slate roofs, I saw the unmistakeable figure of Professor Hovasse, tall and gangly like a Gallic version of the *University Challenge* quizmaster Bamber Gascoigne, walking at a great pace around the open arcades at the foot of the buildings.

Speedily leaving my taxi, I ran in pursuit, never quite managing to catch up with him as he turned the corner into a further arcade full of chic art galleries, jewellery shops and restaurants. Finally, at the house bearing the brass plate, *Maison Victor Hugo*, he came to a halt and, reaching him at last, I rushed forward to introduce myself.

The Hugo family moved to a second-floor apartment here, at No. 6 Place Royale (as the Place des Vosges was called prior to the 1848 Revolution), in October 1832, and for more than a century it has been preserved as a museum. It was the scene of Adèle Hugo's earliest memories. Three years after arriving here, at the age of five, and described as 'very advanced' by her older sister Léopoldine, she started school at Mademoiselle Briant's, a short walk away at No. 17 Place Royale.

Jean-Marc Hovasse and I entered a nearby brasserie where he kindly bought me a plate of *dorade* and we talked in English, as his command of my language is superior to my spoken French. He was still in his twenties when he was commissioned to write a single-volume biography to commemorate the bicentenary of Hugo's birth in 2002. His publisher hadn't been expecting what turned out to be only a first instalment, totalling at a conservative estimate some half a million words, covering the years to 1851 and Hugo's departure from France into exile. Hovasse describes his publisher as 'very understanding' – as indeed he must have been, as he ended up accepting a plan for three fat volumes for the entire life. Two have been published so far, and Hovasse is writing the third. It's become something of a cliché to suggest that a weighty, heavily researched biography will never be superseded, but in the case of Victor Hugo at any rate it's very difficult to believe that anything on this scale will be attempted again. Is he obsessed, I asked Hovasse? He smiled and waved his hand as if to bat away the question, but after a moment's thought replied, 'I think I must be.'

Literary biography in France, Hovasse explained, is generally written as 'a sort of novel'. There isn't any requirement for specialist knowledge, only sympathy – or antipathy – for the subject. The English model, of what he calls 'faultless erudition' and 'sound annotation', is much closer to what he is trying to achieve.

In an article published as a kind of declaration of principle when the first volume of his *Victor Hugo* appeared, Hovasse compared a good biography to successful surgery, which 'can only be done by a real specialist'. His priority has always been to chart what he calls the 'essential interaction' between the life and the work. 'I simply can't imagine', he said, 'writing the biography of a writer without fully taking into account his texts, all his words, published and unpublished.'

Later, on the train back to London, I reflected that Hovasse's refusal to sacrifice the work in favour of the life – a worthy objective that stands at the heart of any worthwhile modern biography of a writer – owes something to the legacy of Sainte-Beuve as a critic. It was Sainte-Beuve, after all, who argued that nothing one might be able to find about an author was irrelevant to an understanding of his writing. '*Chercher l'homme dans l'oeuvre*' – 'look for the man in the work' – was his mantra, an approach later decried by Proust, who dismissed Sainte-Beuve's biographical criticism as 'literary botany'.

Hovasse is disinclined to judge Victor Hugo. Instead, as he wrote in his article, he hopes, as objectively as possible, to present his reader with all the elements necessary to form his own judgement. In the course of our conversation, one thing had surprised me, and that was when Hovasse said that he had never found himself out of sympathy with Hugo.

'Not even', I asked, 'when his attitude as a father meant that he tried to keep Adèle Hugo confined to home on the Channel Islands, unable to marry a man of her choice?'

'But that was the way in which unmarried women of her class were treated in the nineteenth century.'

I had wondered about the extent to which the sight of his younger daughter growing up might have revived painful memories for Hugo of her mother's affair with Sainte-Beuve. However, Hovasse emphasized that there is plenty of evidence in letters and Adèle's own journal of an affectionate relationship between father and daughter. She recalled him teasing and tickling her as a toddler, while in a poem from *Les Contemplations*, written when Adèle was twelve, Hugo tenderly depicts his two daughters sitting at a gateway to a garden, the elder, Léopoldine, as a swan, and Adèle as a dove: 'Beautiful, alive, they catch the light of the sun.' In a marble urn, a bouquet of carnations 'with long, fragile stems' looks at them, 'fixed and living in turn',

And shivers in the shadows where it appears to be
A flight of butterflies frozen in ecstasy.

Jean-Marc Hovasse had thoughtfully asked Gérard Audinet to join us for coffee. Audinet, dark and stocky with black-rimmed spectacles, is the Director of both the *Maison Hugo* in the Place des Vosges and Hauteville House, the Hugo house of exile in Guernsey, where he has been spearheading a major project of renovation. Audinet's background is in the visual arts, having worked for 20 years for Paris's Museum of Modern Art. After lunch he offered to show me the new exhibition at the *Maison Hugo* centring on the Hugo family as a family of artists.

Passing through the body scanners that have been in operation since the 2015 terror attacks on Paris, and into the ground floor area, where tickets and souvenirs are sold, we climbed to the Hugos' apartment on the second. If the house at Villequier could be said to be 'Léopoldine's museum', the Place des Vosges site is very definitely the headquarters of Victor Hugo Incorporated, a national monument to France's 'noble poet' in the French capital that Hugo once referred to as 'the city of cities'. Maybe his poetry isn't memorized as it once was, and perhaps the novels are too daunting in length, too complex in scope and detail, to win over a popular modern readership. Yet there can be no doubt of Victor Hugo's eternal place in the cultural zeitgeist, not least through the multiple retellings of his stories for stage, television and film.

What happened next rather proved this point. A youngish female teacher was having trouble controlling her group of unruly teenagers. They lay sprawled on the stairway, shouting vague obscenities at one another, and obstructing sightseers attempting to climb the stairs with outstretched legs and rucksacks.

Suddenly the air was filled with the sound of a light soprano voice. The teacher was singing a song from the musical of *Les Misérables*. It was 'On My Own', an anthem of unrequited love performed in the show by the impoverished teenager Éponine, whose feelings for Marius are unreturned. The effect was instantaneous. The singer's pupils were silenced in open-mouthed astonishment, a silence only broken by the round of scattered applause into which they burst at the conclusion of the song. As I passed up the stairs and looked down I caught the teacher's eye. She appeared as startled as everyone else at her impromptu rendition.

Today the second floor is arranged and decorated to evoke different periods of Victor Hugo's life. An ante-chamber depicts his ancestors and family, including his father, the Napoleonic General Léopold Hugo. It covers the years of his marriage and the birth of his children, leading up to the period of his early literary successes in the 1820s. The Chinese drawing room preserves the décor of Juliette Drouet's own house of exile from the Guernsey years, displaying both Hugo's inexhaustible appetite for antique bric-a-brac and his talents as an interior designer. His humorous drawings line the walls: a Chinaman dozing off in a rowing boat, a red-eyed devil sitting, arms folded, in an urn. The final room recreates Hugo's bedroom in the Avenue d'Eylau, the Paris address where he spent his final years.

Charles Dickens thought the Hugos' apartment was like the props room 'of some gloomy vast old Theatre'. Some visitors in Hugo's lifetime already viewed it as a museum, with its profusion of antique sculpture, Sèvres porcelain and magnificent tapestries. Still others saw it as a version of a Gothic fantasy, the light pouring through the stained glass of an ogee window and casting a rainbow of surreal colours onto the carved oak chairs.

The *salon rouge*, the walls covered in red damask and dominated by David d'Angers' 1838 marble bust of Hugo – the existence of which alone, Hugo complimented the sculptor, would guarantee him immortality – is no longer in its original position, currently occupied by the Chinese drawing room. However, its recreated grandeur is a reminder of the spectacle of evening parties at the Place Royale apartment, when distinguished writers, artists and musicians crowded into its rooms – in spite of the inadequate refreshments on offer – to pay court to Victor Hugo.

For a moment I imagined one of them, Franz Liszt, throwing back his head and pounding the piano keys playing a Beethoven funeral march. A divan surmounted by a kind of dais once stood on a large platform at one end of the room. Hugo didn't actually ascend this improvised throne, but its presence was in keeping with the aura of kingship that clung to him. 'The man seemed so great,' wrote one observer, 'that I saw around him only men who were infinitely small.' To the novelist Stendhal, Hugo was '*determined* to be extraordinary'. Hugo's utter conviction of this superiority was to bring him a growing list of enemies, affronted by such unconcealed egotism. No wonder he would inspire the poet Heinrich Heine's neologism *Hugoiste* – defined as an extreme form of egoist.

More difficult to recapture in the ordered, cordoned-off world of the museum are the less public moments of domestic life that form the subject matter of poetry from these early years at the Place Royale. In one poem, '*Date Lilia*' ('Lilies in Tribute'), Hugo set out to defuse the rumours about his wife's affair by paying tribute to Madame's virtues as a wife and mother. She was his 'pride', his 'trust', his 'refuge', the 'purity above my head, /The secret marble figure by my head' (Sainte-Beuve's review scoffed that Hugo was throwing a pinch of 'lily-dust' in the reader's eyes). He went on to say that if either he or her children 'start to fall', she 'helps them with her hand, me with her heart'. In the summer of 1837, all Madame Hugo's maternal feeling and nursing skills were to the fore when seven-year-old Adèle was taken gravely ill with typhoid fever. She was twice bled with leeches, and for a time the worst was feared. Even after she began to recover, her convalescence was protracted. Adèle's attendance at her first ball the following February, when she was described by Léopoldine as wearing a little red skirt with a black velvet bodice, signalled her return to health.

The poster for the exhibition I'd come to see showed a photograph of Victor Hugo towards the end of his life. His beard was white, he wore a benign smile and his arms were wrapped around his grandchildren, Jeanne and Georges, the children of his dead son Charles, whose affectionate company lit up his old age. He looked engaging, to all intents and purposes like a welcoming Santa Claus in his grotto. On display was work in the arts – painting, drawing, photography, music – of five generations of the Hugo family, from examples of designs by Hugo himself, to prints by his mathematician nephew Léopold, to buttons created by his great-grandson François for the fashion designer Elsa Schiaparelli, right down to paintings and photographs by present-day members of the Hugo clan.

What came across most strongly to me as I made my way around the exhibition was a sense of the oppressive burden of a great name. Many of the members of this family struggled to escape from the shadow of their illustrious progenitor. Perhaps only Jean Hugo, another of Hugo's great-grandsons, famous for the avant-garde originality of his paintings, managed to break free.

On one wall hung a group of framed music manuscripts, their black ink long since faded to watery brown: Adèle Hugo's musical compositions. Gérard Audinet explained the headache they'd given him as he'd tried but failed to get them performed for the opening of the exhibition. So, more than 150 years after they were composed, these settings of various poems, including works by Adèle's father, still await their first performance.

It was summers spent as a young child in the early 1830s with the Bertin family at the Château des Roches that first encouraged

Adèle's musical gifts. This fine house was situated high up in a valley close to the village of Bièvres, in countryside 20 miles or so outside Paris. The journalist Louis-François Bertin lived here with his two sons and his daughter Louise, a musician and poet.

The enchanted setting of Les Roches, far removed from the dusty boulevards of the city, had a beneficial effect on the Hugo parents and children – though Madame Hugo had an ulterior motive for the 'two leagues' she claimed to walk each day. She was keeping assignations with Sainte-Beuve at the local church (Hugo may have grown suspicious as he noted that despite all this daily exertion, his wife was visibly putting on weight). Not to be outdone, on subsequent visits Hugo installed Juliette Drouet 'in a prison cell of love', two and a half miles away at Metz, where they left letters and poems for each other in the hollow of a tree.

Hugo wrote thanking Louise Bertin for 'such delicious evenings by your piano, with the children playing all about us'. When Adèle's attention could be diverted from her fascination with the cows grazing in the great park surrounding the house, she and Léopoldine would beg Mademoiselle Louise to perform for them. Louise Bertin was already working on an opera based on *Notre-Dame de Paris*. Entitled *La Esmeralda*, with a libretto by Hugo, it concentrates on the love story between Esmeralda (who is spared execution) and Captain Phoebus, and significantly reduces Quasimodo's role. As Louise had been physically handicapped from birth and was unable to stand, rehearsals were supervised by Hector Berlioz, but the short run of performances was a humiliation for her: the leading soprano lost her voice; there were cries of accusation from the audience that the opera was in fact by Berlioz; and on the final night a near riot broke out. Despite living for 40 years more, Louise Bertin never wrote another opera.

For Adèle, this very early introduction to the piano developed into serious study of the instrument throughout her teenage years. By her early twenties she was attempting her own compositions. These would earn commendations for their 'grace' and 'originality', as well as 'their remarkable poetic sentiment', from the Professor of Composition at the Paris Conservatoire, Ambroise Thomas.

Displayed on the walls of the *Maison Hugo* was one of Adèle's melodies, for which her father had done the signal honour of providing some verses. You can see how the swift, darting path of her notes might have suggested to him the quality of birdsong, as he imagined a bird flying 'through the space /where love catches fire'. The words are written in Hugo's own hand.

Further back along the display was another collaboration between father and daughter. On this occasion it was Adèle setting to music the three songs of the child revolutionary Gavroche from *Les Misérables*. It isn't clear whether further adaptation was planned, but there is no doubt that more than a century before *Les Mis* swept London and Broadway, Adèle was the first to exploit, in a small but definite way, the musical potential of Victor Hugo's famous novel.

Then there are the lives that are cut short and have little or no chance of self-expression.

Like the house at Villequier, the apartment in the Place des Vosges is filled with mementos of Léopoldine: her cashmere shawl and kid gloves, her napkin ring engraved with her family nickname Didine, a painting of her first communion at the age of 12, in the autumn of 1836, wearing the dress made for her by Juliette Drouet from one of her old organdie gowns.

Léopoldine was serious-minded, discreet enough to handle the fraught and complex relationship developing between Hugo's wife and mistress, and doted on by her father in letters that suggest at times an impassioned lover rather than a watchful parent. In the wake of her mother's affair with Sainte-Beuve – which was certainly on the wane by 1836 – Léopoldine had become her father's closest confidante. It was almost inevitable therefore that her falling in love with Charles Vacquerie, brother of Hugo's chief disciple Auguste Vacquerie, whom she met on summer visits to Villequier at the end of the 1830s, and to whom she became engaged shortly before her eighteenth birthday, in July 1842, should rouse Hugo to fits of jealous opposition.

In the end he gave way, having for a time disguised his determination not to lose Léopoldine with insinuations about the unsuitability of this son of a ship-owning family as a husband for the daughter of one of literature's immortals. The marriage went ahead in Paris on 15 February 1843. 'I haven't gone a quarter of an hour without thinking of you,' Hugo wrote to Léopoldine after a month. 'I know you are happy, I rejoice in it from a distance, and with a melancholy pleasure.'

In May, Madame Hugo was staying with the young couple and writing home that 'Villequier is magnificent now. The water gives life to everything.' Before he left Paris with Juliette Drouet to embark on their tour of south-west France and Spain, Hugo spent a short time with Léopoldine and her husband, apparently reconciled at last to their union: 'I feel I must thank you, my good Charles, for the happiness you have given me . . . I saw my daughter happy in you, and you happy in her. Remember my children, that that is paradise. Live in it, both of you, until you die.'

On my way out of the *Maison Hugo* on the afternoon of my visit, I noticed the portrait of Léopoldine by Auguste de Châtillon, which hangs in the *salon rouge*. I retraced my steps to take a closer look at it. Completed the year before her first catechism, it shows Victor Hugo's elder daughter at the age of eleven. She sits on a Chinese-patterned chair, a Book of Hours open before her, with a tiny red flower behind one ear to match the colour of her dress. She has turned to the spectator with an intense, devotional look.

Back at home I checked various reference books for further information about the painting. One detail stood out. The words on the pages that Léopoldine has been reading, and against which her hand gently brushes, are from Psalm 116, commonly used in services for the dead:

The cords of death entangled me, the anguish of the grave came upon me; I was overcome by trouble and sorrow.

The water in his eyes glinted as it caught the light. As the tears spilled over and down his face his head dropped and he looked away. But he'd seen me looking at him, and in a split second turned to confront me with all the old violence in his speech – more violent in sheer force than actual profanity – showing that he felt embarrassed by this sudden exposure of his grief.

Or perhaps unmanned by it.

'What the hell are *you* staring at?'

Someone sitting at the kitchen table had mentioned Caroline. She was my father's daughter from his second marriage, following his divorce from my mother. Born prematurely late one summer, suffering from a hole in the heart, Caroline had barely survived until the following Easter, dying after eight months in Great Ormond Street Hospital. Much of Caroline's short existence was marked by a struggle to put on weight and to breathe free of the chronic coughing and wheezing produced by the fluid congestion in her lungs. I may be idealizing her appearance in long retrospect when I describe her as pretty like a tiny doll, black-haired and dark-eyed, with lengthy, extraordinarily graceful fingers. I like to think, though, that in this instance memory isn't playing me false.

'You'll be pleased to hear that your ½ sister, Lady Caroline, has now topped 6lbs,' my father had written to me when, at a little over two months, the baby finally began to gain weight. Sadly her progress didn't last long. In the New Year an operation on her damaged heart went badly wrong. Her brain was briefly deprived of its oxygen supply and fatal complications ensued.

Following Caroline's death, my father avoided all mention of her. Undoubtedly this was a strategy designed in part to protect the feelings of my stepmother. But it was also evident from the handful of occasions when her name did surface that this particular wellspring of emotion was a deep and turbulent one for him. As far as I know he never visited his daughter's grave after her tiny white coffin was lowered into the ground, and never told us where it was.

Biologically I was my father's son. Notwithstanding all our dissimilarities there was never any doubt about that. Two pressing questions, though, had preceded my birth. One was whether my parents would stay together long enough to conceive me. The other was whether I would bear the paternal surname. For among the inducements to persuade my mother to marry him my father had offered to change it. However, despite coming from a family of plain-sounding Hills and Clarks, or because she relished something a bit more exotic, my mother opted for the rather more outlandish label of 'Bostridge'.

As I was growing up my father regarded me quizzically, as if he found it difficult to believe that he could have produced a boy so different from him in appearance, manner, tastes and interests. My total lack of aptitude for ball games was perplexing. His witnessing of my longing at age seven to play with dolls belonging to a friend's sister sent him raging from their house. Clearly remedial action was urgently required to toughen me up. I was presented with a pair of boxing gloves and a punch ball. When I failed to show sufficient aggression to knock it for six I was taken to judo classes, where I generally ended flat on my back staring at the ceiling.

By the time I reached my mid-teens and asked that we spend one holiday together walking in the footsteps of the Brontë sisters at Haworth, he must have realized the game was lost. Over dinner one evening while we were away, he raised the subject of my sexuality for the first and only time. The exact words he used and the tone in which they were delivered – which I assume, or rather trust, to have been semi-humorous – are lost to me, as is my reaction, if any, to what he had to say. But the gist of them was that if I was gay he'd kill me. Two decades later, in my final face-to-face conversation with my father, days before he fell down dead in the street, he accused me of being overly secretive with him about my life. At that stage in our relationship I could do no more than turn to look at him with the kind of bemusement with which he'd so often treated me.

His template of masculinity derived not from his own father, a spare, bony man of few words, but from his maternal grandfather, a footballer from the early days of the professional game in the years immediately before the First World War. John 'Tiny' Joyce, who played as goalkeeper for a number of clubs, including Millwall and Tottenham Hotspur, was a great hulking bear of a man. I look at him in team photos, standing four-square in his grey goalie's sweater, and experience a strong sense of genetic disinheritance. He seems to represent the kind of alpha male that I've been in flight from all my life.

On Saturday afternoons, aged four or five, I was pushed by my father through the turnstiles to stand alongside him on the terraces at Millwall football ground. Its address at Cold Blow Lane aptly conveyed the intimidating bleakness of the surrounding industrial wasteland. The home crowd, chanting and screaming abuse at the opposing supporters, more than lived up to the club's reputation as one of the most feared in the country.

Following the match, the extended Joyce clan gathered in my grandmother's kitchen to celebrate or commiserate with one another over the outcome. Those Saturdays, I see now, were important to my father. Like many others who have aspired to something better and possessed the drive to achieve it, my father remained ambivalent about his working-class origins. Football provided an uncontroversial meeting ground with his family, an easy and accessible path back to his roots.

My father's reinvention of himself has always seemed to me to be touched by the miraculous. He grew up in urban poverty. His family were so poor, my maternal grandmother once told me, still incredulous at the idea, that they used newspapers for tablecloths. Investigation of the address given as my father's birthplace on his death certificate showed that it was a cover for the local workhouse infirmary.

His eventual transformation into an affluent businessman, living in a comfortable suburban home, was undoubtedly aided by his moment in history. A bright boy who won a scholarship to grammar school, he'd been evacuated during the war to a middle-class family near Guildford. Later, as the 1960s broke down barriers of class and deference, and the speed of social change accelerated, he became part of a generation whose eyes were firmly fixed on a new horizon where opportunities seemed limitless and money was there all but for the asking.

In another turn of the wheel of social mobility, he sent me to a school with a reputation as one of the leading establishments of its kind. In truth, Westminster School, in the mid- to late 1970s, didn't live up to its hallowed name. It was finding its feet after a period of decline, fighting a rearguard action against the prevalence of drug abuse among its pupils, and biding its time waiting for the more old-fashioned teachers to retire. For me the privileged access, several mornings a week, to the sanctified loveliness of the Abbey went a long way towards making up for the deficiencies of O-Level English taught by a foreign language master; of German taught by a foreign national with erratic English; or of being part of a class shut in a room for 90 minutes while the History teacher communed with himself, reading aloud from a book and occasionally emitting moues of criticism of its author: 'Wow', 'Gosh', and – cue the stern climax – '*Steady . . .*'

Nevertheless, Westminster offered a passport to many things, not least Oxbridge. The mere presence of the school name on the application forms could be enough to guarantee even mediocre applicants a place. And for my father the simple fact of having been able to send a son to a public school proved that he was doing right by him. Indeed, in material terms he was always generous, never denying his children anything that it was within his power to give them.

Yet he cannot be the hero of my own story. His violent temper disqualified him. 'Don't you realize that your children are frightened of you?' someone once asked him in my presence. I was in my late teens by then and watched him feigning surprise. Even today I still find myself grappling with the apparent paradox: that he could at times be such a warm, loving, physically affectionate parent, intent on giving his child a sense of protection and security; but then, with no red warning light, his mood would change, turning him into a noxious, intimidating bully. His powerful physical frame meant that a slap across the face from him, or a thrashing across his knee with his belt or hand, was hardly something that could be lightly shrugged off. Inanimate objects weren't safe either. Sometimes, returning from church choir on a Sunday morning, I found the breakfast table overturned, and a sharply fragmented mosaic of smashed china scrunching on the floor beneath my feet.

In the best 1960s tradition of working-class boy made good, my father was a practised womanizer. Men gave rise to his insecurities, whereas an attractive woman encouraged him to call on his abundant reserves of charm, emphasizing his suave handsomeness. My biographical skills were honed at nine, ten, eleven, eavesdropping in doorways, listening to my parents' arguments about his infidelities, trying to piece together the story of their disintegrating marriage. With my mother at my side, egging me on, I slid my hands into the pockets of the Savile Row suits hanging in a long row in my father's wardrobe, daring myself to find what we both knew might be there: the evidence of an illicit liaison. It was like a lucky dip. Occasionally the search yielded a jewellery receipt or a telephone number. I'd ring the number. A woman would answer and I'd hold on just long enough to form a mental picture of her from the sound of her voice, and to hear the note of panicked irritation in it when she received no response down the other end of the line.

At eleven, I was part of a prep school trip to the châteaux of the Loire Valley. I never saw them. At our first stop in Ostend I rushed out of the hotel across the busy main road and was hit by a car. It was entirely my own fault. I'd misjudged the speed of the oncoming traffic and my ability to reach the other side of the road in time. A blue Mercedes caught me on my right flank and I was flung forwards 18 feet, arriving face down on the tarmacked surface of the road. For the rest of that week shopkeepers along the promenade kept customers enthralled with dramatic descriptions of the extraordinary sight of the English boy flying through the air like some prepubescent Superman (a misprint in the school magazine described me as having been knocked over by 'an oar', considerably lessening the impact of the report of my accident, as well as mystifying many readers).

Luckily I escaped serious injury. I'd lost a front tooth and my face, staring back at me in the mirror through two black and bruised eyes, was a bloody mess that gave me a terrible shock the first time I saw it, but looked a lot worse than it actually was and healed relatively quickly. I spent a lonely couple of days in an Ostend hospital, left behind by my teachers and schoolmates, who had sensibly decided to move on to Chenonceau without me.

The real stroke of misfortune had meanwhile been occurring in my parents' marriage. On the very day of my accident my mother had received a phone call from the husband of a woman with whom my father had been conducting a not very discreet affair. The call was to tell her that my father was being named as co-respondent in the divorce case he was bringing against his wife. This ill-timed event heralded the end of my parents' relationship, though it was to take four or five years more of attempted reconciliations, divorce petitions and counter-petitions to bring it finally to its long overdue close.

In the midst of his marital crisis, my father flew out to Ostend to bring me home. My glasses had been cracked and twisted in the accident, and without them I could only peer short-sightedly at the familiar, well-built figure entering the ward and making his way to my bed. There was no mistaking, though, the atmosphere of anxious dejection that enveloped him, and I thought long afterwards of the guilt he may have been experiencing at that point. He wasn't an overtly religious man. But he was a superstitious one, arranging my shoes and slippers at bedtime in a neat little row, in some peculiar, obsessive ritual, when he came to say goodnight to me as a child. Looking at his son lying injured in bed, did it cross his mind that my brush with death might have been some form of supernatural intervention for any sins of the flesh he might have committed?

My overwhelming relief at seeing him again was as great as his at seeing me. We clasped each other tightly in a surge of affection on both sides that was never to be repeated.

As I grew older I defined myself increasingly in opposition to him, in what was simultaneously a conscious and unconscious process. The masculine values that he was ready to hand on didn't appear to fit me. I was too much repelled by the bullying violence of them. Scratch away at my father's veneer of superficial polish – the bespoke suits and expensive shoes – and you might uncover a coarser vein expressing itself in foul, wounding language that shocked and outraged me well into adulthood. Reacting against his behaviour turned me into a shyer and more withdrawn individual than I might otherwise have been, and also accentuated the fey, effeminate elements of my physical and emotional character, earning my father's mocking rebuke in his nickname for me: 'Princess'.

I provoked him too when my early interest in history solidified into a determination to write not about the great movements and male protagonists of our island story – Magna Carta perhaps, or Oliver Cromwell (a favourite of my father's after he read John Buchan's biography), or the history of the British Empire – but to concentrate on the lives of women. He may have seen this coming. On a visit to his office at the age of six, I'd been taken to the nearby bookshop, Hatchards in Piccadilly, where he'd bought me a copy of the early nineteenth-century children's classic *Little Arthur's History of England* by Maria Callcott. As far as he was concerned it might as well have been called *Little Martha's History*. For rather than the patriotic history it contained, it was the sad tale of Maria Callcott's permanent invalidism after she suffered a burst blood vessel, outlined in a brief introduction, which transfixed me. 'You're only ever interested in the romance of the thing,' my father would say, dismissing the historical projects I showed him with a contemptuous curl of the lip. If he were alive now he would no doubt be saying something similar about my fascination with the story of Adèle Hugo.

A decade ago, the diaries of my Westminster headmaster were published. John Rae, always referred to in reverent Arnoldian tones as '*Dr* Rae', was a charismatic figure. He loved to swirl around the cloisters in his red canonical gown, and was generally given to striking poses. In the middle of a lesson on seventeenth-century France, he would turn his favoured profile to the light and exclaim, in a deliberate echo of the Sun King Louis XIV, '*L'école, c'est moi*'.

In one diary entry Dr Rae described a meeting with my father. It's always surprising to see oneself captured in print through another person's eyes. But maybe I wasn't surprised enough to find that my father had referred to me throughout their conversation as 'my daughter'. I was never man enough for him, and yet ironically I'd become a stand-in for one of the most important elements taken from him and missing from his life.

At night the grief-stricken cries of Madame Hugo could be heard coming from the apartment in the Place Royale as she sat gazing at the dark tresses cut from the head of her drowned daughter.

For the first time the young Adèle Hugo comes clearly into focus. At 13, cruelly deprived of the love and guidance of a devoted elder sister, she was the family member bravely refusing to be overwhelmed by bereavement and offering solace to the others. 'It is she who consoles,' wrote her brother Charles, 'or who seeks to console by her reflections, which are always profound and full of wisdom.'

The loss of Léopoldine was a perpetual agony for her father. In darker moments Hugo saw her death as a divine punishment meted out to him for having left his wife and children to set off on his travels with his mistress. Desperately trying to free himself from all the tragic associations, he distanced himself from Juliette Drouet, reimmersed himself in family life and, by the end of 1843, had begun a relationship with a woman who, still in her early twenties, was not much older than Léopoldine herself.

Even the first syllable of this woman's name – Léonie – sounds like an aural visitation from the dead. Léonie Biard was unhappily married to the painter François-Auguste Biard. She sounds like a spirited individual. Several years earlier she had accompanied her husband on Gaimard's scientific expedition to Spitsbergen, the Norwegian archipelago in the Arctic Ocean, the first woman to take part in an exploration of the Arctic. Hugo wrote that he loved her beyond the power of words to tell, and when he did attempt to describe his love to her, in letters and poems, the words he used were strikingly reminiscent of those he'd once written for Juliette, who'd been left looking sorrowfully in the mirror at her worn face and prematurely white hair.

In the summer of 1845 the affair proved a public embarrassment for Hugo and a source of acute trauma for Léonie. The pair were caught in flagrante delicto by a private detective hired by Léonie's husband. Biard was merciless and pressed charges for adultery. Only Hugo's recent elevation to the peerage allowed him to claim immunity from prosecution, though he was ridiculed widely in the press. For Léonie the consequences were far harsher. She was arrested and imprisoned for two months.

To his remaining daughter Hugo sent tender words as Adèle and her mother began a series of annual pilgrimages to the graves at Villequier. Hugo could not bring himself to join them until 1846, three years after the drownings, but he asked Adèle to return with a blade of grass or flower for him from her sister's grave. Signing himself 'Ton petit père', he told her that he wanted her to laugh, to play billiards and nain jaune [the card game 'Yellow Dwarf'], to eat like an ogress – and to love him.

Despite Hugo's cheerful tone, the funereal atmosphere at Place Royale was inescapable, and must at times have felt overwhelming. The writer Théodore Pavie recalled Adèle at this time, beautiful in her mourning clothes, sitting in the apartment surrounded by portraits and other sacred relics of the doomed couple who had disappeared beneath the waves.

Balzac had been merely the first to remark on Adèle's beauty as she entered her teens. A bronze medallion by the young sculptor David d'Angers, a family friend, shows Adèle at the age of 15, displaying her proud Roman profile, her thick ropes of dark hair coiled up decoratively around her head.

Adèle's first romantic kiss came not long afterwards, with Auguste Vacquerie, her father's most devoted admirer and the brother of Léopoldine's husband, Charles, who had died trying to save his wife. It took place, appositely enough, in the garden at Villequier. Adèle was 16, the same age as Léopoldine had been when she first met Charles, Vacquerie more than a decade older. Later Adèle would write that he loved her 'madly'. She could appreciate the symmetry in their potential union even to the extent of reflecting morbidly that she might one day share his grave at Villequier, united in death beneath the rose bushes like Léopoldine and Charles. Marriage to Auguste would also, she believed, please her father and win his approval. Later she would realize that by marrying him she risked sacrificing her own identity to that of her dead sister.

Did Adèle feel the force of parental pressure in allowing Auguste Vacquerie to court her? In a flimsy notebook preserved in Paris, constructed by Adèle from paper that's nearly transparent, she has made a sketch of Vacquerie. His lank hair and his figure, straight as a line, give him all the spindly allure of a garden rake.

But Adèle had another love whom she hoped for in these teenage years, beside whom Auguste Vacquerie appears pale and dismal. Jean-Baptiste Clésinger was the sculptor whose *Femme piquée par un serpent* ('Woman Bitten by a Snake'), modelled by the courtesan Apollonie Sabatier, caused a scandal at the Salon of 1847, making the artist notorious throughout Paris. While in Paris I'd visited the Musée d'Orsay to take a look at this work of art sneeringly dismissed by the painter Delacroix as a 'daguerreotype in sculpture'. It's immediately apparent why Delacroix reacted in this way. Clésinger's depiction of the female body, curvaceous and provocative and making no attempt at disguising the cellulite rippling above Madame Sabatier's thighs, is sexually explicit to a degree unrivalled by other portrayals of the female nude at that time.

Adèle later recalled experiencing a crush on Clésinger, not long after that first kiss with Vacquerie, and not long before the sculptor seduced and married another teenager, Solange, the daughter of the writer George Sand. Clésinger's reputation as an uncouth drunk, spending his way through his wife's dowry, was widespread. But for Adèle his genius, allied to his association with a potent whiff of sexual danger, remained irresistible. It suggested a different kind of existence, far removed from the relatively passive, acquiescent one she might have with Vacquerie. A life of violent, fiery passion, a life lived to the full, though one that might end in some defiant act of emotional self-immolation.

However, the revolutionary events of 1848 suddenly and dramatically cut across the Hugo family's lives, changing their course forever.

That June saw four days of intensive fighting in the streets of Paris, with government troops firing on barricades manned by militant workers. The apartment in the Place Royale – briefly called the Place de la République before reverting to its older name, the Place des Vosges – was overrun by rioters. Madame Hugo, Charles, François-Victor and Adèle, together with their servants, escaped just in time. They hurried over cobbled streets stained with blood and took sanctuary in the town hall, and afterwards with a neighbour. Victor Hugo was at the Constituent Assembly, to which he had been elected earlier in the month, having spent hours helping to co-ordinate the military efforts needed to break the barricades. A rumour quickly spread that his home was ablaze. Later, after it was established that this wasn't true, the contents of the apartment were discovered to have been largely undisturbed by the mob. The early drafts of Hugo's new novel, *Les Misères* ('The Miseries'), for which he'd just signed a contract, remained on his desk where he'd left them. Nevertheless, Madame Hugo refused to return. Temporary lodgings were found in the rue d'Islay before a permanent move was made to a house in the rue de la Tour-d'Auvergne. It was to be the Hugos' final family home in Paris.

At the beginning of her twenties, Adèle Hugo would set herself a programme of reading from her father's works and marvel at the extent of his journey from monarchist to republican. As recently as February 1848, when the king, Louis-Philippe, was forced to abdicate against the background of mounting economic crisis in France, Victor Hugo had supported the continuation of the Orléans monarchy through a regency led by the widowed Duchesse d'Orléans on behalf of her infant son. He had personal reasons enough for doing so. As well as ingratiating himself with Louis-Philippe, to whom he owed his peerage and the king's own protection in trying to hush up the Biard scandal, Hugo had become a devoted admirer of the Duchesse.

However, the revolutionary crowds invading the Chamber of Peers during a debate on the constitutional crisis made it abundantly clear that France had done with the Orléans dynasty and with the monarchy itself. The Second Republic was declared on 26 February and the poet Lamartine took his place at the head of a provisional government.

A decade earlier Victor Hugo had posed himself a question about the role of the poet in society: should he become part of the crowd and direct himself towards social questions, or move away 'from our tempests' and into 'nature's reposeful embrace'? Hugo had followed the path to greater political influence. When the peerage was abolished by the provisional government, he got himself elected to the Constituent Assembly to keep a voice in deciding the shape of the nation's future.

He remained wary of republicanism, though. It might lead to anarchy, to a re-enactment of the revolutionary Terror, adding the word 'Death' to the 'noble motto' 'Liberty, Equality, and Fraternity'; or it might result in 'the sacred participation by all Frenchmen now living . . . in the principles of Democracy'. For Hugo it was too soon to tell.

And so in those June days of 1848, Victor Hugo bravely – some said suicidally – walked to the barricades as a Representative of the People with the task of restoring order, opposing what he saw as 'a revolt of the people against themselves'. At the same time, he was horrified by the shedding of 'decent and noble' blood on both sides, and shocked by the savage reprisals taken by the provisional government against the rebels. The government extended the state of emergency and passed measures to ban certain newspapers and retain the death penalty, both matters of pressing concern to Hugo.

Into this dangerous moment in French history, as the country waited on a new constitution and the election of a president, stepped Louis-Napoléon Bonaparte. He was an unprepossessing figure, short and thick-set, speaking with a stammering German accent. He was also inscrutable, with no discernible gift for anything other than his ability to be bold and decisive in action. He was, as Karl Marx famously wrote, nothing more than 'a grotesque mediocrity' playing a hero's role. However, as the nephew of Napoleon I, Louis-Napoléon possessed the magical name that could still rouse voters to ecstasy. He would become, in the words of Alexis de Tocqueville, 'a dwarf on the crest of a wave'.

As a candidate for the presidential election, Louis-Napoléon sought Hugo's support, assuring him that he was 'a man of liberty, a man of democracy', and promising furthermore that if elected he would introduce legislation to alleviate poverty. That summer, Hugo, together with his two sons and Auguste Vacquerie and Paul Meurice, had started a newspaper, *L'Événement* (The Event). It was very much a family affair. Its contributors included

Madame Hugo and Adèle – while the fashion and society notes were by none other than Léonie Biard. No one was fooled by Hugo's claim that he had no part in it. The paper was a useful propaganda tool, reflecting his politics and beliefs, not least his decision to support Louis-Napoléon's candidacy in the election. On the eve of the poll *L'Événement* published a single-page supplement that contained nothing but Louis-Napoléon's name repeated a hundred times.

In December 1848, Louis-Napoléon won a landslide victory as President of the Republic for a four-year term.

And yet in just three years Victor Hugo would be on the run. Louis-Napoléon had reneged on his promises and embarked on a programme to increase his power. The self-styled Prince-President introduced legislation to disenfranchise over a third of the electorate and censored the press and the theatre. As Hugo grew more critical of the new regime, his family were targeted. Both Charles and François-Victor were imprisoned for months in the Conciergerie for condemning capital punishment and flouting the new law restricting the press.

In the summer of 1851, while Louis-Napoléon's demand for a second term of office was debated – and rejected – Hugo delivered a pungent attack. He reminded his audience of how far short this new Napoleon fell from the greatness of his illustrious namesake: 'Because we have had Napoleon le Grand, must we now have Napoleon le Petit?!' The next day, Hugo wrote in a private note to himself, 'Republicans open your ranks and let me in!'

By December 1851 an air of tension had settled over Paris as it waited expectantly for what already seemed long overdue: the *coup d'état* that would bring Louis-Napoléon absolute power. On the 2nd the city awoke to find placards announcing the dissolution of the Assembly and a new constitution giving the President full powers. The army was placed at strategic points around Paris and opposition leaders were arrested. Resistance was minimal despite attempts by Hugo and other members of the committee of resistance to go into the working-class quarters of the city and urge the setting up of barricades. Troops with cannon and musket fire easily crushed what uprisings there were. Within days, rebellion in Paris and the provinces had been halted.

With his life – or at the very least his freedom – in jeopardy, Hugo turned to Juliette Drouet, who more than proved her devotion. She found hiding places for him, deceived police and sentries, set spies off on the wrong trail – and, finally, on 11 December, arranged his escape to Brussels by train from the Gare du Nord. Hugo was disguised as a printer's compositor, a working men's cap pushed down low across his brow.

Where was Adèle during all this? Looking through her letters to her father delivered by Madame Hugo on two trips to meet Hugo in Brussels, I see there is one in which we can recognise her shiver of reminiscence as she recalls 'that terrible night when they [the police] came to take you'. It was like a nightmare, she continued, a bad dream from which she was relieved to be awakened.

For the first half of 1852 the lives of Adèle and her mother followed a monotonous pattern, centred on their daily visits to Charles and François-Victor at the Conciergerie. The two women occupied one room in their house, heated by a coke fire, to conserve funds for an uncertain future. A few friends came to see them. Adèle began to keep an intermittent record of her daily life to while away the time. For the rest they wandered around Paris like ghostly remnants from the past, with no firm future as yet to inhabit. Despite keeping their heads down they did not pass unrecognized. On one occasion a precocious five-year-old boy accosted Adèle in the street and told her that he liked her because she was pretty and kind, even though her father was 'a red'.

It was a hard life for a young woman, Madame Hugo reminded her husband. At the beginning of January Adèle hadn't received a single New Year's present. 'I told her to congratulate herself for seeking joy only in moral satisfaction,' her mother wrote sanctimoniously.

Madame Hugo hoped that the family would settle in London, and encouraged Adèle to start learning English in preparation. But in the spring, to the two women's intense disappointment, came the news that Victor Hugo had decided on the island of Jersey for their new home, where at least French was spoken. 'Jersey is a charming place,' Hugo wrote to his daughter, his 'poor angel'. 'There we will have the sea, greenery, magnificent nature and, what is best of all . . . the intimate circle, the family; all the joy of the hearts that love each other.'

In June most of the contents of the house in the rue de la Tour-d'Auvergne were put up for sale by public auction. A queue of carriages lined the street. Inside, the crowds jostled one another to handle Victor Hugo's paper knife or take a seat in his armchair. All the Gothic furniture and bric-a-brac that had once adorned the Place Royale apartment was sold. Only a few possessions were retained, including Hugo's bed and the Sèvres dinner service once presented to him by Charles X. A shadowy figure was noticed at the open window, as buyers surged around her, 'a patch of whiteness, calmly, attentively, looking out in silence over the city which must be left the next day'. It was Adèle.

Hugo comforted her with the thought that they would soon be reunited. All together again in Jersey they would wait 'for the end of the bad play that is being performed at the moment, and we will bless God who, having taken away our country, leaves us our family'.

Six months earlier, Adèle had sent her father a ringing declaration of her belief in him, with the assurance that his heroism had won him esteem and admiration all over the world. Then the young woman, who may or may not have been accepted by Victor Hugo as his own, summoned up the feeling that was sustaining her in these difficult times and wrote of her pride in being his daughter.

4

Ghosts

The sea was at low tide on a warm midweek afternoon in the final days of August. The holiday season was almost at an end. The broad expanse of sand was devoid of a single individual, save for one sturdy-looking woman wearing an unseasonal mackintosh who left a neat trail of footprints as she walked diagonally across it, throwing a ball for her dog. I noticed her, turned my head briefly, and when I looked again she had gone.

I'd come to Jersey to search for another of Victor Hugo's homes. Only this time there was a difference. For in Jersey there is no museum to his memory. The house at Marine Terrace, on the outskirts of the capital St Helier, to which he and his wife and children moved in the summer of 1852, marking the first stage of their exile from France, is no longer standing. However, where it had once stood, and exactly when it had disappeared, were proving surprisingly difficult to ascertain.

Attempting to find answers to these questions I'd visited Jersey Museum in the centre of St Helier, not far from Liberation Square where the annual commemoration of the end of Nazi Germany's occupation of the island, in 1945, is held each May. Brightly lit displays showcased 250,000 years of history, right back to the time when Jersey was still connected to the mainland of France. These outlined the ways in which the island was fought over by England and France during the Middle Ages, leading to Jersey's eventual emergence as a British Crown dependency in the thirteenth century. There were interesting modern sections about life under German rule. There was also more information than seemed strictly necessary about the 1980s BBC TV series *Bergerac*, in which a maverick detective drives around the Jersey countryside in a snazzy Triumph Roadster solving crimes left open by the island police. But to Victor Hugo's residence in Jersey there was no more than a passing reference.

A member of staff suggested that I consult the Jersey Heritage website. My search produced an extraordinary photographic record documenting the fate of the Hugo house. Here were photos of Marine Terrace's later incarnation as a hotel. Owned by an English family, the Roses, once the Hugos' landlords, the Maison Victor Hugo opened its doors to guests in the latter part of the nineteenth century and operated as a hotel until the second half of the twentieth. By the late 1970s the building had fallen on hard times. It was empty and dilapidated and a target for vandalism. Photos show it surrounded by dumped cars. In 1978 a demolition squad moved in. A team of contractors is photographed standing triumphantly in the wreckage of the house, its glassless windows revealing the broken timbers of the roof, open to the sky. Then, in the next shot, the ground is levelled and the house is suddenly gone. A single pathetic photo, the final one in the collection, is of a door saved 'from the former home of Victor Hugo', as if someone at the last moment had come over all sentimental in the wake of such wholesale destruction.

Many of us might consider it scandalous that a house of such cultural significance, the home of a great writer, where some of the greatest French poetry of the nineteenth century was written, should have been summarily dispatched with no apparent efforts to save it. But modern Jersey has always displayed if not an antagonism to all things French then certainly an air of indifference towards them. A plan, ten or so years ago, to build a bridge to link the island to the northern coast of Normandy disappeared almost as soon as it was mooted, while French speaking in Jersey has been in steep decline for years. Adèle Hugo may have announced patriotically, soon after arriving in St Helier, that 'Jersey is a bit of France which has been stolen by England' – adding that 'Jersey is actually French but legally English' – but even in her time French influences were on the wane. In light of this it seems hardly surprising that the historic home of Victor Hugo had been razed to the ground without protest.

Having established the site of the house, I set out to find it. Walking from the centre of St Helier through an underpass pulsating with thundering traffic, I emerged into a small winding street of houses that led to the coastal area known as Grève d'Azette. Sitting on the boundary of St Clement, this is the smallest but most densely populated of the twelve parishes of Jersey. It didn't take me long to identify the former position of the Maison Victor Hugo. The vast, ugly, steel-and-concrete apartment block that has taken its place, trying vainly that afternoon to hide in the grey shadows cast by the afternoon sun, is still known by its name.

Judging from daguerreotypes of the 1850s, the outlook to the sea remains strikingly unchanged after all these years, apart, that is, from the addition of an unsightly electric pylon at one end of the beach. Auguste Vacquerie, who shared the family's exile at Marine Terrace, remembered how at low tide 'there was only a flat beach whose flatness extended as far as the eye can see, bespattered with innumerable small chocolate-coloured rocks which would make one believe that an untidy Gargantuan had passed by'. As I made my way across the sand I paused to sit on one of these rocks, looking back momentarily at the powerful sunlight reflected in the enormous windows of the apartments, before starting to read Adèle Hugo's account of her arrival and early months in Jersey.

Adèle and her mother, accompanied by Vacquerie, who had become for Hugo 'as one of my children', reached St Helier on 31 July 1852. They sailed on board a Royal Mail packet from Southampton. 'Rocks, more rocks, and then in the distance the shore that bears the name of Jersey,' Adèle wrote as they approached the island. For his part Vacquerie gloomily, and unfairly, noted St Helier's resemblance to the first Napoleon's island of exile, St Helena. They booked themselves into the Hôtel de la Pomme d'Or and began the search for lodgings. On the first day 'an impertinent Englishwoman' shut the door in their faces. Meanwhile they waited anxiously for Victor Hugo's arrival from Belgium.

On 5 August he appeared at last. It was eight months since Adèle had seen her father, during the terrifying period when Hugo was dodging arrest at the hands of Louis-Napoléon's police. With him was her brother Charles, freed since the beginning of the year from imprisonment in the Conciergerie. François-Victor, released a bit later, was still in Paris, enamoured, to his father's dismay, of a pretty vaudeville actress, Anaïs Liévenne. He wouldn't be joining the rest of the family until the end of September.

Travelling incognito to Jersey on a separate boat, for the sake of propriety, was Juliette Drouet. She had shared Hugo's banishment in Brussels and continued steadfast and loyal, despite her complaints of his frequent absences, his occasional indifference to her, and of feeling increasingly like 'a squirrel in a cage' as she uprooted her life once more and struggled to find a place to live that she could afford. Flaubert's remark about the Hugo–Drouet affair, in a letter written the following year to Louise Colet, his own longtime mistress, appeals to me. Its watery imagery, after all, is well suited to lovers stuck on an island. 'I love the long passions,' Flaubert observed, 'which patiently cross and in a straight line against the currents of life, like good swimmers against deviation.' True, the patience was mostly on Juliette's side, but she had already proved herself a champion at negotiating savage, erratic currents.

Hugo embraced his daughter and turned to address the crowd of Jerseymen, Englishmen and other political refugees from Louis-Napoléon's regime gathered on the quayside. There were around 300 *proscrits*, as they were known, on the island: doctors and lawyers in large numbers, as well as artisans, shopkeepers and tailors. Not all of them were French. Jersey also provided political asylum to Poles and Hungarians and several other nationalities. But the largest proportion of these political emigrés had been proscribed and expelled from France by Louis-Napoléon following his December *coup d'état*. Some of them would figure in the pages of the journal that Adèle was to begin working intensively on in the months ahead, as Victor Hugo became their leader and frequently a moderating influence on their intrigue and clandestine activities. General Le Flô, formerly of the French legislative assembly, the philosopher Pierre Leroux, who had introduced the word 'socialism' into French political discourse, spending hours in Jersey working on an agricultural experiment for recycling sewage, and Sándor Teleki, Hungarian soldier and aristocrat, were to be among regular visitors to the family.

Back at the Hôtel de la Pomme, Hugo delivered another speech to the French *proscrits*, ending with the stirring conclusion that their cause would triumph in the end. 'They shouted twice, with my father: "Vive la République",' Adèle recorded. That evening Hugo gave a reading from *Napoléon-le-Petit*, his fierce indictment of the new Prince-President's regime. A million copies were about to go on sale worldwide. Smuggled into France, sometimes in the lining of clothes, or hidden in a tin of sardines or bales of hay, the pamphlet would be a runaway success. Nevertheless, in just four months the Second Empire would be declared and the newly proclaimed Napoleon III ride in triumph into Paris.

Within a fortnight the family and their household of four servants had found their Jersey home. No. 3 Marine Terrace was large and white-painted with small sash windows and a flat roof (the pitched roof came later) that made it resemble, in Hugo's words, 'a clumsy white cube'. The house was divided into two, with separate gardens. In one half lived the Hugos. Next door, with his wife and four sons, was their landlord Thomas Rose, a friend of the artist J. M. W. Turner. The street entrance led to the road from St Helier to Gorey and a landscape of vibrant green fields. The uncultivated garden at the back opened out onto a vast terrace, 50 by 40 feet, overlooking Grève d'Azette with a view to the sea.

When the tide was low and the weather fine the coast of France could be glimpsed. On a clear night the lighthouse in the harbour at Saint-Malo was visible in the distance, standing firm like a beacon of hope for the future. When the tide rose to its height, the sea violently pounded the terrace wall. A dyke had been constructed to save the low-lying area of St Clement from flooding, with large, whitened tree trunks planted in the sand along a stone pier. As the ocean 'writhed, roared, swirled', wrote Vacquerie, 'the wood of the dyke took revenge for shipwrecks by breaking up the exasperated wave.'

From his second-floor room at the back of the house, Hugo watched as the foam threw 'its white muslin on the rocks'. When the tide retreated he observed the horses on the beach pulling carts loaded with seaweed, and women combing the sands searching for valuables. Grève d'Azette was a popular bathing spot. Hugo often swam there, though in the summer of 1853 he was caught by a wave and narrowly escaped being swept away and drowned.

Adèle recognized that her father had realised one of his dreams at last: 'to be on an island and have the sea at his feet'. Madame Hugo told her husband that a rock was 'an admirable setting' for him, with 'your fame, your mission, your personality', and wrote that she understood that his family 'which exists because of you alone, should be sacrificed not only to your honour but also to the image you present'.

At the same time, Adèle's mother was also concerned that exile was least well suited to her daughter, 'whose moral health does not need this heroic remedy'. Now 22, Adèle had exchanged the bright lights of Paris, leaving behind the prospect of the city's artistic and musical diversions, for windswept beaches and, for all the joy she felt at being reunited with her father and brothers, a sense of isolation that would only grow with the passing of time.

Still, there was enough at first about her new situation to engage her interest. Soon after arriving at Marine Terrace, the family went into St Helier for an outing to the theatre. By comparison with Parisian theatres, the Theatre Royal was cramped and poorly lit. But they were received with ceremony and seated in the Governor's box, the lead actor paying homage to Victor Hugo before the entire audience. In October 1852 Adèle went to her first Jersey ball. She dressed completely in white, carrying a snow-white bouquet to complete the ensemble, 'and her individual bearing', wrote her proud mother, 'made a great effect although surrounded by . . . English beauties'. The following February she attended the Grand Fancy Dress Ball at the Queen's Assembly Rooms. Adèle, with her long dark hair pomaded, dressed in the style of a lady of the court of Louis XV.

By omnibus the Hugos set off on sightseeing tours to Jersey landmarks, like Mont Orgueil Castle, whose medieval battlements had once protected the eastern side of the island from French invasion. On another occasion they boarded a *bateau à vapeur* (steamboat) to sail round the coastline. At Gorey Hugo was spotted by a Spanish tourist who exclaimed, 'How happy I am to see the greatest poet of our time!' At St Brelade's Bay they visited the tiny church, probably the oldest Christian site in Jersey, with its granite interior and fishermen's chapel. Somewhere here, in the mass of graves crowding the churchyard, overlooked no doubt by the Hugos, is the burial place of Gilbert Imlay: American revolutionary soldier, entrepreneur and lover of the English feminist Mary Wollstonecraft, who was tormented and nearly destroyed by her feelings for him.

Jersey's supernatural traditions combined to make a strong impression on the family. According to Adèle, there wasn't a rock or ancient ruin that wasn't said to be haunted. This may have been vaguely on my mind as I stumbled across the sands in the dark one moonless night during my stay and noticed a small ring of sparkling lights at my feet, like a miniature firework display. As it continued to throw off an eerie glow, resting for half a minute as if it were recharging its batteries before starting up again, I half began to wonder whether I hadn't stepped by accident inside a luminous ring inhabited by fairies or some other spectral creatures. The receptionist at my hotel merely looked bemused when I told her about the encounter, and I only discovered much later that the light was indeed produced by tiny creatures, a rare type of glow-worm rather than something of otherworldly origins.

However, you don't have to travel far inland in Jersey to come across prehistoric sites, associated with centuries of ghostly legends (Hugo erroneously identified these sites as Druidic, when in fact they dated back much further, to the Neolithic Age). Cromlechs, menhirs and dolmens, or passage graves, constructed from stones and boulders thousands of years earlier, were common features of the landscape. Not far from Marine Terrace, the Mont Ubé dolmen had been excavated on flat land several years before the Hugos' arrival. Many of these stones were reputed to be haunted. A Grey Lady, a druidess, was said to have sacrificed her father on the altar stone of one dolmen, while another murderess, a White Lady, was reputed to haunt Mont Ubé.

Among the Hugos' favourite places for excursions were the caves at Plémont on the northern shore. To Adèle they were 'one of the marvels of the world . . . Imagine immense carved rocks in the form of a cathedral . . .' The first time her father attempted to descend from one of the rocks he quickly climbed up again, claiming to be suffering from vertigo. However, before long he was scrambling up and down rocky surfaces, as Jersey's landscape became the backdrop for a series of photographic portraits of him. These were the work of Vacquerie in collaboration with Charles

Hugo, who in the spring of 1853 travelled to Caen to train with the photographer Edmond Bacot. The 60 or so daguerreotypes of a rather portly Hugo must be among the earliest author photographs. Hugo pioneers a variety of poses, not surprisingly without the slightest hint of self-consciousness. In some he folds his arms in a gesture of defiance or thrusts a hand Napoleonically through a small opening in his jacket; in others he adopts a more creative posture, his head resting thoughtfully on a hand or a finger on a cheek. Seated on top of the Roche des Proscrits, near Marine Terrace, looking far out to sea in the direction of France, he is a man of destiny.

Family and friends offered other subjects for the camera: Madame Hugo, reading a volume of her husband's poetry, hiding her increasing girth in the folds of a toga; Charles and François-Victor fencing outside the conservatory; Vacquerie's cat, caught from behind in a moment of repose.

Four solo portraits exist of Adèle in Jersey. The earliest, from the spring of 1853, is the one with eyes cast down that I'd first seen in the museum at Villequier. Is she shy of catching the new contraption's eye, or is she trying to avoid the sun's glare?

The others, like the pose with the parasol seen earlier, were familiar from Villequier too. They can't be precisely dated, and resist being placed in a chronological order. What can one read into them except to say that in the left-hand one (on page 97) Adèle seems remote, older even, wearing a bored, sullen expression: was Vacquerie taking the picture? In her pretty, patterned dress she is more alert, and almost questioning of the observer. The photos give us the imaginary possession of a moment, but little more.

Music formed the main pastime in the evenings at Marine Terrace. Schubert was sung, and Ede Reményi, the young Hungarian *proscrit* and violin virtuoso, performed. In Paris Victor Hugo had been known to refer to the piano as a 'wooden brute', but now his attitude softened towards his daughter's playing. Adèle dedicated long hours to practising and to working on her own compositions: 'charming, original music', according to Vacquerie, 'which she has created all by herself, far from the Opera, far from the Conservatory, springs spontaneously from nature and from the heart'.

Each family member's daily regime centred on their individual writing projects, so much so that Marine Terrace came to resemble a literary production line. Madame Hugo, 'in great confusion', was beginning the memoir of her husband that would take her a decade to complete. Charles and Vacquerie individually wrote plays and together planned, but never completed, a book about Jersey, illustrated with their photographs. François-Victor wrote nostalgically about Normandy and translated Shakespeare. Hugo himself unleashed a torrent of words with an intensive programme of writing.

Adèle's journal, begun in Paris in the spring of 1852 while waiting for definite news of what the future might hold, contained her first tentative steps of self-exploration. 'How can I explain what has been going on in me for some time?' she asks herself in its opening lines. The rudimentary code was designed to allow her to set aside any inhibitions and write freely about her dreams of love, her confidence in her own beauty and flirtatiousness, her talents as a musician, and her wish to be a worthy daughter to Victor Hugo.

Within months, however, her journal had suddenly taken on a new and overwhelming focus: her own father. It was now to be an up-close, day-to-day portrait of Victor Hugo, recording his reminiscences of the past, his views on contemporary politics and literature and his interactions with his family as well as with the wider circle of exiles on the island. The primary impulse behind this recasting of Adèle's journal was probably Hugo's. He'd tried to persuade Juliette Drouet to keep a diary to occupy her time in Jersey, but she'd managed it for only a month before transferring her energies to the twice-daily love letters she sent him.

Adèle's undertaking was to be more ambitious and time-consuming. In her waking hours she was rarely to be without a pen or pencil in hand, taking down her father's never-ending flow of talk: the long monologues during which he brooked no interruption, or the dialogues with his wife and sons and assorted visitors, whose arrival at Marine Terrace Adèle registered with the precision of a court circular.

The dedication underpinning the enterprise is extraordinary. How did it work in practice? Clearly, as is apparent from the surviving manuscripts, Adèle scribbled notes of ongoing conversations. The inky mess of the facsimile page I'd seen at Villequier wasn't an indication of a mind in disarray, but of the haste of composition. Later Adèle would go back over the pages, reconstructing her text and filling in details, like proper names, that she'd been unsure of and left blank. To allow her a breathing space, other members of the family sometimes stepped in and continued taking notes on her behalf. They also provided background information and descriptions of incidents she might have missed or forgotten. Nevertheless, Adèle was the principal author of what she took to calling the 'Journal of Exile', and on her shoulders rested the responsibility of maintaining a full and accurate record. If her attention wandered she was soon pulled back to the task in hand, as this mealtime exchange shows:

Victor Hugo . . . But the English cavalry, who have the finest uniforms in England, tend their horses and do nothing else, and do it so well that . . .

Adèle (to a servant) Can I have some eggs?

Mme Hugo Ask for them later: write down what's being said.

Victor Hugo . . . so well that the English infantry used to insult the cavalry and the foot soldiers told the mounted men they were fine soldiers, required only to look after horses . . .

One parallel that springs immediately to my mind is James Boswell's journal account of his tour of the Scottish Hebrides with Dr Johnson, 80 years earlier. Like Adèle Hugo, Boswell wrote rough notes of his subject, Dr Johnson's conversation, afterwards diligently transforming them into journal form. However, although Johnson read Boswell's journal as it was being written and corrected it where necessary, he had little alternative but to allow Boswell the freedom to include any indiscreet and unflattering details he chose. Adèle's journal, by contrast, was overseen by Victor Hugo, its subject, and amounted in effect to a work of dual authorship. He was the guiding hand behind it, reading and correcting her prose, offering advice on her writing style, inserting passages of his own, while occasionally scolding her when she omitted something he considered significant.

Despite all the time, effort and concentration involved, Adèle evidently relished this collaboration with her father, of becoming, in a sense, his pupil. She may well have viewed her work on the journal as a means of establishing a new closeness with him. As someone with literary ambitions of her own she felt honoured that 'the poet of genius' should come down from his throne to criticize her 'very plebeian literature'.

The poet of genius was experiencing an astonishing burst of creativity. Adèle mentions family conversations about the idea of launching hundreds of balloons, emblazoned with the title *Napoléon-le-Petit*, across the Channel into France, in order to advertise Hugo's pamphlet attack on Napoleon III. But for Hugo the new Emperor was only cooked 'on one side'; it was time 'to turn the Emperor over on the grill' and continue the attack in poetry. That first winter in Jersey he completed 3,000 verses of a new collection, boiling with righteous anger at the events set in motion by the *coup d'état* of December 1851. He paused to reflect sorrowfully in one poem on the grief of a grandmother laying out the body of her small grandson, caught in the government troops' rifle fire and killed with two bullets to the head. Initially the book had trouble finding a title, as various possibilities were put forward only to be rejected. Finally, as Adèle records, *Châtiments* – in English, *Chastisements*, *Castigations*, even *Thrashings*, capturing the violence of the French word – the title she favoured, was decided upon.

From political invective Hugo's poetry took on a more lyrical voice. *Les Contemplations* are full of nostalgia for past love, of mourning for his dead daughter, and of a newfound, visionary belief in the harmony of creation. The lengthy process of writing, ordering and reordering poems, old and new, to fit a complicated structure, was to occupy Hugo for much of the rest of his time in Jersey.

Ever since I first came across the book, on one of my earliest visits to Villequier, a single poem has stood out for me. *Magnitudo Parvi* ('The Greatness of Small Things') is long and dense, but at the same time powerfully transfixing. At night, as the poet walks along the ocean shore, contemplating the evening sky and landscape, he sees through the darkness the flicker of a shepherd's fire. Like the exiled Victor Hugo, the shepherd is an outcast, cut off and isolated from society. Yet even though he lives a life of solitude and simplicity, the shepherd can come to an intuitive understanding of God and the mystery of the universe. The message Hugo is sending here, not least to himself, is abundantly clear.

The poet is accompanied on his walk by his 'beloved' daughter, an 'angel with a woman's look'. We understand in the scheme of things that this is Léopoldine, whose death will shortly irrupt upon the sequence of poems, overthrowing the natural order. However, in reality, as Adèle's journal reveals, the daughter who shared evening walks along the terrace and seashore with her father, pointing out the stars in the night sky, was Adèle. In the poem she has been simply airbrushed from the scene and replaced by her dead sister. If there's an unseen, ghostly presence hovering around the poem it's not Léopoldine's, it is Adèle's.

Coming off the beach I took a different route back into town, managing this time to avoid the onslaught of heavy traffic. Eventually I found myself in St Helier's Royal Square. This is the historic centre of the capital, home to the Royal Court, the principal court of justice for both Jersey and Guernsey, and to the States chamber and other government departments. Office workers, the men in rolled-up shirt sleeves, relaxed in the late afternoon sun and stood drinking outside the pubs and cafés on the far side of the square. Uncertain of which direction to go in, I made my way up towards the Victorian cast-iron market hall, drawn by its conspicuous, maroon-coloured gates, where a market worker was stacking crates of unsold oranges. From there I turned into Halkett Place and wandered along streets lined with small shops and businesses until almost by accident I came upon the address I was looking for.

Belmont Road was part of a small residential area erected swiftly and cheaply in the mid-1830s. Today it's a lengthy thoroughfare with mostly white-painted, three-storeyed houses on both sides. No. 24 is one of the larger of these, with an imposing front door, its exterior painted a pale green with windowsills and mouldings in a darker shade of the same colour.

I stood on the opposite side of the street for a while, taking in the house's appearance and trying to imagine a moment from its past.

On a June evening in 1854, a young man stepped into Belmont Road from no. 24. He was 22 years old and lived there as a boarder with his widowed mother in rooms on one of the three floors. Given his subsequent reputation for being immaculately dressed, he was perhaps smartly, even stylishly, turned out. It was too late to catch the horse-drawn omnibus in the direction of St Clement's. Instead, if he had a few pennies in his pocket, he could have hired a hansom cab or fly. Or if time was on his side and the weather fine, he may have decided to amble along the coastal road to his destination.

The young man's name was Albert Pinson, and he was on his way to Marine Terrace to take part in a séance.

Albert Andrew Pinson. The question rattles around inside my head every time I think about him: how is it possible to unravel a love story, even an unconventional, one-sided, unrequited one – which is what everyone takes this to have been – when we know so little about the male half of it? For Albert Pinson is the man who very nearly isn't there.

None of his letters have come to light, and so it's impossible to capture any trace of his voice echoing down the years. There is no known painting or photograph of him, and all we have to go on is Adèle's brief description of his physical appearance in her journal. Even there the words she writes give little away about him and what it was that had such a magnetic effect on her. Pinson in his twenties is described as blond with sideburns (*favoris*), and possessing childlike, almost feminine features (in his colouring and relative lack of facial hair he must have formed a marked contrast to her dark-haired, hirsute brothers). One thing about him that does strike her are his ravishing (*ravissante*) blue eyes.

Pinson's motives in his relationship with Adèle are one of the mysteries at the heart of this story. She pursued him from the moment she met him. But over the course of a decade he also chose to remain in contact, often close contact, with her, even after he left Jersey to join the militia and then the army and went for long periods without seeing her. At some point he may even have wanted to marry her. Accounts of their relationship, based on nothing more solid than hearsay, agree that on his part money, or rather the lack of it, was the determining factor in his attraction to her. Does he then fit the stock character of the penniless adventurer? Must he inevitably be cast as the villain of the piece? Are these destined to remain rhetorical questions?

The rumour mill that was hard at work in the wake of Victor Hugo's death in 1885, revealing the existence of the mad daughter, and which started up again, 30 years later, following Adèle's own death, offers some tantalizing glimpses of the English lieutenant in fleeting, eyewitness accounts of him published in newspapers.

Living up to the promise of his surname, James Gossip, owner of the Granville Street bookstore in Halifax, Nova Scotia, Pinson's first foreign posting, told one reporter that Pinson had been 'a sort of dude in dress'. This impression was confirmed by the testimony of an old army colleague of Pinson's, Guy Mannering, when another newspaperman pursuing the story caught up with Mannering in retirement in Chicago. Pinson was 'a great dandy', Mannering said, and was jokingly known as 'the Count' by his brother officers. Warming to his theme, Mannering remembered that Pinson was reticent about his age. 'He used to dye his hair and long moustache [the moustache was obviously an embellishment from Pinson's army days, but what an appropriate adornment for a villain], and even went so far as to paint his face so as to hide the crow's feet.' He is portrayed as quite a ladykiller, especially when 'arrayed to astonish the belles of a garrison town'. But he's also a 'taciturn man' who 'always passed as a bachelor and resented any insinuation that he had ever been married'.

A repeated strand in memories of Pinson is that he was 'a lover of the turf': in other words, passionate about horse racing. In Halifax, Nova Scotia he was said to have ridden as a gentleman jockey in the races that took place on the Common, the grassy expanse that the military garrison used as pasturage for its horses and livestock. Hand-in-hand with this go recollections of his heavy gambling at the racecourse, with the result that 'he was always hard up'. There appears to be general agreement that Pinson didn't come from a wealthy background, and that his father was a Church of England clergyman.

But then an alternative version pops up in other newspaper accounts that turns this version on its head. Pinson's father was indeed an Anglican clergyman living in Jersey. However, he was also rich, looked down on the Hugos for not being rich enough, and further disapproved of them because they were – in nominal terms only – Roman Catholics.

Sometimes, in my frustration at failing to get to grips with anything more substantial, I've found myself longing for the certainties of fiction and the pleasures of following the arc of a character. The two fictional characters I invariably pick on as representative of Albert Pinson are both in their way stereotypes, and pretty negative ones at that. Yet in the hands of great writers they acquire a flesh-and-blood believability that all the surging doubts surrounding a shadowy real-life figure from the past can never provide.

One of them is Sergeant Troy, Thomas Hardy's dashing soldier villain from *Far from the Madding Crowd*, who proves irresistible to the heroine Bathsheba Everdene, with unhappy and ultimately tragic consequences. 'Brilliant in brass and scarlet', vain, impulsive, and described as 'vulnerable only in the present' – which turns out to mean that he marries Bathsheba having jilted his pregnant true love Fanny Robin at the altar – Frank Troy is known as 'a walking ruin to honest girls'. The temptation to see Pinson reflected in Hardy's creation only increases when Troy bets on the horses at the autumn races and loses £100 of Bathsheba's money.

The other handsome cad is Morris Townsend from Henry James's *Washington Square*, published in 1880, six years after Hardy's novel. Townsend is the quintessential fortune hunter. He pursues Catherine Sloper, dull and unprepossessing, but destined to inherit a vast income from her father, Dr Austin Sloper. Dr Sloper opposes the match, recognizing, like the reader, what lies at the root of Townsend's interest in his daughter, behind all the silky blandishments of his courtship. The book has always been my favourite James (James's stroke of genius is to make Catherine's father, with his contempt for his daughter's lack of beauty and gracefulness, the source of an even more powerful cruelty than that of the scoundrel suitor). It takes on a renewed significance when in the odd, despairing, moment I imagine Albert Pinson as Townsend. Moreover, in the anecdote that inspired *Washington Square*, told to James by the actress Fanny Kemble, the original Townsend, Kemble's own brother, happens to have been 'a young ensign in a marching regiment'. He was very handsome, 'but very luxurious and selfish, and without a penny to his name'.

But escape from this world of make-believe and it is still possible to nail down a few hard facts about Pinson. Plain, unadulterated facts that often beg more questions than they provide answers. Facts that open up gaps into which you pour your own speculations, fantasies, and alternative scenarios.

Inexplicably, in all the years since my first interest in the subject, I'd managed to overlook some of the scores of public records – census returns, baptismal and marriage certificates, school records – which have gradually become available on the internet (mind you, so has everyone else writing on the subject). The day after my visit to the beach I typed the name Albert Andrew Pinson into the search engines on various ancestry sites, and then spent the rest of the week sorting through all the positive identifications, false leads and duds this threw up.

The resulting picture clears a path through the thickets of half-truth and rumour. The Pinsons were a wealthy family from Dartmouth in Devon. Albert's great-grandfather Andrew Pinson was partner in a successful merchant company established in the 1760s, trading salted fish across the Atlantic with the Canadian coastal province of Newfoundland. It was a lucrative business, though not without its dangers. Sailing across the ocean from Dartmouth to their company's base in southern Labrador, members of the family often battled terrible storms that wrecked their ships. They also constantly faced the risk of their cargoes being pirated by rogue traders or confiscated by foreign powers trading in the same waters.

The business inherited by Andrew Pinson, Albert's father, in the early years of the nineteenth century, had suffered some diminishment from family feuds and bank failures, but was still a going concern. Andrew's first wife died in 1824. Two years later he married again, to Jane Tuson (née Capon), the widow of a solicitor from Ilchester, in Somerset.

At this point the branches of the family tree start to bend noticeably under their collective weight. Andrew's first marriage had produced four children, and so too had Jane's. In 1827, the year following their wedding at St David's, Exeter, Jane gave birth to their first child, a daughter, Julia. Jane was pregnant again in November 1831 when an unexpected tragedy occurred: the sudden death of Andrew Pinson at the age of 46. Like his own father, Andrew may have drowned on one of the company's ocean voyages.

Albert Andrew Pinson was born at Townstall, a small suburb of Dartmouth, three months after his father's death, on 14 February 1832 – Valentine's Day, appropriately enough. He was baptized in December that year at the parish church of St Clement's.

Jane Pinson inherited her late husband's estate, limited though this appears to have been (Andrew's will refers to his bequest to his wife as only a 'little property'). Andrew's children by his previous marriage continued to benefit from their grandfather's, the first Andrew Pinson's, will. Having been born long after their grandfather's death, neither Julia nor Albert Andrew, Andrew and Jane's children, stood to gain under the terms of this.

A boy who never knew his father, brought up in his earliest years by a widowed mother, living in circumstances where money was short: this was Albert Pinson's introduction to life.

Yet whether or not she had to scrimp and save to do so, Jane Pinson managed to enrol her son at the age of nine in a reputable boarding school. St James Collegiate School in St Helier, Jersey, founded not many years before by Dr Vincent Thompson, a graduate of Trinity College, Dublin, advertised itself as 'a Preparatory Academy for the Universities and the Naval and Military Colleges'. In 1841 Albert Pinson was recorded as being one of 39 boarders there.

The decision to send young Albert to school in Jersey arose from Jane Pinson's move, not long after her husband's death, to the Channel Islands. Two of her sons by her first marriage were by 1834 attending Elizabeth College in neighbouring Guernsey, which may offer some explanation of why she chose to live close by. Some time in the latter half of the 1830s Jane married for the third time. Her new husband was an Anglican clergyman living in Jersey, the Revd Charles Templer. Like the Pinsons, Templer was originally from southern Devon, which suggests that he could have been a family friend or acquaintance. The army comrades who described Albert Pinson as the son of an Anglican clergyman were not that far off the truth. He was the stepson of one.

By the time of the 1851 census, taken on 30 March that year, a small family unit was residing in the boarding house at 24 Belmont Road in St Helier. Jane Pinson, now Jane Templer, her husband the Revd Templer, and her son Albert, aged 19. Like Adèle Hugo, Albert had suffered the loss of a sister. Julia, his only sibling (as opposed to his half-siblings), briefly married to Edward Askew Sothern, an actor who performed at St Helier's Theatre Royal, had died the previous year from tuberculosis.

On that March day, 24 Belmont Road was crammed with occupants. The landlady, Mrs Aaronsen, a young widow with three daughters and two sons, all except one of school age, was probably renting out rooms in order to make ends meet. She also had three visitors staying with her on the night of the thirtieth, one of whom described his occupation as that of a comedian, so maybe the house was ringing with laughter.

This is as much as can be deduced from the census form. Nothing more. You feel so close to a moment from the past and then frustratingly the door slams shut on you, leaving open the question of how Albert Pinson, his mother and stepfather came to be living in such reduced circumstances. And those circumstances were about to worsen. Within two years the Revd Templer would be dead at the age of 65, leaving Jane a widow for a third time.

Further questions rapidly accumulate. What had Albert been doing in the years since he left school? Presumably the Templers hadn't the money to pay his fees as a gentleman cadet at Sandhurst or Woolwich, but why then was he not employed in some other way? The column beside Albert Pinson's name for 'Rank, Profession, or Occupation' is left resoundingly blank.

Here my imagination takes a leap. Supposing Jane Templer doted on the son who'd never known his father to the extent of slipping him (without the knowledge of his stepfather) what little money she had to spare, which Albert proceeded to lose on the horses? Or worse: supposing the Templers' sad situation was a direct result of having to pay off the work-shy Albert's debts incurred at the racetrack?

In writing about other people's lives, you learn to be wary of your imagination. For the imagination tugs you irresistibly in the direction of tying up all those tiresome loose ends to make something neat and tidy, something that almost inevitably conforms to a familiar, and invariably stale, plotline. Meanwhile the rational part of oneself remains earthbound, grudgingly recognizing that there are aspects of any individual's life – never so much as guessed at – that are irretrievably lost to time. But it's the ongoing tension between the imaginative elements and the stamp of factual truth that gives the best biographies something of their lasting power.

We do know for sure where Adèle Hugo first encountered Albert Pinson – or at least where he first caught sight of her. According to a letter Adèle wrote a decade later to her father, she was sitting on a bench on the Terrace overlooking the beach at Grève d'Azette, absorbed in reading a book. She didn't notice Pinson as he strolled along the sands beneath her. However, looking up he saw her, and – here Adèle's letter swells to a romantic crescendo – from that day on he was in love with her.

Other evidence, as we'll shortly discover, suggests that this first sighting occurred sometime in the autumn of 1852, not long after the Hugos' arrival at Marine Terrace. On the lookout for other places and occasions where Adèle and Pinson's paths might have crossed, I couldn't help noticing that Pinson's home in Belmont Road was just doors along from the Queen's Assembly Rooms, where Adèle attended the Fancy Dress Ball and occasionally went to concerts. The Assembly Rooms were also the scene of a bazaar held at the end of February 1853. This had been arranged to raise money for the poorer *proscrits*, partly to discourage them from returning to France under the amnesty recently granted by Napoleon III. Madame Hugo wrote to her sister Julie Chenay about the response of the Jersey ladies, who demonstrated unexpected and generous enthusiasm for the occasion. Knitwear, embroidery and fabrics of all kinds 'rained down on us'. There were pennants displaying the words '*Vive* Victor Hugo' and 'Honour to the Proscrits'. Five hundred people attended and £160 was raised. Both Madame Hugo and Adèle ran stalls.

More intriguing is Adèle's journal account of a day at the Jersey races, in June 1855, for the annual Queen's Cup on Gorey Common. Curiously, throughout her lively description of the event, which runs to several pages, she doesn't give any indication of whether she was actually present on that day, or who accompanied her if she was.

Was she instead drawing on memories of the same race, perhaps a year or two earlier? She writes that 'it is not a steeple-chase for horses; it is a steeple-chase for women', and with a Parisian's gimlet eye for fashion describes 'delicious sky-blue hats' worn with 'superb green dresses' which, she notes tartly, are a fashionable style 'only in the countryside'. Some of the ladies, decked out in reds, greens and yellows, resemble parrots. As for the young men watching the race from the grandstand, they are a collection of 'beaux, English dandies, cretins, collectors of cretinous cravats, surmounted by side-whiskers (usually red)'. Could one of these dandies with side whiskers have been Albert Pinson? Had he and Adèle managed to slip away to Gorey – not far from Marine Terrace – so that he could show her the delights of the turf?

I'm racing ahead of myself, though. Further back, at the end of 1852, during the Hugo family's first Christmas in Jersey, Adèle's secret journal, the few coded pages into which she poured her own private thoughts, contains a reference to a mysterious 'Monsieur P.', whom she has yet to meet. This 'P.', it's safe to say, is Albert Pinson.

In the final days of that December, Adèle had taken advantage of her mother's absence in Paris to continue a flirtation with the boy next door. John Rose, the eldest of the landlord Thomas Rose's sons, was pining for Adèle. She was largely indifferent to him but, in the manner of young women with limited experience of the amorous advances of young men, she was enjoying the sport of playing with his feelings, acting 'the little coquette', while resolving 'to be loved, without loving'.

The stern reportage of the main part of the journal, in which Adèle is generally a listener and rarely an active participant, has been replaced by a much more relaxed and intimate tone in which she plays the heroine of her own story. She goes next door, dressed to kill, resplendent in a red gown under a black cloak, a veil of tulle over her head. Her expression of confidence in her own beauty is surprising – she is 'ravishing, dazzling' – not least because it provides such a contrast with her muted, passive presence in the bulk of the journal.

John Rose borrows Adèle's portrait and hangs it above his bed. They read to each other, as he is meant to be teaching her English and she improving his French. He pointedly chooses Casanova's *Memoirs* and reads aloud from some of its bawdiest passages. 'The lesson over', Adèle records, 'he said to me, Mademoiselle kiss me, I will not, I assure you, make the slightest resistance. Start with me, finish with P.'

Rose and his brothers had sometimes mentioned Monsieur P. to Adèle. 'They say that he is in love with me,' she notes, but she is unimpressed and unwilling to stay to meet this mysterious stranger one evening when P. is expected at the Roses' for dinner. Instead she continues to flirt with John Rose, and is captured in a passionate embrace. 'His lips, not having had time to relax, met mine in a second kiss. So I ran away very quickly, without saying a word, without turning my head.'

The incident set off warning signals, and Adèle remembered some words of Balzac about one thing leading to another. She feared that to encourage John Rose further might result in her becoming his mistress or – worse – his wife. The Rose family, who had been cheering John on from the sidelines in his pursuit of Adèle, were surprised by her rebuffing of him, and assumed that this was because she was already promised to Auguste Vacquerie. However, despite the memory of the 'intoxicating kisses' she and Auguste had shared seven years earlier in the garden at Place Royale, and despite Vacquerie's intense, brooding presence constantly hovering over her, Adèle's feelings for him had cooled. They had simply 'not developed', Adèle stated matter-of-factly in her journal.

Adèle's resistance to marriage was by this time clear. In my ignorance, I'd always thought of nineteenth-century women from the French middle and upper-middle classes as possessing more freedom in their relationships with men, and in their choice of husbands, than their counterparts across the Channel. In fact, young French women from bourgeois families were much more constrained. At times their status within the family amounted to little more than that of a chattel. A young woman's movements, following the completion of her education, were strictly regulated.

She would not normally leave home unless chaperoned by an older woman, usually her mother or grandmother. A marriage was nearly always arranged for her. Romantic attachment was immaterial and had little or nothing to do with it. Once married, a husband owed his wife protection; she owed him her obedience.

Adèle regarded all this as a humiliating prospect. In March 1853 she received her first proposal of marriage and promptly rejected it. Admittedly, her suitor's hand was a 'little wrinkled', as he was 45, double her age. Three months later the possibility of another proposal appeared on the horizon. 'A white bouquet mixed with a spray of orange flowers was sent her,' Madame Hugo informed her sister. But Adèle 'immediately gave the gallant knight the cold shoulder'. Madame Hugo regretted this, as 'the marriage would have had some advantageous aspects'.

Why should she lose her name and give herself 'a master', Adèle responded when her mother despaired of her ever finding a husband – 'I who am so proud to call myself Mademoiselle Hugo, I who am free, so calm and happy in my home!' Adèle had read some of the early novels of George Sand (the pen name of Amantine Lucile Aurore Dupin), absorbing their feminist ideas, especially their implicit protest against the repression of women and their presentation of marriage as a form of slavery. She would also have been aware of Sand's own life as an emancipated woman. In her twenties Sand had left her husband to live a Bohemian life in Paris, telling him as she went that she would go where she pleased, without having to render an account to anyone. Adèle herself envisaged writing a book about female emancipation, an idea she predicted 'no one would laugh at in a hundred years'.

Victor Hugo's vision of freedom for women was in some respects wider than Sand's as, unlike her, he argued for women's civil and political rights, including the right to vote (amazingly a right denied to French women until 1944). In July 1853 Hugo spoke at the Jersey graveside of a female *proscrit*, Louise-Anselme Julien, who had died of consumption, and declared that 'the eighteenth century proclaimed the Rights of Man, the nineteenth will proclaim the Rights of Women'. Yet, in a way that was to have far-reaching consequences for his daughter's future, Hugo stopped short of extending that vision to one of personal freedom for women. Perhaps it was his romanticism that stood in the way, but for Victor Hugo family, and a woman's place within it, remained fundamental. As he told Adèle, a woman's role in life was to get married. It almost goes without saying that he meant to someone he considered suitable.

As for Adèle, her principled rejection of marriage would not long survive the arrival in her life of Monsieur P. – Albert Pinson.

So there's no clue as to precisely when Adèle and Pinson met. Certainly by the early summer of 1854 he was a regular visitor to Marine Terrace. Sometimes he was invited to dine with the Hugos. Throughout that summer and early autumn he was also present at seven séances at the house, as the assiduously maintained records of these occasions reveal. I wonder whether he was surprised the first time he was ushered into the parlour, seated in semi-darkness at a table, and asked to place his hands on top of it. Maybe Adèle had forewarned him about this new-fangled, after-dinner activity, which often stretched into the early hours. Probably he was already aware of the current spiritualist craze for table-rapping – *tables tournantes*, or table-turning, as it was known – which had originated in the United States and was proving a sensation in Paris and other parts of Europe.

It was from Paris, nine months earlier, in September 1853, that spiritualism had entered the lives of the inhabitants of Marine Terrace, in the shape of Delphine de Girardin, a writer and old friend of Victor Hugo's. After dinner on the first evening of her stay in Jersey, Madame de Girardin announced that she wanted to turn the tables. Hugo refused to take any part in the experiment. Initially the table obstinately refused to move. Declaring that the spirits weren't like cab horses, 'obedient to the whim of those who hire them', but would come only when they felt like it, Girardin purchased a three-legged circular table from a St Helier toyshop and pressed it into service. Again there were no results. Finally she placed the smaller table on top of the four-legged square one. On 11 September, with Hugo involved in a séance for the first time, the table began to rap out answers to questions – once for an A, twice for a B, and so on; this was not a speedy process – ultimately silencing sceptics among the assembled company.

Flippantly, I can't help thinking of these visits of the spirit world to the Hugo home as akin to the characters and plot of Noël Coward's 'improbable farce' *Blithe Spirit*. In this scheme of things, Madame de Girardin takes the role of the eccentric medium Madame Arcati and Hugo is the writer Charles Condomine, whose initial response on being told that there is someone from the other side who wishes to speak to him is to ask them to leave a message (actually, as the author of several comic plays, one of which, *C'est la faute du mari*, 'It's the Fault of the Husband', has a decidedly *Private Lives*-ish flavour, Girardin would have relished Coward's comedy).

Delphine de Girardin was a chatty, enlivening presence for a household starved of much evening entertainment, and of political and literary gossip from the French capital. But for her, table-rapping was not merely a parlour game. There was a dark seriousness, even a sense of urgency about it. She was suffering from the cancer that would kill her two years later and had already yielded, so she said, to 'the charm of death'. For the Hugo family, the first communication from the dead on that September evening could not have been more welcome – or more astonishing and disturbing, like a gust of icy wind unexpectedly blowing through the house. The table trembled, moved sideways, jumped (tables didn't really turn). 'The Book of the Tables', kept by assorted members of the family, and the account in Adèle's journal agree in essential details and report the following exchange:

> *Mme de Girardin* Who are you?
> *Table* Ame Soror [sister soul].
> *Hugo* That is sister in Latin . . .
> *Charles Hugo* I have lost a sister.
> *Mme Hugo and Victor Hugo hold back their tears.*
> *Hugo* Are you happy?
> *Table* Yes.
> *Hugo (profoundly moved)* Where are you?
> *Table* Light . . .
> *Hugo* Are you happy when I mingle my prayers with your name?
> *Table* Yes.

Promising that she would soon return, the spirit departed.

Vacquerie, initially averse to table-turning, dismissing it as an 'opium of weak souls', had 'distinctly felt' Léopoldine's presence, and became a committed participant in future séances. Madame Hugo said that she had long held communion with her dead, and that the table had come to tell her that she was not suffering from illusions. Adèle wrote simply that it was beyond doubt that 'There is a spirit in the table'.

Hugo himself became fully persuaded of the reality of the spirits and of the phenomenon of the tables. In the course of the next two years at Marine Terrace, calling to the souls of the deceased through the darkness became a regular evening pastime, as the table-rapping intensified and a roll call of more than a hundred spirits floated through the house. They included Plato, Dante (who confessed to admiring Hugo's poetry), Shakespeare, Racine, Isaiah, the prophet Muhammad and Jesus Christ (criticizing Christianity and spelling out the need for prophets of a new religion, of a kind advocated by Hugo in his poetry). Some were abstractions: Criticism, Drama, the Novel. Some spoke in prose, others in verse that might conceivably have been written by Victor Hugo. All of them conveniently communicated in French.

Just occasionally Hugo was troubled about the true nature of these visitations. Were the spirits genuinely who they said they were, or were they another, third party? At first he had wondered whether they might even be 'ourselves multiplied by emotion?' Charles Hugo had quickly established himself as the outstanding medium – in opposition to François-Victor, who remained a confirmed sceptic and was decried by the rest of his family for being 'a man of the nineteenth century' rather than of the future – but were the communications he awakened simply his own thoughts amplified by 'magnetism'? That there was something more complex at work than the movement of the table by a dominant participant is obvious. It's especially telling that while Hugo interrogated the spirits, he rarely touched the table himself, suggesting that some kind of extra-sensory perception was involved, with Charles acting as an effective transmitter of his father's thoughts. However, simply exposing the phenomenon as a hoax is futile. The fact is that Hugo, together with other members of his family and circle, believed that they were communicating with the supernatural (unlike another great poet of the time, Alfred Tennyson, who was certain that 'God and the ghosts of man' would have chosen something other than 'mere table-legs' through which to speak to us).

It's too cheesy a pun to say that Albert Pinson entered into the spirit of things, though this is exactly what he did. At the first séance he attended, on 7 June 1854, the spirit making contact through the table was a member of his own family. Not Julia, his recently deceased sister, as one might have expected, but another, more distant relative:

Charles Hugo Who is there?
Table Frater tuus [your brother]
Charles Hugo You are not my brother. Are you Pinson's?
Table Yes, Andrew.

This Andrew Pinson was Pinson's half-brother, one of his father's children by his first marriage, who had mysteriously disappeared more than a decade earlier after joining the merchant navy. No one in his family had any idea of what had happened to him. Pinson continued with another question, speaking in English this time, and received an answer, also in English. He got up from the table visibly moved and requested that neither the questions nor the answers be recorded, since they were 'family matters'.

Five days later Pinson was back at the table; this time Hugo wasn't present. The young man's bilingualism was becoming useful. Lord Byron appeared, and with a violent shake of the table obstreperously refused to recite any of his poetry. Sir Walter Scott – an old favourite of Hugo's, and of Adèle's, as she hoped to set Scott's poem 'The Lady of the Lake' to music – was more obliging, and dictated to Pinson two lines of verse of a distinctly pessimistic nature, expressed in an irreproachable English: 'Vex not the bard; his lyre is broken, /His last song sung, his last word spoken.'

The words of the dead spirits were acting beneficially and formatively on Victor Hugo and his writing, softening the effects of bereavement, giving shape to many of his ideas and intuitions, and allowing him a glimpse into the infinite and a confirmation of the idea of the transmigration of souls. But this invoking of the spirit world had stirred up something mysterious, even wantonly uncontrollable, something that was held responsible for a series of baffling occurrences at Marine Terrace.

A baker's boy, approaching St Luke's Church, opposite the Hugo house, witnessed a white figure, motionless and in flames. Returning home at two in the morning, Charles and François-Victor found the drawing room locked and its windows brilliantly illuminated, as if by dozens of candles – though the next morning there was no sign of candles or a lamp having burned. The White Lady, adopted by Adèle as the guardian angel of Marine Terrace, announced at one of the séances that she would appear at the front of the house at 3 a.m. At precisely that hour, the front door bell rang. Could someone have been playing a trick? No one answered the door.

Meanwhile Hugo was disturbed by strange tappings on the walls of his room. His papers were shuffled about by some unseen hand.

And cries and piercing shrieks could be heard at times echoing through the house, above the roar of the ocean.

They are silent, my ghosts.

Once, a departing figure, one of a pair of Victorian women wearing identical crinolines, who I believed or knew to be sisters, turned to me, as if to speak. Her mouth opened and formed an 'o'. She closed it and tried again. Still no sound. I remember her voluminous skirts brushing against the furniture as she left my room. But it was a noiseless rustle, and these women, like all the other unaccounted-for presences I'd grown used to seeing, didn't suddenly dissolve through doors or walls, as ghosts are supposed to. In a way I've never been able to define or describe to my own satisfaction or anyone else's, one moment they appeared to possess a material existence, the next they did not. They simply disappeared into the silence.

This absence of verbal communication generally left me wondering what on earth the purpose of these night-time visitations could be. I had no clue about the identity of any of these ghosts, so it seemed unlikely that they could be making an act of reparation for some lifetime's wrongful deed, or had some urgent message to impart to me. There was one exception to this. On a freezing winter's night I had sat bolt upright in bed, my body coursing with fear and my attention riveted by the sight of my father's disembodied head coming towards me from the other side of the room. The expression on his face, unrelentingly grim, was as frightening as the fact of his sudden physical manifestation, years after his death. A look of admonition was perhaps discernible in his eyes, but what all these ghostly presences gave off, like some invitingly familiar scent, was an overriding impression of curiosity. They kept staring intensely, unblinkingly, at me. Aghast and rooted to the spot, I stared back. It could be that the moment I was unable to keep up my part in this staring contest, the mysterious connection was lost, the apparition vanished, and I found myself once again alone in my bedroom.

But while I held their gaze I seemed to pay close attention to every detail of their physical appearance. Afterwards I was able to recall it all with pinpoint precision: the lines and veins on a face, the tarnished gold of a ring on a finger, the fabric and fold of a dress. Staying at a friend's house on the Kent coast, I was awoken in the early hours by a middle-aged man holding a guttering candle a few inches from my face. He was clad in a long nightshirt and on top of his head he wore a nightcap, its bobble dangling carelessly over his shoulder. The terror he instilled in me at that moment was real enough, but retrospectively what lies imprinted on my mind, like the photographic image on an old glass plate, is the intricate embroidery work, the sweeping floral design in raised stitch work, that decorated the pleated hem of his cap.

These ghost-seeing experiences were at their height during my mid- to late twenties, only gradually subsiding in the course of my thirties and becoming much scarcer thereafter. Initially regarded by me with a frisson of excitement, they soon became a source of dread, as my sleep was interrupted two or three times a week by strange phantoms lurking in the shadows or tripping lightly over the floorboards. I had started off by congratulating myself on possessing some kind of paranormal power. Now I began to wonder, ever so tentatively at first, what they betrayed about my mental condition.

My brother, a classical tenor, was singing the role of Peter Quint, one of the ghosts who haunts the governess, in a production of *The Turn of the Screw*, Benjamin Britten's opera based on the famous ghost story by Henry James. He gave an interview to the London *Evening Standard* that was headlined with a provocative quote from him: 'I'VE NEVER SEEN A GHOST BUT MY BROTHER HAS.' My father took umbrage on my behalf, incensed at what he clearly considered to be a breach of confidence about something that the outside world might potentially judge as shaming. 'People will think you're mad, or well on the way to becoming so', he rang to tell me, in typically plain-speaking fashion. Although he would not have known it, my father was of one mind on the subject with the novelist Walter

Scott. Scott wrote that anyone who claimed to have seen a ghost was pathetically unbalanced, the victim of 'some lively dream, a waking reverie, the excitation of a powerful imagination, or the misrepresentation of a diseased organ of sight'.

Henry James's tale of the inexperienced governess who arrives at a grand country house to take care of two young children and becomes increasingly convinced that a former manservant and governess, both dead, are trying to possess the souls of her charges, has become a useful repository for all our equivocal feelings about the nature of unexplained apparitions. Are the ghosts the governess sees real, or are they products of her imagination? Do these apparently supernatural phenomena have any independent existence, or are they a totally subjective human vision?

If my own encounters were visions, resembling some magic lantern show of the unconscious, what I could say with an inward conviction of absolute certainty was that they were no figment of a dream world. I saw them while I was wide awake, with my eyes resolutely wide open.

Into my life at this time came a Cambridge scientist keen to treat me as a test case, and to use all the powers of experiment and deductive reasoning at his disposal to establish the source of my nocturnal disturbances. Graeme Mitchison's scientific interests were prodigious, encompassing molecular biology, physics and neuroscience. His enormous bulbous forehead, inherited from his great-uncle, the scientist J. B. S. Haldane, which I took as denoting his sheer weight of braininess – to say nothing of the clarity and celerity of his thinking – made it difficult at times not to think of him as the fount of all reason.

In collaboration with the illustrious Francis Crick, one of the discoverers of the structure of DNA, Graeme had embarked on a study of dreaming, developing the theory that dreams are essentially meaningless. To Crick and Mitchison, we dream in order to forget. Far from being the process by which we make order out of the chaos of our experience, dreaming, according to their theory, is simply a dumping ground for all the unwanted material we accumulate in our daily lives.

Graeme was certain that my ghosts were dreams, visual hallucinations belonging to the rapid eye movement period of sleep during which the sleeper's emotional state is heightened. I was equally certain that they were not, and we debated the subject back and forth. I repeated over and over that I was awake and in a state of clear perception whenever I saw a face staring back at me. Graeme's own facial expressions during these verbal assaults – never mockery or ridicule, for he was far too gentle and sympathetic an individual for that, but quietly registering doubt – indicated that he remained to be convinced.

The clinching argument, as far as I was concerned, against any notion that dreaming was the key to explaining these apparitions, was the overwhelming element of surprise that accompanied my every encounter with them. This was in definite contrast to any dream I've ever had, in which, no matter how terrifying, absurd, or surreal are the images conjured up by sleep, a sense of shock or awed surprise is always precisely what's missing. We reached a stage where Graeme wanted to attach EEG scalp electrodes to my head to monitor the brain's electrical activity as it transitioned into sleep. I resisted playing the part of his guinea pig, not least because I was beginning to realize that it wasn't only my unconscious he was interested in dabbling with.

In the 30 years since, there's been renewed interest among researchers about that tantalizingly brief period between sleeping and full wakefulness, when reality begins to warp and the cerebral cortex is said to produce hallucinations of a vivid and arresting power. Nowadays there's even a scientific term for this relatively rare, and still incompletely understood, condition: hypnopompic hallucination (though actually the name was introduced as far back as the first year of the twentieth century).

These hallucinations, or spectres of the self as they could be called, might indeed be mistaken for ghosts. You can see how, to a receptive mind, they could easily reinforce a belief in the supernatural. But is that all there is to it? Or does the mind in these moments gain access to a spiritual or supernatural realm?

Once your sense of reality has been upended, you no longer look for certainty in such things. What I do believe is that any ghostly tale should remain resistant to strict interpretation. For me, to use a phrase from James's *Turn of the Screw*, it shouldn't tell 'in any literal vulgar way'.

———

Critics of the *tables tournantes* were adamant that these séances were no innocent parlour game. Inviting unruly spirits into your home was only asking for trouble, and might in some cases lead quite literally to madness. Women especially, with their alleged susceptibility to nervous attacks, were considered to be prone to mental disturbance following prolonged exposure to the tables.

Excluded from the activities at Marine Terrace, Juliette Drouet was suspicious of their possible effects. From her lodgings nearby, at the Green Man public house, she made fun of spiritualism, rapping out 'a most affectionate good night' to Victor Hugo, her 'beloved Toto'. But she wrote also of her concern, signalling a caution that there was 'something dangerous to reason in this sort of playing about, when it is taken seriously'.

The tables posed an additional threat, to decorum and social well-being, according to commentators who cared about such things. The extinguishing of lamps and candles and the plunge into darkness at the start of a séance could only act as an encouragement to lax moral behaviour, putting women, and in particular well-bred young women, at risk. On a warm August evening in 1854, Adèle Hugo felt Albert Pinson's leg pressed against hers under the table. It awakened 'a thousand desires in her blood' and confirmed her in the 'certainty of loving, of being loved'. Later they kissed.

Something about their attraction of opposites fascinated her. Addressing Albert in the private pages of her journal, she explored the paradoxes implicit in their relationship:

Englishman, you love a French woman; monarchist you love a republican; blond, you love a brunette; man of tradition, you love a woman of the future; materialist, you love a woman of ideas.

So why do I love you, can you tell me?

As late summer turned into the first weeks of autumn, Albert Pinson continued to be a guest at the Hugos' lunch and dinner tables, as well as at the *tables tournantes*, contributing the occasional remark to the perennial discussions about Napoleon III and his imperial ambitions. Scrutinizing Pinson closely, and observing that Adèle was unable to hide her feelings for him, Auguste Vacquerie was eaten up by the bitterness of rejection. 'For eight years', Adèle reported Vacquerie as telling her, 'I, who am a man of genius, have deployed my talents to make you love me. I give up. I cannot do the impossible.'

However, the sight of Pinson giving Adèle his arm as they left the dining room together further enraged Vacquerie, making him 'green' with jealousy. Having failed to make Adèle jealous in turn by flirting with Margaret Allen, an English friend of the Hugos visiting Marine Terrace, Vacquerie resorted to physical assault. Alone with Adèle on the Terrace, he insulted her appearance – she was too skinny, he said, and her arms were like spindles – before spitting in her face and delivering a sharp kick to her backside.

Auguste 'makes my life impossible', Adèle wrote, understandably enough, in despair. 'God cannot have meant anyone to put up with what I endure.' Far more devastating, though, was the news of Pinson's imminent departure from Jersey. He had decided to enlist in the 3rd West Yorkshire Light Infantry, a regiment in the militia, and would be leaving for England shortly.

Much later the rumour surfaced that a magistrate's ultimatum had forced Pinson's hand because of the debts he'd incurred gambling on the turf: join the army or else be sent to debtors' prison. This could have some basis in truth, but seems unlikely, given that new recruits to the military reserve were selected on the basis of their being without a single blemish on their character. Candidates were carefully interviewed prior to attestation, and great lengths gone through to check police, bankruptcy and debtors' records.

Having fallen into disuse at the end of the Napoleonic Wars, the British army's militia force had been reconstituted as recently as 1852, partly in reaction to Napoleon III's coup, which had revived age-old fears of French invasion. Volunteers were engaged for five years. Training was for 56 days on enlistment. Militiamen then returned to civilian life, reporting for several weeks' further training during each subsequent year. The pay was a pittance, though it could act as a useful supplement to civilian earnings.

Pinson was joining a militia regiment at a time when recruits were eagerly sought to compensate for the loss of trained men to the regular army, to serve in the Crimean War. He was commissioned as an ensign, the lowest rank, but promotion to lieutenant came quickly, by the spring of 1855. What Pinson must have calculated on – that the militia would serve for entry by the back door to the regular army – did indeed prove to be the case. With the deaths of so many commissioned officers during the war, at Balaclava and Inkerman, to say nothing of the losses incurred through the rampant spread of disease, the army would allow a fixed number of men from the militia to transfer as officers to the regulars without having first to purchase a commission. In this way Albert Pinson circumvented his lack of family funds and the need to take the traditional route into the officer ranks of the British army through the hallowed portals of Sandhurst or Woolwich. In April 1856, just as the Crimean War was being brought to a close with the signing of the Treaty of Paris, he would enter the army as an ensign in the 16th (the Bedfordshire) Regiment of Foot and begin his ascent through the ranks.

All this was lost on Adèle. How could Albert even think of deserting her, given their manifest love for each other? Her one objective now was to make him stay in Jersey. While the rest of the household was asleep, she removed the smaller table from the parlour, carrying it up to her room on the first floor. Here she began to consult the spirits, seeking their advice in matters of the heart in her own private séances, allowing the table to function as some kind of spinning agony aunt.

Her mediumship was not on a par with that of her brother Charles. There were long gaps and silences, and impenetrable responses impossible to interpret. But on many occasions she believed herself able to reach the ghost of her elder sister. Léopoldine counselled Adèle with sympathy, revealing herself to be fully in support of her great passion for Pinson, and telling Adèle exactly what she wanted to hear.

Despite his 'insults', his 'threats' and 'blows', Adèle remained full of pity for Vacquerie's situation, and of guilt at having 'masked' the death of her love for him. She didn't want to treat him badly, and was worried about her mother's reaction when she received the news of this definitive break. For Madame Hugo had long favoured Auguste as a possible husband for her daughter.

The table was having none of this. Vacquerie must be sent from Marine Terrace.

'Why do you tell me to throw Auguste out of the door immediately', Adèle countered, 'when Albert loves me so little and doesn't pretend he'll come back?'

If Albert did love her, she continued at a later session, why had he been overheard telling Charles Hugo of his plans to marry a pretty fourteen-year-old orphan? The remark had hurt Adèle, 'implausible as it was', and if true would mark 'the absolute death of my love'.

The table's response soothed her. Albert had no intention of marrying the young girl, and had said this only to make her jealous.

By late September 1854, Albert Pinson had left Jersey to join the West Yorkshires at their headquarters in Doncaster. The table's assurances that 'cheerfulness, spiritedness, and tenderness' would be enough to put a stop to his departure had proved far off the mark. A new, more frantic campaign was now embarked upon to persuade Pinson to renounce his commission and return home to Adèle. And for the first time there was a strong element of menace behind it.

The table evaluated various possibilities. Adèle could try making Albert jealous, with Vacquerie (whose own dispatch from Marine Terrace had been given a stay of execution by Madame Hugo), or with Jules Allix, the young *proscrit*, banished to Jersey for his part in a plot against the Emperor, who made no secret of his attraction to Adèle. Alternatively she could threaten Albert with her suicide. Or she could inform him that she was pregnant with his child.

This last option made me sit up smartly when I read about it, in the decoded transcriptions of Adèle's séances: so she and Pinson had started having a sexual relationship. But where could their lovemaking have taken place? Surely not in the cramped boarding house quarters Pinson shared with his widowed mother? And not amid the claustrophobic atmosphere of Marine Terrace, with its constant stream of visitors, either?

Which of Adèle's threats was actually communicated to Pinson? All or none of them? It's impossible to tell, for at this point the boundary between reality and fantasy, in the narrative of Adèle and Pinson's relationship, starts to blur and erode like a chalk drawing dissolving in the rain.

From her conversations with the table, it's evident that Adèle was writing innumerable letters to Pinson, and submitting drafts to the spirits for their sanction. How many of these were sent is a mystery. Presumably most of them were destroyed, but she appears nonetheless to have kept up a correspondence with Pinson back in England, aided by Margaret Allen, her English friend, who acted as a courier for Adèle's letters when returning home.

In one surviving draft letter, dated 28 December 1854 – and it is only a draft, with no evidence that it was ever sent – Adèle justifies her actions, including the threat of her death by her own hand, by maintaining that Pinson had 'to be torn away from the army at all costs' for his moral and physical well-being. She reveals that in an earlier letter she had taunted him with the news that she was having his child, but would be marrying someone else, 'a handsome and very spiritual young man', unless he renounced his commission.

This stratagem, if it was ever put into practice, clearly hadn't worked. The idea of marriage to Pinson, which Adèle had earlier rejected because of her attempt 'to hold myself up as an example for my sex', now seemed to be the one sure way of trapping him. 'He needs to have money,' the table prompted, and in the scrap of another draft, this time undated, she placed the fortune she would receive on her marriage, 40,000 francs, an income of 2,000 a year, squarely before him as a bargaining counter:

You will resign your commission, we will get married, and with my dowry you will buy a more important, lucrative, more brilliant commission as a line officer. No one can accuse a man who leaves the undangerous militia for a commission in the line of being a coward.

Albert didn't take the bait. That much is obvious, though little else is. He was intent on an army career, for certain, but how exactly did he respond to Adèle's harassment? Frustratingly, there's no way of knowing. All one can say is that her behaviour appears to have proved no obstacle to him seeing her again. Adèle's journal mentions the prospect of a reunion in mid-January 1855, just at the point when Pinson's initial phase of training in the militia ended and he was free to return home. Throughout the rest of that year he would have been able to come and go from the English mainland back to Jersey, to stay with his mother – apart from a short intermission for further training – pretty much as he chose (so he probably did fill the role of Adèle's companion on that day at the races on Gorey Common in June 1855). And besides, there's evidence that they continued to correspond whenever they were apart.

For the time being, though, Albert Pinson silently exits the story as suddenly and as unobtrusively as he entered it. At times my inability to flesh him out has made him appear like a figure in the background to, rather than in the forefront of, the actions and feelings he inspired. At others it feels almost as if he had the ability to blend into his surroundings, biding his time, concealing his hand.

After two years, the household séances at Marine Terrace came to an abrupt end in the autumn of 1855. Interest in them had been waning for several months. Madame Hugo declared that she was tired of sharing her house with spirits. Vacquerie was warming to the idea that these so-called 'spirits' were really spectres of the self, emanations from the individuals present at the table.

For Victor Hugo, conversations with the supernatural had served their purpose. He had completed nearly all his religious and visionary poetry for his new volume, Les Contemplations, and was about to write a long poem addressing Léopoldine directly, without the table's intercession. In 'A Celle qui est restée en France' ('To the

One Who Stayed Behind in France'), he asks her, 'In your life do you see ours?'

The culminating blow for further activity at the tables was the descent into madness of one of the séance participants. Jules Allix, the *proscrit* attracted to Adèle, was overtaken by delirium and despondency, and sat immobile murmuring, 'I have seen things this night'. In the course of the next few days, he punched both Charles Hugo and Vacquerie, declared himself to be God and Vacquerie the Devil, and smashed up his sister's house. Allix was interned in the hospital at St Helier for four months. (He was always an eccentric young man, advertising his invention of an early form of wireless communication using two snails, placed in boxes, who were said to have created an indivisible bond through copulation.)

Not long afterwards, the simmering tensions between the *proscrit* community and the islanders, the British government and Napoleon III's France, Britain's new Crimean War ally, reached boiling point. At a public meeting in London, in September 1855, Félix Pyat, a French exile living in England, read out a letter attacking Queen Victoria in crude and personal terms for her recent state visit to Napoleon III in Paris. Published in *L'Homme*, the newspaper of the exiles in Jersey, the letter caused enormous offence among Jerseians, with their intense loyalty to the Crown. The long-term resentments against the political refugees, fanned by French agents, exploded, and the islanders demanded their immediate departure from Jersey.

Victor Hugo hadn't endorsed Pyat's letter, but he championed those who did. On 27 October Hugo's expulsion was ordered and he was given just a week to make arrangements to leave Jersey. The family's new destination was the neighbouring island of Guernsey, another 'rock lost in the sea'. Hugo went first, accompanied by François-Victor and Juliette Drouet. Charles Hugo joined them two days later. As the steamer made its way across stormy waters, Hugo looked back to see only a whitish line on the waves. Jersey appeared to have sunk in the storm.

Madame Hugo, together with Adèle and Vacquerie, was left behind to supervise the packing of 35 pieces of luggage. On 8

November, after three years in Jersey, they finally left for St Peter Port, Guernsey's capital. For one perilous moment, a tin trunk containing the manuscript of the completed *Les Contemplations* and drafts of the book that would become *Les Misérables* dangled above the rough sea before being lowered into the boat.

In her final months at Marine Terrace, Adèle had begun to take stock of her life. Once she had been free, she wrote sadly in her journal, looking back on her final years in Paris, but now she was 'a slave to duty'. In her most depressed moments she saw herself returning to France only when her hair was white and wrinkles had hollowed out her forehead.

'Exile seems to weigh heavily on us', she continued in a further entry. In Guernsey she would feel the deprivations of this way of life more strongly still as the saltwater waves of banishment broke once again over her head.

5

Absences

The Hugo family's new home was 20 Hauteville Street, an undistinguished three-storeyed mansion in the upper reaches of St Peter Port, where the houses give the appearance of scrambling on the backs of one another to get a view of the small bustling harbour and the open sea. They were to remain there for just under a year. Meanwhile the publication in April 1856 of *Les Contemplations* brought Victor Hugo renewed popular acclaim and unexpected commercial success.

I'd been into the British Library to call up a copy of the first edition. It opens to a drawing of Hugo seated on a rock, watching the sunset, with a picture in the clouds of Léopoldine supported by angels. The two-volume work went on sale in Paris, as well as Brussels, after Napoleon III's watchdogs were assured that its contents were uncontroversial and contained nothing more than 'pure poetry'. Readers demanding the book crowded bookshops, and the initial printing was practically exhausted in a day.

Hugo quickly earned 20,000 francs in royalties. Using this sizeable sum he purchased a house further up the street in which he'd been renting. No. 38, a larger Georgian mansion, eventually renamed Hauteville House, was to be Hugo's inviolable sanctuary, his 'English castle' where he could raise the drawbridge at will. For, as a landowner, according to the island's laws, he could never face expulsion again. Hugo had little expectation now of returning to France, and the house in Hauteville Street offered him the opportunity of creating a lasting home that would bear the unmistakeable stamp of his taste and personality. Soon it was alive with the banging and sawing of construction as workmen laboured at a snail's pace to put into effect Hugo's ambitious scheme of interior decoration. The result of several years' work would be a feast for the eyes, 'a genuine autograph in three storeys', as his son Charles called it: nothing less than a material embodiment of Hugo's fantasies and of his imagination, as well as a shrine to his own genius.

A colourful garden was planted, full of the nodding fuchsia that flourished in Guernsey's fertile soil and subtropical climate. Juliette Drouet was not of course forgotten. Hugo rented a small villa for her, La Fallue, close enough to Hauteville House for Juliette to be able to observe her lover at his toilette every morning, a naked apparition washing himself down in a tin tub on the terrace.

EXILIUM VITA EST – 'Life is Exile' – was the Latin motto that Hugo had carved above the entrance to his new dining room. This and other such mottoes distributed throughout the house sometimes give the impression of a prisoner leaving graffiti on the walls of his cell. In one sense Hugo was a prisoner. His self-respect would never allow him to go back to France while Napoleon III remained in power. 'When liberty returns, I will return,' he said. But Guernsey was also his refuge as well as his 'probable tomb'. He prized his 'splendid solitude', perched on a rock. He imagined himself, 'in this great ocean dream', gradually turning into 'a sleepwalker of the sea'. Observing the vast foaming waves and huge scudding clouds beneath his window, he saw himself ending up as 'a kind of witness of God'. At a more practical level, the benefits of this isolation to his writing were obvious, not least, he maintained, because a month's work in Guernsey was the equivalent of a year's worth in Paris.

For the rest of the family, the prospects were far bleaker. This putting down of roots strengthened their sense of incarceration, and fear that exile was being transformed into a permanent state of existence. Furthermore, that exile was being lived out on an island that is geographically much smaller than Jersey, and where the monotonous rhythms of everyday existence were closer in the 1850s to those of a provincial town than to life on the Continent. At no more than 9 miles long and 5 miles wide, Guernsey felt cut off and adrift, a sensation only intensified when the seasonal mists and fogs descended and created an impenetrable barrier to the outside world.

François-Victor described winter in Guernsey as 'six months of imprisonment in a bucket of water'. He acknowledged that they were in 'the dark period of exile' where it was difficult to see the light at the end of the tunnel. When he spotted the steamboat from his window he longed to jump aboard and disembark on land where you didn't always have 'to turn on your feet'.

Both he and Charles made periodic efforts to rattle and loosen and free themselves from their chains. For Adèle the situation was much worse. Unlike her mother and brothers she possessed no hard-won right to leave the island from time to time to come and go as she pleased. 'In little Guernsey you must withdraw and live within yourself,' wrote one visitor to Hauteville House, who paced around the island 'in genuine despair' at his temporary confinement. A kind of moody introspection, symptomatic of her distress at Albert Pinson's departure, would be Adèle's pattern of behaviour for the rest of the decade and beyond.

In the meantime, however – and with her mother's connivance – she would plot her first attempts at escape.

News that Hauteville House had reopened its doors as Guernsey's most popular tourist attraction, following an 18-month restoration project, galvanized me into making plans for a visit. R opted to join me, but then unwisely left the travel arrangements in my hands. Instead of flying I'd decided that I wanted to lean over a ferry rail filling my lungs with the salty air, watching the propeller blades churn the sea into foam as we approached the harbour at St Peter Port, maybe envisaging the King of the Auxcriniers, Hugo's green spectral fish with the warty face of a man, who he imagined haunted these waters.

Too late we discovered at Poole that the ferry service to the Channel Islands didn't operate during the winter months. R suppressed his irritation at this turn of events rather too well, which only increased the anger I felt at my own disorganization and stupidity. At the last moment we bounded onto a train at Bournemouth and, arriving there, took a taxi to Weymouth, having established that its ferry service to Guernsey would be running first thing the next morning.

Weymouth bore the down-in-the-mouth appearance of an out-of-season seaside town. Loud music blared from the clock tower along the esplanade, and the net curtains of a row of terraced boarding houses looked worn and grimy and unlikely to survive a wash. We booked into a hotel on the front that boasted of its connection to the resort's nineteenth-century heyday. The Duke of Clarence, later William IV, had once lived there. But the walls of our bedroom were paper-thin, and we spent a disturbed night listening to the couple next door arguing in crystal-clear audition about the number of glasses of wine the man had drunk at dinner. Apparently, as we became only too fatiguingly aware, he'd exceeded his statutory two. They'd fall asleep only to awaken with the hourly chimes of the town clock – or so it seemed – bringing with them more ferocious escalations of their row. By the time we boarded the eight o'clock ferry the next morning we were bleary-eyed and flagging in energy. Arriving in Guernsey almost a day later than intended, we forfeited more of our time for exploring St Peter Port in order to sink down into the soft mattress of our bed in the luxurious Old Government House Hotel.

Not far from the hotel, in Candie Gardens, is Jean Boucher's statue of Victor Hugo, unveiled with great ceremony just weeks before the outbreak of the First World War. It was a gift from the French government in gratitude for the hospitality shown by the islanders to Hugo during his time in Guernsey. Hugo is shown striding against the wind, on a ruminative walk, as if he is seeking inspiration. The hotel itself, which opened for business not long after the Hugos' move to Hauteville House, has an uncomfortable association with the most troubled years of Guernsey's history, the German occupation that lasted for much of the Second World War. After the German army invaded the island in June 1940, the hotel was used initially as a military headquarters. Later it was converted to a *Soldatenheim*, a place of recreation and relaxation, where German officers and NCOs could enjoy their leave. Once we became aware of this it was difficult to shake off the shadowy hand of the past. Throughout that weekend, our conversation kept returning to the so-called 'model occupation' of the Channel Islands, the phrase a polite disguise for the real story of deportations to internment camps, of ever-tightening anti-Jewish measures, and of widespread incidents of collaboration with the enemy.

The question also kept coming back to me of the degree to which Victor Hugo had anticipated the world conflicts of the twentieth century. Would he have been surprised to find St Peter Port overrun with German soldiers? Probably not, I thought. In 1871, in the aftermath of the Franco-Prussian War, which finally toppled Napoleon III and left Paris in a state of siege, Hugo had warned of the potentially tragic consequences of France's acceptance of Germany's humiliating peace terms. He saw it as paving a path to a future war in Europe, encouraging the newly unified Germany's imperial ambitions while leaving France hungry for revenge.

The war of 1870 proved a serious setback to Hugo's dream of European federation. But his faith in the idea of a United Europe – naturally one in which French would be the dominant language – remained undimmed. In the garden of Hauteville House he planted an acorn. It sprouted into an oak tree, which he christened the 'Oak of the United States of Europe'.

On our tour of the house, later that day, the guide pointed out the tree through a downstairs window. Back in Britain, the great misbegotten Brexit saga was stumbling on towards yet another false climax. We looked at the dying tree, its wilting leaves and cracked brown bark discernible even at a distance. The symbolism was so obvious it didn't require anyone to put it into words.

We made our ascent to Hauteville House, pausing on the way to catch our breath and peer along the offshoots of mysterious alleyways, which occasionally afford a tantalizing glimpse of the sea. The house's restoration, partly funded by a three-million-euro grant from the luxury goods billionaire François Pinault, has returned the exterior to an appearance of its original sand and lime coating. This has been achieved by painting the brick façade slate grey and giving it an additional patina effect. Indoors a team of dedicated conservators has painstakingly brought this Aladdin's cave back to life. They've rescued its contents from damp, manufactured fabrics to match scraps of originals, strengthened the building itself, and everywhere made the eccentricities of Hugo's design shine like new.

Tourists, local people as well as 'a plethora of English colonels and American reverends', were already flocking to Hauteville House in Hugo's lifetime. During his absence from home one summer, not long before his return to France at the end of his years of exile, Hugo recorded that almost a thousand visitors had seen over the house. This is a figure that slightly beggars belief, but which nevertheless gives some indication of the curiosity his creation inspired. Our guide was a charming young Frenchman, handsome and compactly built, who kept glancing nervously at his reflection in the mirrors we passed on every floor. In many shapes and sizes, oval, long, convex, concave, some with the stains on the glass painted over with a pattern of flowers, these mirrors are often placed to face one another, giving one a sense that the heavy, and at times suffocating, atmosphere has been captured and intensified in the space in between.

We were received in the front entrance hall. Directly opposite the door is what Charles Hugo referred to as the 'frontispiece' of the house: a composition supported by a Corinthian column containing a pair of terracotta statues, with bottle bases providing a murky filter for the light, evoking memories of *Notre-Dame de Paris* and of the novel's own frontispiece by the painter and engraver Célestin Nanteuil. To my surprise, inserted in the wood panelling at the bottom are the two David d'Angers medallions, one of a youthful Hugo, the other of the 15-year-old Adèle. Unavoidably, his younger daughter must have come to mind every time Hugo entered the house.

Like so much of the rest of Hauteville House, the décor of the hallway is a product of afternoons spent by Hugo rummaging in the island's antique and junk shops, buying up old furniture, carvings, hangings, pictures and porcelain. He launched a 'chest hunt', and in all 60 chests or coffers were conveyed in carts back to the house to be dismantled and transformed into new and elaborate structures by his carpenter Peter Mauger, according to Hugo's design. Occasionally Hugo put himself to work, planing or carving a piece of wood. The original function of an object was more often than not ignored. He turned a Chippendale chair upside down and made it part of a pelmet; he amputated table legs and used them for banisters. Similarly, no respect was given to style or period. One mantelpiece was constructed from components dating from the Middle Ages, the Renaissance and the reign of Louis XIII. And yet, out of all these discordant elements, all the clashing patterns and surprising juxtapositions, a unifying harmony has somehow been achieved.

You walk from room to room, along dark corridors hung with the Sèvres porcelain presented by the last Bourbon king, and enter the dining room where the Delft tiles trace an interwoven *V* and *H*, or the blue drawing room where the motto *EGO HUGO* is carved on the fireplace. Barely for a moment are you able to forget Hugo's presence. The house is decorated and furnished almost entirely in his own image. Everything about it is redolent of his past memories and his personal symbolism. Nothing, it seems, has found its place by accident.

What must it have been like to live oppressed by the tyranny of someone else's taste? In a house that is a monument more than a home, that has its own language, formed from layer upon layer of associations, but not one that necessarily speaks to you? At least the billiard room, I suppose, catered for the leisure time of the young men of the household. Opening a concealed door in the panelling of the ground-floor tapestry room, I came upon the tiny space used by Charles and Vacquerie as a photographic studio. The dead weren't overlooked – *ABSENTES ADSUNT*, 'Those Absent are Present', proclaims one carved motto – and in Hugo's new design Léopoldine's water-stained dress was now displayed in a glass-fronted cupboard. I asked, though, to see the bedrooms of Adèle and her mother, shown on the plan as situated at the front on the first floor, overlooking the street, only to be told that they were never open to the public.

Hauteville House has been compared to a stage set, a reminder for Hugo of his theatrical past. And many pieces – the oak gallery's majestic four-poster bed, for example – do indeed resemble large-scale props that seem to have strayed in from some climactic scene in a theatre production.

Others, beginning with Madame Hugo, have seen the house as a poem of sorts – paid for from the proceeds of Hugo's more orthodox page-and-print collection. The theme of this particular poem is pointed to in the inscription on the headboard of the four-poster: *NOX MORS LUX*, 'Night, Death, Light'. Hugo had conceived the house as a journey from dark to light, symbolizing his belief that light and freedom could only be attained through darkness and struggle. And so you move from the funereal blackness of the oppressive lower levels, thick with tapestries and heavy oak, up through the more ornate decorative style of the first and second floors, until finally you reach the dizzying brightness at the top.

Here you find a glass conservatory. This 'six-foot-square crystal palace' was added to the roof in late 1861 and early 1862. It gives 'upon the sky, and on immensity'. Writing in his look-out, as the conservatory became known, at two black wooden standing desks, Hugo would eventually begin the lengthy process of revising *Les*

Misérables. He slept on a narrow bed in the small adjacent attic. His diary, with its coded notations in Spanish and Latin, makes it clear that he wasn't only sleeping here, and that he enjoyed sexual relations with the chambermaid – Rosalina, Coelina, Marianne, to name just a few of the servants over the years – who occupied the room next door.

On the morning of our visit the crystal cage dazzled us with its brilliant sunlight, just as Hugo had intended. Looking out across the clear blueness of the sky and down to the rippling ocean beneath, we watched small cruisers and passenger ferries sailing past Jersey, Herm and Sark, and focused our attention for a moment on the coastline of France. How often, I wondered, did Adèle find her way to the very top of the house, away from the stifling gloom below, and long for her freedom and for a different kind of life while dreaming of being reunited with Albert Pinson?

There she stands, pasty-faced, listless, in her father's study. Her hands drape weakly over an enormous chair occupying the foreground, forcefully representing her absent father. Without this support one can't be sure that she would manage to stay upright.

Equally the chair seems to serve as a barrier, cordoning her off from the outside world.

Surrounding her are treasures from her father's art collection. On the wall are works by Corot and Millet, displayed under a Chinese silk hanging. To her right are Egyptian funerary artefacts in a glass case. In view of her lifelessness, she could easily be passed off as simply another object in her father's collection, mummified and entombed.

This young woman isn't Adèle Hugo. She's Hélène Rouart, portrayed by Degas in her early twenties in his painting *Hélène Rouart in her Father's Study*, now in the National Gallery in London. The painting was begun in the mid-1880s, three decades on from the Hugos' exile in Guernsey. Yet, regardless of its separation in time, Hélène's depiction appears to echo Adèle's predicament as an unhappy, possibly ailing, daughter of a nineteenth-century patriarch.

Hélène's father was the industrialist Henri Rouart: amateur painter, collector, financial backer of the Impressionists – as well as lifelong friend of Edgar Degas. He and Degas had been at school together and, years later, during the Franco-Prussian War, Degas served in the French army as a lieutenant under Rouart's command. Right-wing, nationalistic and openly anti-Semitic, the two men's shared political views were a world apart from Victor Hugo's.

Not long after sitting for this portrait, Hélène married and left home. Her husband Eugène Marin was an engineer like her father and took over the management of Rouart's hollow iron factory. Beyond the fact that Marin died prematurely, leaving his wife a young widow, Hélène's life was uneventful. She had their three children to look after, never remarried and spent her later years devoting herself to her own painting.

Degas' *Hélène Rouart* was one of the first works of art I remember studying closely as a teenager. On visits to the National Gallery today I rarely miss the opportunity to return to the room where it's hung and puzzle over it. For it is something of an enigma. Hélène was already engaged when it was painted. However, Degas, who fussed over the painting for almost a decade, decided in the end not to show his sitter wearing an engagement or a wedding ring.

But beneath the layers of paint on Hélène's left hand there is the ghostly shadow of what may be a ring. Did Degas paint out her ring, and, if so, why? Is he suggesting that she remains in a sense her father's possession, that Henri Rouart will always be the only man in her life?

There is a more fanciful interpretation. Admittedly it's one that goes against Degas' well-known reputation as a misogynist. Hélène appears cut off from her surroundings, gazing into the distance, almost in a state of entrancement. On the eve of her marriage, is Degas allowing her to dream of another kind of life, a different set of possibilities?

It began with, of all things, a twisted neck.

Adèle had spent the summer of 1856 pleasantly occupied in preparing her new bedroom and swimming at Fermain Bay, a secluded beauty spot accessible along a cliff-top path from St Peter Port. She had also been busy with her music. That May her setting of her father's poem '*Nuits de Juin*' ('June Nights') was performed in a public concert by the soprano Augustine Allix, Jules Allix's sister. This short lyric – 70 years later the basis of one of the young Benjamin Britten's earliest compositions – captures the midsummer night hours when 'the sweet and pale dawn, as if waiting to break, /Wanders at the bottom of the sky the whole night'.

On Saturday, 6 December, though, her neck pains were suddenly joined by far more serious symptoms as Adèle fell gravely ill with a severe attack of gastroenteritis. She was delirious with a high fever. In the early hours of Wednesday, the doctor treating her, Dr Terrier, announced to her horrified family his fear that she wouldn't last the morning. Her father spent the night at her bedside and was there at daylight when the crisis passed and 'she breathed and looked at us again'. By Christmas Day Adèle was out of danger. A long convalescence lay ahead.

Adele's excessive thinness, commented on by Vacquerie when he ridiculed her spindly arms, suggests that she may have been suffering from anorexia, a condition that would certainly have compromised her immune system and increased the likelihood of gastric problems. But to François-Victor it was clear that his sister's illness originated in 'an attack of nerves'. This idea of nervous depression was confirmed by Dr Terrier in his diagnosis. His patient's 'weakness, heightened sensitivity, pallor' were attributed by him to an 'excess of work' and 'lack of distractions'. Didn't anyone at Hauteville House suspect that Adèle's prolonged separation from Albert Pinson – since the spring of 1856 an ensign in the British army after his spell in the militia – must also have played a part in her breakdown? If they did, no one said so.

Dr Terrier's 15-page report, 'Some precepts of hygiene for the use of Mlle Adèle Hugo', prescribed the abstention for six days a month from literary or musical work, together with a regime of late rising and daily walks. Adèle was to cut down her sugar intake and drink beer instead of wine. 'I recommend the game of billiards,' Terrier wrote, 'but I believe perhaps that Mlle Hugo may be put off by tobacco smoke.' He advised her to overcome this distaste as the smoke billowing around the billiard room was far from unhealthy for her.

To celebrate his daughter's recovery, Victor Hugo wrote a short poem addressed '*À ma fille Adèle*', which he presented to Adèle on New Year's Day 1857. It instantly strikes one as rather a morbid gift for a woman recovering from such a close brush with death. Essentially it's a companion piece to one of the poems written for Léopoldine in *Les Contemplations*. In '*Demain, dès l'aube . . .*' ('Tomorrow, as soon as day breaks . . .'), Hugo describes himself travelling to Villequier and laying a bouquet of holly and heather on his dead daughter's tomb. This new poem does at least confirm the natural order of life's expectations after the tragic earlier reversal, that the child will outlive its parent. Hugo remembers watching the baby Adèle as she slept, stripping leaves of jasmine and carnation over her coverlet. One day, he tells her, it will be his turn to sleep, a sleep 'so shadowy, so gloomy, so wild and deep'. Then she will return to his tomb

the tears, prayers and flowers,
That I bestrewed by your cradle.

Both Hugo parents kept up a united front to the outside world, insisting on their children's 'serene' acceptance of the hardships of exile. Courageous and proud, Adèle understood the grandeur of persecution, her mother wrote to one friend towards the end of 1855. Five years later, in a letter to the critic Jules Janin, Madame Hugo would still be describing her daughter in similarly grandiose terms. Adèle preferred 'a rock to the pleasures of her age because her father inhabits that rock. She takes joy and pride in playing her part in this great and austere existence.'

However, behind this front, Madame Hugo was increasingly anxious about the warning signals sent out by her daughter's illness, and early in 1857 chose to confront her husband with the situation. She did so not face to face, where her words might fail to make an impression, but in writing, where she could take full and uninterrupted control of the argument.

It was inevitable, she told Hugo, that Adèle would fall prey to depression again. She saw indications of it already. Adèle was 'powerless and unarmed'. Discouraged for the time being from immersing herself in her music, their daughter had little else with which to occupy herself. A garden to tend and some tapestry work to do, her mother reminded him, was scarcely enough mental stimulus for a young woman of 26.

A further letter took Hugo to task for criticizing Adèle for loving no one but herself. Madame Hugo's response was forthright. 'Adèle has given you her young womanhood without complaint. Is that what you call self-centred?' If she seemed temperamentally cold, she added, that was hardly surprising. 'Who knows what she has suffered, may still be suffering, as she sees the future turning its back upon her, as she reckons up the tale of years to come, knowing full well that every tomorrow will be a replica of every today?'

Madame Hugo's solution to her daughter's problems was straightforward. Adèle must be allowed to travel and derive what benefits she could from a change of scene. As her mother, Madame Hugo was intent on devoting herself 'entirely to the poor child's interests'. But beneath this undoubtedly genuine concern was a bid for her own freedom. If she couldn't get her husband to quit Guernsey, then she would do so with their children, little by little.

Hugo accused his wife of conspiring to leave him. She forgave him for such an 'abominable thought'. Nevertheless, she made it clear that while submissive to him she could not be 'absolutely his slave'. He recognized only too well the signs of revolt and threw obstacles in her path, baulking at the expense that travel would entail, and questioning the necessity of the two women visiting Paris. She was quick to reassure him. 'I admire you and you are my great experience, that's why I belong to you . . .' But, she added as a caution, 'you must not abuse this declaration . . . You have to think about the other sufferers.'

It was François-Victor who stepped in to salvage their plans, finally winning Hugo's consent to a six-week trip. On 18 January 1858, mother and daughter left Guernsey by the morning steamer for Paris, via Southampton and Le Havre. The best way that she could repay him for his diplomatic efforts on her behalf, François-Victor wrote to Adèle, would be for her to reappear at Hauteville

House, 'very fat . . . very pretty, very gay, an Adèle who is the sister I dream of . . . So be happy, my child!'

Over the next few years a pattern was set. As François-Victor predicted, these visits abroad would become almost an annual event. And, just as regularly, assurances in each instance would be given by Madame Hugo about the date of their return to Guernsey, only for these to be reneged upon once they were safely away, and prolongations – repeated prolongations – to their stay agreed. The first French trip, originally arranged for a matter of weeks, was extended several times, so that Adèle and her mother didn't return until the first week of May. Reading Madame Hugo's letters to her husband, I can't help applauding from the sidelines her smooth manipulation of him. She was spoiling Adèle, she informed Hugo in April, and Paris was doing their daughter good, but of course her own place was always to be close to him. Adèle wrote her father a 'charming' letter. She was clearly enjoying herself, and asked him to pay for a corset in the latest fashion that she wanted to buy. He agreed on condition that it didn't cost more than 30 francs, as he was feeling 'very poor' at present. The expense of the ongoing works at Hauteville House was mounting. Radical changes to several rooms in their absence meant that mother and daughter must have blinked in amazement at the transformations they encountered when they got back home.

The pain of their desertion, as Hugo saw it, was intensified by his sons' discontent. Charles pleaded for his father's consent for a leave of absence from their island isolation. François-Victor hurt his father by describing him as 'a gentle tyrant' in preventing them from taking a break from life in Guernsey, though the attractions of Emily de Putron, a young local woman with whom he'd fallen in love, were mostly enough to keep him there. To Adèle's considerable relief, even the faithful Auguste Vacquerie had had enough and departed at the end of 1858, deciding to pursue his literary career in Paris.

For Hugo there was also a very real sense that his time might be running short. In the summer of 1858, not long after the two Adèles returned from Paris, he fell seriously ill. He was suffering from an attack of anthrax that would keep him bedridden and convalescent until October (and resulted in him growing a beard for the first time as a protection for his throat, so that he began to resemble a bewhiskered sea captain).

Emerging from his sick room, Hugo faced all the familiar arguments from his wife about the need to rescue Adèle from the claustrophobic atmosphere at home. Their daughter was once more increasingly silent, closeting herself in her room, and tiring herself at the piano. 'Be convinced of one thing,' Madame Hugo wrote to him, ' . . . as soon as my daughter is out of the woods, I will devote my old age to yours. Until then you will understand that I am all in Adèle.'

On 11 May 1859, Madame Hugo and Adèle, accompanied by Charles who remained with them for the first fortnight, left St Peter Port, bound for London for a month's stay. What she told him about the improvement in Adèle's condition, Hugo wrote to his wife a week later, gave him great pleasure. No doubt he was thinking of Adèle's declining prospects in the marriage market as she neared 30 when he continued by asking that their daughter make progress on two fronts: as a woman of the world and as a woman of the household. 'She has all the qualities of pride, serenity, and strength. What she needs to add are qualities of being useful and kind.' He finished by asking Madame Hugo to tell Adèle that he loved her very much. 'If she could see my mind constantly turned on her, I'm sure she would do whatever I tell her.'

The two women were expected home on 11 June. Madame Hugo requested an extension to the end of the month as Adèle was 'so happy' in London. Then, in the last week of June, came another request, this time from Adèle, asking for a further delay to 11 July. Again Hugo assented, telling his 'good little Adèle' that he would send her mother the necessary additional funds.

This was far from being the end of the postponements of their return. On 7 July Madame Hugo wrote to her husband that Adèle had a heavy head cold and that consequently they would leave for Guernsey in just over ten days' time. It was Hugo's birthday, his fifty-seventh, on the 21st, and he was sure that his wife and daughter wouldn't want to miss the celebration. He was to be miserably disappointed.

Instead Hugo received a birthday letter from Adèle. She sent him a kiss, enquired about the piano that François-Victor was meant to be hiring for her, but otherwise told him nothing about her activities in London. Moreover there is a trace of something peremptory in her tone. She brings her brief letter to a close 'because I'm afraid of running out of time and paper; and what are letters made of if not of these two?'

Another letter from Adèle at the end of July announced that they would be staying 'a few more days in London', on account of the resources for music that the capital offered. 'You know, dear papa, the keen taste I have for music by instinct and reason. This aspiration towards an art is part of the strength and serenity you wish to see in me.'

Meanwhile, in a desperate attempt to bring the two women home, Hugo had seized on the news 'that the Thames stinks and poisons London in the summer'. The problem, arising from untreated human waste in the river and the consequent fears of waterborne disease, had reached its peak in the scorching heat of the previous summer, when the hideous stench had sent people fleeing from the city. Work on a new sewage system had begun, but the threat to Londoners' well-being was still present. Her health was more important than Handel, Hugo told Adèle. 'London is full of pestilence at the moment . . . Hurry now to return.'

His warnings were blithely ignored. 'I see only flourishing beings here,' Adèle replied, before informing Hugo that he could expect to see them again at the end of the following week.

This expectation yet again proved false. The desperation to bring Adèle and her mother home renewed itself in a more farcical form of persuasion as François-Victor set off for London on 4 August as his father's envoy, hoping to succeed where Hugo's entreaties had failed. He was no more successful. On 25 August, as his mother and sister applied for their eighth extension, François-Victor returned to Hauteville House – alone.

At long last, on 6 September, Madame Hugo and Adèle disembarked from the steamer at St Peter Port. They had been absent for just a week short of four months, four times longer than originally agreed.

When Madame Hugo left for France again in the first days of February 1860, she did so unaccompanied. In Paris she was reunited with old friends, dealt with family frictions arising from her sister Julie's unhappy marriage to the engraver Paul Chenay, visited George Sand in the rue Racine, and collected contributions for the charity bazaar she was organizing in aid of Guernsey's poor children.

But she was also on a private mission: to bring back to Guernsey the man she and her husband viewed as a possible husband for Adèle. On 19 March she duly returned to Hauteville House with Alfred Busquet in tow.

Busquet was 40, a journalist, and latterly a published poet. From my internet searches he appears to have been another of the faceless beardies who populate the lower rungs of French nineteenth-century literature, leaving little impression on posterity. He was, however, an old friend of François-Victor's, a cousin of Vacquerie's, and he moved in the right literary circles. Furthermore, as a potential son-in-law he immediately recommended himself to Victor Hugo during his stay by searching for copper bric-a-brac for the house around St Peter Port, and by agreeing to make various purchases on Hugo's behalf once he was back in Paris.

Adèle evidently wasn't taken with Busquet. She had been impressing her father with the 'charming' music she'd composed, so much so that he'd invested in a second-hand piano for her sole use (the other one, mainly for show, was transported to the tapestry room). She wasn't about to acquiesce in her parents' choice of a suitor, though. Reading Victor Hugo's notebook for the period of Busquet's three-week visit, you can see that Hugo held out hopes of an announcement, but that by the time Busquet shook his hand in farewell in the second week of April, nothing had materialized. Five months later, a visit from Busquet's parents to Hauteville House delivered the knock-out blow to all idea of Adèle marrying their son. Terse entries in Hugo's notebook record the delivery of an 'overture' from Alfred Busquet, followed by Adèle's 'refusal' and her 'strong dissent'.

Opening the tin trunk that contained his manuscripts, Hugo had fished out the early versions of his unfinished novel, *Les Misérables*, which he'd broken off from 12 years earlier as Paris erupted into violent revolution.

For almost seven months he pondered his reasons for writing a book about 'the wretched', the lives and living conditions of the poor. He plotted the ways in which he might bring the stories of ex-convict Jean Valjean, Cosette, the beautiful young girl he rescues from poverty, Marius, the Republican student who falls in love with her – and all the rest – to a satisfactory conclusion. A bad bout of laryngitis in December 1860 reminded him once more that his time might be limited. He prayed to God in the last days of the year 'to order my body to hang on, and to wait until my mind is done'. In January 1861 he resumed the writing of this, the century's longest novel – 1,500 pages in some modern editions – with a superhuman burst of energy that enabled him to lay down his pen on his first draft in just six months.

Nevertheless, continuing worries about his health persuaded him to accept his doctor's advice that he needed a holiday. In the last week of March, in the company of Juliette Drouet and his son Charles, Hugo left the Channel Islands for the first time in a decade. A trip to London for a medical consultation was followed by a relaxing stay in Brussels, and then two months' intensive writing in a room at the Hôtel des Colonnes, 15 miles outside the city, at Mont Saint-Jean, overlooking the site of the Battle of Waterloo. For Hugo, Waterloo was the 'founding' event of the nineteenth century. It was to be the subject of the novel's lengthy historical digression and he needed to see the overgrown battlefield for himself.

At the same time, Madame Hugo had gone to Paris to seek help for her failing eyesight, with the intention of reuniting with her husband in Brussels later that spring. Adèle and François-Victor remained at Hauteville House with their aunt Julie Chenay. Adèle was assembling her musical compositions in the hope of eventually publishing them. François-Victor was toiling away on his umpteenth volume of Shakespeare. The original plan, that brother and sister should have their own holiday by spending several days together on the Isle of Wight before joining the others in Brussels, speedily evaporated when François-Victor decided that he preferred to remain behind in order to be with his love Emily de Putron. Instead, in early May, Adèle departed for the Isle of Wight with her maid Rosalie Philippe. She had arranged to stay in lodgings at Ryde on the north-east coast of the island, a fashionable town that had grown in popularity since the arrival of Queen Victoria at nearby Osborne House a decade earlier.

The news that his daughter had departed from Guernsey without a family member to chaperone her first perturbed and then angered Victor Hugo. He would have been still more upset had he discovered what happened next: that having settled in Ryde, Adèle promptly sent Rosalie packing, back to Hauteville House. Alone in her lodgings, Adèle reported on the establishment's 'execrable' food and 'mediocre' standard of comfort, but otherwise her letters to François-Victor and her mother were short on any information about her welfare, or how she occupied her time, beyond her declaration, ringed with bitterness, that she knew 'so well how to be bored without saying anything'. Madame Hugo was worried about her daughter, but resisted pressure from her husband that she should cut short her time in Paris, find Adèle on the Isle of Wight and bring her to Brussels. Neither did François-Victor see why the task of escorting his sister must fall to him by default.

In the criss-cross of family letters on the subject, you can see that along with all the anxiety for the safety of an unchaperoned woman of 30, travelling by herself in a foreign country, is the fear of what the outside world might think about such a disregard for convention. Even so, in the absence of anyone willing to collect and bring her to Brussels, Adèle made her way on her own. She reached London from Southampton on 11 June, sending word of her safe arrival to her mother, who was soon to leave Paris for Brussels. 'You will be in Ostend tomorrow morning,' Madame Hugo replied, confirming the arrangements. 'From what I can see, you will have spent a day or two in London. As soon as the innkeeper has given you this letter, ask him about the departure times for Brussels and come to us immediately because I can't wait to see you again.'

The family – minus François-Victor, and with Juliette Drouet discreetly left behind at the Hôtel des Colonnes – were reunited in

Brussels on 18 June over lunch at 26 rue de Louvain, the address where Charles had found rooms for his mother, sister and himself. It was a momentous date for Victor Hugo: the forty-sixth anniversary of Waterloo. With lunch over, Hugo returned to Mont Saint-Jean to immerse himself again in *Les Misérables*. The end of the novel was in sight. At 8.30 on the morning of 30 June, with sunlight streaming through his bedroom window, he wrote the final words. However, as he informed Hetzel, his publisher friend, before this 'Leviathan' could be launched 'on the high seas', he was going to revise and reread everything. 'A last, major, serious incubation, and then I'll say – Go!'

Years ago I visited Waterloo, and saw the sculpted lion sitting atop the vast conical mound that forms Europe's first purpose-built war memorial. More recently I've been to the house in the rue de Louvain, hardly altered since the family gathered there in 1861, and also to Victor Hugo's eventual Brussels home at the Place des Barricades, marked with a plaque. For me, though, the strongest associations of Brussels will always be with Charlotte Brontë and the painful story of her unreciprocated feelings for her beloved teacher, Monsieur Heger. Seen through her eyes Brussels becomes a city filled with reminders of hopeless love. The Pensionnat Heger, the school where Charlotte studied and taught and fell in love in 1842–3, its foundations now buried at the foot of the Belliard steps. The Park, where she tried to walk off her misery during a long summer vacation. And the Cathedral of Saint Michel and Sainte Gudula – acknowledged by Victor Hugo as 'the purest flowering of the Gothic style' – where she, daughter of a Church of England clergyman, found herself driven to unburden those feelings to a Catholic priest by entering the confessional box.

The glaringly obvious had been staring me in the face. I'd been aware, of course, that there was something missing when I'd read the letters and started to outline the sequence of events in my mind. What *had* Adèle been doing during those weeks on the Isle of Wight? Who had she seen? Was there some significance to the day or two she'd spent in London, pointedly referred to by her mother?

The figure of a man is there in the shadows. Albert Pinson.

Once I'd accepted that Adèle must have met or spent time with Pinson in the summer of 1861 a number of suppositions slotted into place. The bare bones of his army career are there in the annual *Army List*. This shows his first appearance in the regular army in April 1856 as an ensign in the 16th Regiment of Foot. In March 1858 he was promoted to lieutenant and joined the second battalion of his regiment in Ireland, first at Limerick, and then from 1859 to 1861 at Newry on the historic boundary between County Down and County Armagh. For some weeks in 1860 he also trained as an Instructor of Musketry, at the army's school at Hythe in Kent. In April 1861 – to get our bearings, a month before Adèle went to the Isle of Wight – he transferred with his battalion to the army garrison at Aldershot in Hampshire. This was the vast training camp for British soldiers, established in the wake of the Crimean War.

Lieutenants.
2 Isdell, Charles W.
2 Street, George
2 Russell, Thos.
1 Westby, B. H.
1 Le Feuvre, L. *I. of M.*
2 Pinson, Albert A.

A division of regular troops was permanently based at Aldershot, and it represented an important home command. The accommodation was spartan, no more than row upon row of wooden huts, but there were off-duty diversions for officers, including horse racing

(Pinson flashes by in a report in the *Aldershot Military Gazette* in the summer of 1861, taking part in a hurdle race on his horse, the suggestively named Crinoline). Inevitably, given the garrison's proximity to London, there were also opportunities for pleasure and dissipation in the capital. Officers could easily take the afternoon train to London and get back to camp by an early train the next morning, in time for parade.

It's conceivable that Adèle and Pinson met on the Isle of Wight at some point during Adèle's weeks at Ryde. Perhaps he was able to get leave and take a train from Aldershot to Southampton, 50 miles away, and then a ferry across to the island. Even more probable is that the pair were reunited in London on those two days in June 1861. Is there some secret passing between Madame Hugo and her daughter, something understood in the older woman's words, 'you will have spent a day or two in London'?

I could push it further and hypothesize earlier meetings for Adèle with Pinson. What about the four months she'd spent in London in the summer of 1859? Pinson was stationed in Ireland at the time, and any meeting between the couple would have depended on Madame Hugo's acquiescence in her daughter's relationship with the young English soldier – or at least on her unseeing eye (an unfortunate metaphor, I'll admit, given the problems with her eyesight) – but it's not out of the question. In the absence of firm evidence, one enters what seems like a never-ending circle of possibilities and wishful thinking.

I'd continued searching for information about Pinson. Any scrap I could find to help breathe life into him. Occasionally a surprise popped up on the internet. Not, sadly, a photograph of Pinson himself, but a tiny, blurry one of his mother Jane in old age, in which her facial features melt into the whiteness of her hair and the snowy-white bow tied at her neck. Her straitened circumstances evidently hadn't altered following the death of her third husband, the Revd Templer in 1852. The 1871 census records her residing at a boarding house in London's Paddington area. She died in Kent in 1879, having long outlived three husbands.

Pinson himself lived until 1915, dying at the age of 83 (by an odd coincidence, a matter of months after Adèle Hugo's death at the nursing home in the suburbs of Paris). His last home, where he died, was in South Brent, a small Devonshire village, 20 miles inland from his birthplace at Dartmouth. One summer I'd been giving a talk at a literary festival not far away and decided to take a detour to look at the white-painted house in Springfield Terrace, surrounded by a luxuriant garden, which he'd rented in his final years. Afterwards I wrote to the owners to ask if they knew anything about this previous occupant of their home, and whether its history had thrown up any information about him. I received an enthusiastic response. They had watched Truffaut's *Adèle H.* after receiving my letter and were intrigued by the connection to the man they'd found described in a book on Truffaut in the local library as 'an unworthy and feckless libertine'. But, no, they had nothing to add from their side, though they'd be sure to contact me if anything came to light. Gone in an instant were wild dreams of letters turning up under floorboards or in the attic, buried in the garden, or something just as far-fetched.

Pinson's direct descendants were the obvious people to track down – if he had any. That Pinson had eventually married there was no doubt. Modern biographers of Victor Hugo have generally picked up on the notice from *The Times* of March 1870, recording Pinson's marriage in London, a year after he'd returned from Barbados and resigned his army commission. Hugo copied it into his notebook with a telling absence of comment. Pinson's bride was Catherine Roxburgh, and the following year she had given birth to their only child, a son, Eudo, an unusual name, a bit like a sound memory, I decided, of some medieval duke of Aquitaine or king of the western Franks. To discover whether Eudo, who died in 1934, had had any children I obtained a copy of his will. The swirly script of the legal clerk was practically indecipherable. All I could make out, amid a lot of legalistic verbiage about settlements, indentures, and trusts, was a reference to 'one or more of my issue'. So Eudo had had children.

In an idle moment one day I returned to the internet, having noticed that latterly Eudo's surname wasn't simply 'Pinson', but 'Pinson-Roxburgh'. I typed the double-barrelled name into the search engine and was rewarded with a lucky find. In the parish magazine of a Suffolk village were the names of two Pinson-Roxburghs, with the helpful addition of a telephone number. I rang the number and a middle-aged man answered. Before I could finish explaining the purpose of my call he said, 'You need to speak to my wife as she's the one who's really interested in our family history,' and handed the receiver to her.

Colin Pinson-Roxburgh turned out to be Albert Pinson's great-grandson, Eudo's grandson, and the son of one of Eudo's children, Stanley. However, as he'd said, it was Silke, his wife, who'd investigated the story of her husband's family in some detail. Originally from Germany, she had arrived in Britain in the 1970s as the au pair to a Suffolk family, subsequently meeting and marrying Colin, who lived in the same neighbourhood. Silke had always found family history a stimulating outlet to occupy her spare time. The Roxburghs, Albert Pinson's wife Catherine's family, are well documented. Catherine's grandfather was the eighteenth-century botanist William Roxburgh, famous as the founding father of Indian botany and for his *Flora Indica*, an illustrated catalogue of hundreds of species of Indian plants. During our phone conversation Silke warned me that the other side of the family, the Pinsons, were by contrast much less clearly delineated, but that she was willing to share her findings with me. This was very generous of her, as was her offer to collect me by car from Ipswich Station so that we could drive the 20 minutes or so to her home and talk.

We interrupted the car journey to stop at Eudo's grave, in a churchyard set in open countryside close to the farmhouse where he'd lived for some years with his wife and six children. Like his father, Albert, Silke explained, Eudo had served in the army. Presumably he was invalided out, as he suffered from epilepsy, something I was already aware of from the distressing description of the circumstances of his death entered on his death certificate: that in the course of having a fit he'd fallen forward onto his bedclothes and asphyxiated.

As we circled the tombstone, studying its eroding inscription, I asked Silke what Eudo had lived on after leaving the army. 'The money settled on his mother by her father James Roxburgh at the time of her marriage', was her reply. 'I suppose he was what you'd call a gentleman of independent means.' But, she added, Eudo had faced the dilemma of marrying out of his class. His future wife, Eliza, had at one time been in service, and Eudo appears to have waited until after his mother's death in 1905 to marry her.

Silke and Colin live in a former barn, attractively modernized as a bungalow, with a garden at the front and extending into open fields at the back. It was only March, but lovely and warm as if full of the promise of May. After all the commotion of London I was transfixed by the silence of the surroundings. While Silke prepared lunch, Colin, a retired engineer, quiet but alert and interested, came in to introduce himself. Silke took the lead in our discussion, and I was struck by her rigorous approach to the evidence she'd uncovered in the course of her research, and to the questions it raised. I was awkward at first, discomforted by the idea of passing judgement on Albert Pinson in conversation with his blood relatives, even though the fact that they'd never known him made him as much a dim and distant figure from the past to them as he was to me.

Silke was clear from the outset that what had originally motivated her investigation into Pinson's life was an awareness that so much of what had been written about him, in books and articles on Adèle Hugo and her family, was either based on hearsay – like his gambling debts – or overlooked key evidence – for instance, about his family origins. She admitted feeling sympathetically inclined towards him because of the rough start he'd had in life, born to a widowed mother and never knowing his father. But when I suggested that she and Colin might feel some familial obligation to defend him, they replied in unison, 'Absolutely not'.

After lunch Silke pulled a folder across the table and opened it. 'Have you seen this?', she asked.

It was a photograph of Albert Pinson.

My eyes widened in surprise, and I felt my pulse accelerating. Here at last was a picture of the man with whom Adèle Hugo had fallen in love with such disastrous consequences. Silke had discovered the photo only a week or two earlier in the regimental archives in Bedford. This studio portrait, in which Pinson sports his ceremonial sword, has the name 'A. Pinson' written beneath it on the album page, but is undated. It could well belong to the end of the 1850s, when Pinson was sent with his battalion to Ireland, in which case he is in his late twenties.

He wasn't at all how I'd expected him to look. For a start his colouring doesn't tally with Adèle's description of him in her journal at the beginning of his twenties as blond, though this could easily be a photographic illusion. Nor, less surprisingly, does he bear the slightest resemblance to the callow, clean-shaven youth played by Bruce Robinson in Truffaut's film. Perhaps, though, a man with childlike features, as Adèle also described him, is hidden there, beneath the thickets of facial hair. Pinson has all the appearance of a fully signed-up member of Britain's 'Beard Movement'. From the 1850s expansive whiskers were no longer the sole preserve of bohemian artists, or nascent revolutionaries like the Chartists. Instead, the progress of the beard, alongside the moustache and bushy sideburns, was a dramatic new fashion, signalling a redefinition of masculinity as rugged, potent and authoritative.

Was it imaginative fancy, or did Pinson's pose display an air of nonchalance, in his expression and the careful positioning of his wide-apart legs straddling the chair, that any interested female might warm to?

As I mused on this, Silke was describing Pinson's probable first meeting with his future wife Catherine Roxburgh. From 1859 Lieutenant Pinson was with the second battalion of the 16th Regiment in barracks at Newry, County Armagh, in Northern Ireland. At that time 23-year-old Catherine was living in Newry with her parents, Major James Roxburgh, a recruiting officer for the town, and his wife Sibella. She and Pinson could have become acquainted at any one of the many social engagements in the surrounding area to which young army officers were invited to add a dash of glamour and colour. Silke handed me one newspaper report from July 1859 of 'Festivities at Ballygawley House', which Pinson (inadvertently promoted in the list of guests to the rank of 'Captain') attended. Ballygawley, in a village of the same name, 40 miles further north from Newry, was the home of Sir John Stewart, High Sheriff of County Tyrone. A fire in the 1920s reduced the house to a burned-out shell, but old photographs show an imposing classical-style mansion, with Doric columns, set in its own parkland.

Did the grandeur of such occasions, mixing in Anglo-Irish society, feed Albert Pinson's hopes of moving up the social ladder? And did marriage to Catherine Roxburgh, daughter of a wealthy and influential father, and from a well-connected family, form part of those hopes?

We cannot know whether Pinson first proposed marriage to Catherine during his spell in Ireland in 1859–61. If he did, it's a fair assumption that he was rejected because the Roxburghs were holding out for a better catch for their daughter. However, by the time Pinson returned to Ireland briefly in 1869, a decade later, following his battalion's return from Barbados and shortly before he resigned from the army for good, the situation must have appeared very differently to Catherine's parents. Catherine was 34 and still unmarried. At this late stage, Albert Pinson may have been regarded as something of a godsend, rescuing Catherine from approaching spinsterhood. The couple were married the following spring.

Going back, though, to the early summer of 1861. If I was right and Pinson met Adèle Hugo in London or on the Isle of Wight, soon after his battalion left Newry for Aldershot, then he could well have been seeking her out on the rebound. Perhaps Adèle automatically became a more appealing prospect once Catherine Roxburgh had rejected him and shut the door in his face. Alternatively, maybe there'd been no marriage proposal and it was simply a case of Pinson wanting to keep his options open, of a young man wishing 'to play the field', as Colin suggested.

Either way, neither scenario places Pinson in an especially flattering light. My fermenting prejudice against him was only reinforced by what Silke had to say about his subsequent relationship with Catherine. Within a few years of their marriage and the birth of their son, the couple separated. Pinson was paid the annual sum of £150 – roughly the equivalent of £17,000 today – by James Roxburgh to stay away from Catherine and Eudo. There is a suggestion of acrimony in the terms of the separation agreement and in Major Roxburgh's efforts to ensure that Catherine didn't have to deal directly with her estranged husband.

That settled it for me. A picture had been building in my mind of a vain (as his army comrades had testified), socially ambitious man about town, with an eye for the ladies, a gambler – and now a bad husband and father to boot.

But Silke had another surprise in store.

I'd sensed something tentative in her manner as the afternoon wore on, as if she was withholding something from me, or trying to decide whether to entrust me with further information. Not long before we left for the drive back to the station, she suddenly produced another bit of paper. As she did so she explained that this was a piece of evidence that had been handed down in the family, through Eudo's daughter Dorothy, Colin's aunt. Silke believed that Albert Pinson had preserved it in order to demonstrate to posterity that he'd intended 'to do right' by Adèle Hugo.

It was a marriage licence made out in the names of Albert Andrew Pinson and Adèle Hugo, and dated 13 December 1861.

For the entire train journey home from Ipswich to London I mulled over the significance of this document, quite unable to believe in its existence. For a split second my imagination jumped wildly to the conclusion that Adèle and Pinson had entered into a marriage in secret – before a more rational voice asserted itself to remind me that the entire subsequent direction of Adèle's story derived from the inescapable fact that Pinson had never been her husband. All I could say for certain was that in mid-December 1861 the couple were planning to marry by licence. This was the alternative to having their banns read out in church on three successive Sundays. It meant that, for a fee, the Church of England was willing to allow them to get married quickly and without publicity.

However, to understand anything more, to fit this tiny piece of the puzzle into the general narrative, meant retracing my steps back to Brussels, and to the late summer and autumn of 1861.

His draft of *Les Misérables* completed at the end of June 1861, Victor Hugo had embarked on a holiday in July, zigzagging across Holland in the company of Juliette Drouet. Madame Hugo, for her part, showed no sign of going home to Guernsey, despite her husband's disquiet about anything 'that dissolves our family group'. After several more weeks in Brussels, she and Adèle moved to Spa in eastern Belgium, in the wooded hills of the Ardennes, where they visited the baths and took the waters.

Returning to Brussels in early October, they received a subsidy of 470 francs from Hugo, by now back at Hauteville House, revising his novel and negotiating its sale with the ambitious young Belgian publisher Lacroix. This allowed them to stay in the city for a further month. Adèle had discovered an excellent new teacher, Adolphe Samuel, Professor of Harmony at the Brussels Conservatory. Her studies were going so well that she resisted plans to go with Madame Hugo to Paris in November for further treatment for her eyes until Hugo stepped in to remind his daughter that her 'true place' was with her sick mother. Nevertheless, Hugo showed continuing support for Adèle's music. He wrote some words for the melody of a song she'd composed and sent them to her 'with a great kiss'. He advised her on finding a publisher for her collection of half-a-dozen songs, and emphasized the business side of the relationship. If a publisher was responsible for the expense of engraving her music then he'd be more likely to ensure that it would sell. Notwithstanding this, when Adèle announced that she was more interested in artistic merit than financial success, her father was still prepared to make a contribution towards her engraving costs.

A period of calm appears to be in view. But suddenly, as if from nowhere, a rising current of anger and despair erupts across this surface contentment, creating waves of massive turbulence. Tucked away in the multi-volumed chronological edition of Victor Hugo's complete works – not where one would expect to find it – is a long draft letter from Adèle Hugo to Albert Pinson, written from Brussels on 17 October. Like the earlier drafts addressed by Adèle to Pinson from Jersey, there's no indication that any version of it was ever sent to him. But this time Adèle does mention in her opening paragraph that, in the face of his continuing silence and failure to write and say he's marrying her, she is rehearsing points already made in two earlier letters to him. With repeated blows, she is hammering her message home.

What I didn't take in when I first read the printed transcript of the letter in its original French is that it contains confirmation that Adèle had indeed had that assignation with Pinson in London back in June. She writes that 'The chance and opportunity we had four months ago, probably won't come again', meaning that – for her at least – marriage had been on the cards at their previous meeting. Moreover, Adèle's remarks about Madame Hugo suggest that her mother was being kept abreast of aspects of the situation. According to Adèle, Madame Hugo was anxiously waiting for Pinson to propose to her daughter. Otherwise she will press ahead with an arranged marriage for her with the 'Marquis', 'an honourable gentleman', but a man with 'an angry character . . . [who] will never accept my coldness and resistance to becoming his wife'.

The Marquis is probably fictional – no one else in the Hugo family mentions him – invented in the hope once again of making Pinson jealous. However, Adèle appears to have forsaken her other ploys, of offering Pinson money, or of claiming to be pregnant with his child. In their place, couched in an unrestrained voice that is by turns aggressive, apparently mystified about his behaviour and then utterly despairing, is a threat to end her own life. For Pinson has left her 'in pain'. He has spoken to her 'of love'. But he makes her misfortune by his 'inexplicable silence', by his failure to respond to her letters and say that he will marry her.

> I have a sad story that comes back to me. A young man . . . was one day visited by a young girl; I do not know why the young lady wished him a final farewell; the young man, seeing her withdraw quite calmly, thought it was only a good-bye. Eight days later, when he opened a newspaper, he learned that she had taken poison. The young man never forgave himself and regretted all his life that he'd never stopped the woman while there was still time.

There was still time to save Adèle from a life she described as 'impossible, odious, horrible'. Pinson had only to reply with a letter stating that he was ready 'for our immediate marriage'. If he did not, he'd receive a note of her death and an invitation to her funeral. His letter must arrive in Brussels, at her lodgings in the rue de Louvain, by 25 October, eight days later. She warned him to be sure to post the letter himself. 'The situation is so tense that the slightest mistake of the postman or of the post could cause a delay and consequently a catastrophe.' A 'simple telegram' might be a better solution.

'To our marriage or my death!' were her terrifying closing words.

The existence of the marriage licence, issued within two months of Adèle's letter, shows that Pinson wasn't prepared to dismiss her ultimatum as an empty threat. In the meantime, though, world events introduced a new and critical urgency to his plans. A crisis in Anglo-American relations was rapidly escalating, bringing Britain and the United States to the brink of war. On 8 November a British mail packet, the *Trent*, was forcibly stopped in international waters by the American warship, the *San Jacinto*. On board the *Trent* were two Confederate agents on a mission to win British and French support for the southern states in the American Civil War. They were immediately arrested and interned by the *Jacinto's* commander, Captain Wilkes, acting without instructions from President Lincoln's Union administration in Washington. In Britain Wilkes's actions were widely interpreted as a direct insult to the British flag. Palmerston's government demanded the release of the Confederates within seven days. Otherwise war would be declared and the Confederacy recognized.

While the country waited on tenterhooks for a response from Washington, the army and navy were placed on a war footing. Canada's border with the United States, over 1,500 miles long and thinly fortified, was to be strengthened against invasion, and it was estimated that 10,000 regular troops and ten times that number of militia volunteers would be required to do this. Eleven thousand British soldiers sailed from Southampton at the beginning of December in the first wave of troops to be sent out to Canada. Pinson, with the second battalion of his regiment, would not be far behind, destined for Nova Scotia.

This, then, was the background to the marriage licence obtained on 13 December. In that familiar trope of wartime, Adèle was to be a 'war bride', hurriedly married before her husband left for military service. The wording of the licence informed the couple that in order 'that your reasonable Desires' – some irony there – 'may the more speedily obtain a due effect', their marriage could be solemnized 'publicly and lawfully', and without the proclamation of banns, at the parish church of St Pancras between 'the Hours of Eight and Twelve in the Forenoon'.

St Pancras is the early 1820s, neo-Grecian-style church, with Ionic columns and caryatids – much blackened today by exhaust fumes – that you notice as you drive along the south side of the Euston Road. Adèle is entered on the licence as a spinster of the parish of St Pancras. This counted as her temporary residence. Since late November, having moved on from Brussels to Paris and then to London, she and Madame Hugo had been staying in a hotel or lodgings in Bloomsbury, within the parish boundaries. Pinson is described as a bachelor of Aldershot. As the couple came from different dioceses in the same province of the Church of England, they were able to apply for a 'common' licence from the archbishop of that province. In their case this was the Archbishop of Canterbury. Applications were generally made in person by the prospective bridegroom, though there was nothing to prevent his chosen bride accompanying him to the office in Knightrider Street, Doctors' Commons, near St Paul's Cathedral, where licences were issued.

Being both over 21, Adèle and Pinson didn't require parental permission to marry. A completed 'allegation' would have declared that there was no impediment to their marriage. A 'bond', sworn by the bridegroom and one other witness, pledged to forfeit a specified sum of money if there was shown to be any consanguinity between the couple, or if either of them was pre-contracted to someone else. The sealed licence was handed over to the bridegroom to take to the church in question, giving the clergyman there authority to conduct the wedding service.

A marriage licence was valid for three months. Most couples with licences, however, applied for them on the actual day of their marriage or the day before. Did Adèle and Pinson originally intend to marry in secret on 13 December 1861, and then get cold feet?

If this had been the plan, it was rapidly replaced with another. Adèle would return to Hauteville House and obtain her father's consent to their marriage. Pinson would follow soon afterwards, in good time before he sailed for Canada, and formally ask Victor Hugo for his daughter's hand in marriage.

'I can't wait to see you again, my little father,' Adèle had written in breezy spirits to Hugo in the first week of December. 'My absence seems to me even longer than to you, but at least we can console each other by telling ourselves that it will have been useful to my art and my health.'

As Adèle and her mother left London on 15 December, bells were tolling for the death of the Prince Consort at Windsor Castle the evening before. I imagine Adèle telling herself: Queen Victoria may have lost her Albert, but Albert Pinson is nearly mine.

That optimism wasn't shared by Victor Hugo. On 16 December he recorded in a single line in his notebook the return of his wife and daughter to St Peter Port by the afternoon boat.

Underneath he added, 'Serious worry. P.'

The question is left begging. Why on earth would Pinson agree to marry Adèle in the face of such menacing threats? Up to this point he could have continued his 'inexplicable silence', cut all ties with her, gone overseas and remained beyond her reach. Was it simply his fear that she would carry through her plan to kill herself, and that her death would lie heavily on his conscience, or in some way be attributed to his treatment of her? Or did she have some other kind of hold over him? Earlier attempts by Adèle to sway Pinson with money, in the form of the dowry she'd receive on marriage, seem to have proved ineffective. However, the autumn of 1861 had brought with it the prospect for the first time of Adèle one day being a rich woman. The sale of *Les Misérables* for a record sum to the publisher Albert Lacroix promised her a small fortune after her parents' deaths, as Victor Hugo was quick to inform his wife. Did knowledge of this deal play any part in Pinson's calculations?

Instead, though, it may all have come down to something more fundamental. In the words of Adèle's letter, Pinson had spoken to her of love. While it's impossible to know whether Pinson was ever really in love with Adèle Hugo, we can be pretty sure that sexual attraction played some part in drawing him back to her. 'Often you give your heart, but we take only your body,' Adèle's father wrote in *Les Misérables*, testifying to the paramount importance of sexual desire in men's relationships with women (as he knew only too well). I recollected one of Adele's music manuscripts that I'd seen hanging on a wall of the *Maison Victor Hugo* in the Place des Vosges. It was a setting taken from Hugo's *Les Contemplations*. Hugo complained that Adèle had never bothered to read the book, but he was wrong: one short poem at least had captured her attention. The aptly named '*Chanson*' has been set to music on numerous occasions, most notably by Saint-Saëns in the nineteenth century and by the singer-songwriter Françoise Hardy in the twentieth. But Adèle was the first to compose a melody for it.

There's something in the poem's wistful, sorrowful tone, and resigned though accusatory voice, that makes me wonder whether she saw an image of her own distress in its questioning of someone, presumably a lover, who makes a show of love without offering the reassurance of anything more. The opening stanza asks:

If you have nothing to tell me,
Why do you come so close to me?
Why do you make this smile
That could turn a monarch's head?
If you have nothing to tell me,
Why do you come so close to me?

The final stanza of three is even clearer about the effect that this intoxicating presence has on the writer:

If you wish me to go away,
Why do you pass by here?
When I see you, I quiver:
It is my joy and it is my worry.
If you wish me to go away,
Why do you pass by here?

Remorse for his behaviour towards her could have persuaded Pinson to throw in his hand and agree to marry Adèle. Maybe an even stronger, more complex emotion played its part. Perhaps after all he was overcome with pity at her situation, a woman now over 30, all but imprisoned on an island for long periods of time, desperately waiting for the man she loved to marry her.

This idea of guilt accompanied by pity in the face of an excessive love reminds me of a novel by a bestselling twentieth-century Austrian author that dramatically explores this theme. I'd caught the Stefan Zweig bug relatively late, as new translations of his novellas and short stories piled up, making him again widely read, though never challenging his position, in his heyday between the wars, as among the most popular writers of his time. *Beware of Pity – Impatience of the Heart* is the literal translation of the original German title – was Zweig's only completed novel, originally published in 1939 as war clouds were gathering. Set in a small provincial garrison town shortly before the outbreak of the First World War, it tells the story of Anton Hofmiller, a young cavalry officer in the Austro-Hungarian army. Hofmiller is invited to the home of Kekesfalva, a rich local landowner, where he meets his host's daughter Edith, paralysed some years earlier in a riding accident. Out of feelings of naïve pity, Hofmiller unwittingly responds to Edith's developing passion for him and becomes catastrophically embroiled in a relationship with her that ends in the young girl's suicide.

The novel has been well described as the first sustained fictional portrait of emotional blackmail. The reader grows to dread the tap-tap of Edith's crutches as she heaves herself, 'contorted and witch-like', towards Hofmiller. Her demands that she be loved by Hofmiller against his will assume a disturbing physical dimension as she strokes and caresses him and murmurs that she cannot go on living if he refuses her right to love him.

What appears especially interesting about the novel, in the light of Adèle's relationship with Pinson, is Zweig's recognition that there is a worse torment than suffering the longings of unrequited love, and that is to be loved against your will, 'when you cannot defend yourself against the passion thrust upon you'. In his novella, *Letter from an Unknown Woman*, published almost two decades earlier, Zweig had reversed the situation and portrayed the hopelessness of unwanted love from the perspective of a woman whose depth of feeling is unreturned by the famous writer she falls for. But its degree of empathy and psychological acuity – and its avoidance of easy sentimentality – make *Beware of Pity* the more mature and satisfying work. I couldn't be sure how blameless Pinson was, but Hofmiller's plight gave me a greater understanding of the position he must have found himself in.

> She wants you, she cries out for you with every fibre of her being, with her body and her blood . . . She wants your night and your day, your emotions, your sexual desire and all your thoughts and dreams . . . You don't want to think of her although she is always thinking of you, but that's no use, and trying to run away is no use either, because you are no longer just yourself but

a part of her . . . You are always the captive of someone else . . . never free, unconstrained and guiltless, always hunted, always under an obligation, you always feel her thinking of you.

Zweig's insights into the nature of Edith's love are just as penetrating. At times I thought I saw Adèle in Edith's reflection, never more so than when Zweig remarks that the outcasts of the world 'desire with a more passionate, far more dangerous avidity than the happy. They love with a fanatical, a baleful, a black love.'

And for this kind of baleful, black love to succeed, the clever deployment of artifice and cunning is above all necessary.

At Hauteville House, Victor Hugo had been disturbed by the news of Adèle's proposed marriage. Acting on Madame Hugo's advice, he did the only thing he could do outside of instantly dismissing the idea, and that was to request further information from Adèle about her suitor. Who exactly was this obscure young Englishman with the audacity to present himself as a husband for the daughter of a Peer of France? On 20 December, four days after her return from London, Adèle proceeded to compose a long letter to her father about the man who – this was an ominous sign – she already considered to be her husband 'for every possible reason'.

Adele's timing was scarcely opportune. A few weeks earlier, Hugo's new publisher, Albert Lacroix had arrived in Guernsey to collect the corrected manuscript of Part 1 of *Les Misérables*. In exchange he handed over the first of two tranches of payment for the novel, 125,000 francs in cash (roughly £600,000 today). Hugo was now working to a tight deadline to revise and complete the remaining four parts, while racing to check the galley proofs of earlier sections so that corrections could be sent back on the mail boat which left for Brussels three times a week. An atmosphere of feverish panic had descended on the household, with both Juliette Drouet and Julie Chenay frantically making fair copies of the manuscript as its endless pages left Hugo's desk. 'I'm in *Les Misérables* over my head,' Hugo wrote the week before Christmas. 'I'm sinking, drowning, on the sea floor.'

Adèle's letter, however, was impossible to ignore, not simply because the urgency of its message demanded a speedy response, but because the semi-fictional narrative she had fabricated was as compelling as any novel. For hers was a story of love very nearly succeeding against the odds, with only her father's consent standing in the way of absolute fulfilment.

She described how Albert Pinson had loved her from the first time he'd seen her, as she sat reading on a bench overlooking the beach at Marine Terrace, and of how he'd felt forced to enlist in the army in order one day to be in a position to marry her. He'd left Jersey 'desolate, sobbing, alone', 'but neither separation, nor discipline, nor camps . . . could erase my face from his heart, and the peaceful memory of the young girl reading arose triumphantly from the noises and fanfares of war'.

'After years of labour, courage, work and grief', Pinson had finally been brave enough to approach her and ask for her hand. 'Proud shyness' had prevented him from doing so earlier, 'but possible war and imminent separation tore his heart and made him suddenly bold'. She could not remain 'indifferent to such constancy'. She had loved him and loved him still, but theirs was not a love of 'caprice' or 'fantasy', but one rooted in down-to-earth realities.

Now to practical matters. Adèle confronted the suspicions she knew must be collecting in her father's mind. 'This young man is not marrying me out of self-interest,' she informed him. 'The mere thought of marrying a woman for her wealth would seem to him a terrible insult.' Besides, Pinson had hopes that he'd soon inherit 'a considerable fortune'. In an instant Adèle had created an imaginary uncle, who was 'old and ill and infirm', and on the brink of leaving his nephew some 10,000 francs a year. With Pinson's army pay, increasing over time with promotion, this would create a 'sufficiently lucrative situation' for the couple. Furthermore, she advised Hugo not to worry himself about matters of class. 'This young man also comes from a good family; he must clearly belong to the gentry, because in England the army is an infallible certificate of good birth. Every English officer is a gentleman.'

Adèle understood her father well enough to know that any appeal to his heart or mind would stand a better chance of succeeding if it was laced with a heavy dose of flattery. She soothed his recent fears of illness and encroaching death by reassuring him that he was fit to live for another 30 years – 'and beyond, for God will not destroy a genius like yours . . . You are necessary for the world and for progress.' Of course, no one 'is worthy of the daughter of a man like you', but it was necessary to 'descend from the heights and see the practical side of things'.

Accompanying that descent from the heights was a shift in tone to something darker: a series of warnings couched in terms of the danger of exposure, of the family name, of Adèle herself. 'You are exposing me, and us, to situations which are more than painful,' she told him,

> situations which might disturb life a hundred times more than my present marriage would do . . . I should refuse every suitor for this fiancé who is absent and far away (from absolute necessity). I should never marry another man . . . Consider what I say. See what you are exposing us to . . . Who knows the consequences of the troubles of an unmarried woman? What abyss all this may drag me into, drag us and him? When a member of a family suffers, the whole family suffers, for is it not one body? You say, 'bah! my hand hurts, that's nothing'. Nothing indeed. What will you say when you hurt your daughter?

Saving her masterstroke until last, she invoked the name of Léopoldine. She reminded Hugo that almost two decades earlier he had resisted another marriage, that of her sister with Charles Vacquerie. He had 'disdained that noble young man'. But then one day he'd 'confessed to the whole world that you were proud of him, for that obscure young man was Devotion'.

> The obscure young man whom you disdain today is, perhaps, the Heart.
> I commend Albert to you in memory of Didine.

Adèle's letter had its desired effect. In his notebook, her father judged it 'admirable'. Harassed by work, Hugo was no doubt relieved to have this contentious matter finally settled with a minimum of fuss. He noted the sum that Adèle would receive as dowry: 50,000 francs, an advance of her share of the inheritance that would come to her on her parents' deaths.

Adèle had to work quickly. She probably communicated the news of her father's agreement to Pinson – either at Aldershot or in Jersey (as he may have still had family there) – by telegram. Time was running short for his visit to Hauteville House, to reintroduce himself to the family and gain Hugo's formal consent before the couple made their way to London to be married at St Pancras. In her letter to her father Adèle had envisaged Pinson's departure for Canada as being in two or three months. In fact it was now much closer, only a matter of days away.

Albert Pinson arrived at Hauteville House on Christmas Day 1861. He left abruptly the next day with seemingly nothing decided. He hadn't asked for Adèle's hand in marriage, and no plans had been made for their wedding. What exactly transpired during those 24 hours is a mystery. It's as if the famous island fog has suddenly risen up and muffled the sound of all the voices emanating from the Hugo household. The only insight into what occurred appears in a letter written by Victor Hugo to his wife two years later. Clearly Hugo had been affronted by Pinson's failure to recognize the great honour being done to him by his association with the writer and his family. For a start Pinson had entered the house by the downstairs door and with his head held high. Nor had he greeted anyone. Incredulous, Hugo recalled that the first concern of this prospective son-in-law seemed to have been to make himself 'impossible'.

The biographer's great stumbling block is his desire for lives to make sense, always to make sense. Confronted by his inability to do so, he tries hard not to give way to despair. If I were a novelist, I might invent a number of scenes for that Christmas Day. I'd picture the young English soldier overawed by the décor of this strange home. I'd see him cowed into silence by the approach of the famous writer. I would portray them as meeting at cross purposes, each expecting the other to initiate discussion of the leading subject that has brought the young man here. I could imagine the soldier suggesting privately to his overwrought fiancée that, as his departure is now so imminent, they have no alternative but to postpone their marriage until he is back from the war. Her disproportionate response finally gives him the resolve for the course of action he's been wanting to take all along. 'He had wished to get away from her', Henry James writes of Catherine Sloper's suitor Morris Townsend in *Washington Square*; 'he had been angry and cruel, and said strange things, with strange looks. She was smothered and stunned; she buried herself in the cushions, sobbing and talking to herself.'

However, all we can do here – no doubt like the Hugo parents – is to look on at the blankness of that day with an air of mystification.

On board the transport steamer *Magdalena*, Albert Pinson left Southampton with the second battalion of his regiment in the final week of December. The voyage to Canada was an arduous one in rough winter seas. By the time the ship docked in Halifax, Nova Scotia, almost a month later, the 'Trent Affair' was all but resolved and the risk of war between Britain and America had receded. Nevertheless, the city of Halifax was to be Pinson's home for the next four years. He must have imagined himself safely out of Adele's grasp.

The novelist was keeping a close eye on his daughter. As Adèle relapsed into silence, without a word of explanation for the events at Christmas, Hugo continued with his revision of *Les Misérables*. An addition to the beginning of Book Five shows that negative thoughts of Albert Pinson weren't far from his mind. Cosette, Jean Valjean's beautiful adoptive daughter, is attracted to a handsome young lieutenant from the local barracks who passes by her garden gate. He possesses 'a wasp waist, a splendid uniform, girlish cheeks . . . a waxed moustache', along with fair hair and prominent blue eyes. His face is 'vain and insolent'. When his fellow officers tease him about the girl who's taken a fancy to him, the lieutenant retorts, 'Have I time . . . to look at all the girls who look at me?'

'Bad matches are made in the highest circles,' reflects Hugo. Later in the novel he declares that there is no halfway in matters of love.

'It means either ruin or salvation.' Cosette is saved by Marius's love. She frees herself from her illusions and dismisses the lieutenant in no uncertain terms: 'dull, inane, stupid, feckless, conceited, disagreeable, impertinent and very ugly.' If Cosette had seen through the charms of her lieutenant, was it mere wishful thinking for Hugo to hope that his own daughter might do the same?

1862 was to be the year of the worldwide triumph of *Les Misérables*. The first part was published in April, followed by further instalments in May, concluding with the final four-volume set at the end of June. Madame Hugo was in Paris, acting as her husband's unofficial publicist. Supported by the first major advertising campaign of the modern publishing age, *Les Misérables* received a critical drubbing, but went on to achieve record-breaking sales. The book described by Hugo as having fraternity as its foundation and progress as its summit was a massive popular success.

His intensive writing and publishing schedule behind him, Hugo set off travelling again with Juliette Drouet. This time their itinerary included London, to see the Crystal Palace, a steady progress through the Rhineland and another visit to Brussels, to attend a banquet organised by Lacroix in celebration of *Les Misérables*.

Arriving back at St Peter Port in late September, Hugo could take solace from the near completion, after six years' hard work, of the transformation of Hauteville House, achieved even as his family life continued to ebb away. François-Victor, the favoured son, remained steadfast, but his elder brother Charles had finally made his 'act of secession', moving from Guernsey to settle in Paris, no longer prepared to put up with what he termed his father's 'police supervision'. Madame Hugo was already planning her next extended visit to the French capital. As for Adèle, she had returned to her familiar routine, mostly confining herself to her room with only her piano and her music for companionship.

She had received compliments for her songs, with the exception of the final one, whose harmonies were judged 'bizarre', from Ambroise Thomas, Professor of Composition at the Paris Conservatory. These might have been sufficient to persuade her to accompany her mother to Paris in the spring of 1863, but Adèle chose to remain at home. Instead, in her mother's absence, she faced a further – and final – proposal of marriage. Her suitor was a young Sicilian poet from Messina. Tommaso Cannizzaro, only in his mid-twenties, had been a guest at Hauteville House in February, when he'd won Hugo's approval, and in all likelihood his encouragement to ask for his daughter's hand. On 2 June Hugo recorded Adèle's predictable refusal in response to a letter from Cannizzaro asking her to be his wife.

This latest proposal seems to have spurred Adèle into making a decision. The following day, 3 June, François-Victor reported to his father that he'd made an unexpected discovery in a corridor on one of the upper floors of the house. It was of 'a strange sewn package' containing clothes and papers.

'New symptoms of possible plans', Hugo remarked laconically in his notebook.

Those plans were already hatched. Adèle would shortly be on her way to Canada, without the prior knowledge of her family, or indeed of Albert Pinson.

Early on the morning of 18 June she left Hauteville House, closing the door behind her for the last time. Ostensibly she had decided after all to join her mother and Charles in Paris, travelling from St Peter Port in the company of a neighbour, Madame Evans and her two children. In reality she was bound for Southampton, for a passage to New York on board the steamship the *Great Eastern*, Isambard Kingdom Brunel's leviathan of the high seas.

This stage of the story, in a story filled with absences, affects me more than any other. The shock of the break – the '*violence*' of it, to use Victor Hugo's description – has a visceral impact on me. Part of what is so upsetting is the knowledge with hindsight of the finality of the step. Adèle will never see her mother again. In five years Madame Hugo will be dead, her coffin, unaccompanied by any member of her family, transported on a train across the Belgian border on its way for burial at Villequier. Nor will Adèle ever be reunited with her brother Charles. He'll be dead from an apoplectic stroke at the age of 44, within a decade of his sister's departure. In abandoning her family and home, I wonder whether Adèle was rehearsing her own sense of abandonment: by her father, through his liaison with Juliette Drouet, in his dedication to Léopoldine's memory; by her mother, during her affair with Sainte-Beuve.

For me, running in parallel as I think about this, still possessing the power to interrupt my train of thought, is the memory of myself aged eleven being told by my father one night that my mother was leaving us. She didn't, as it turned out. She looked at the door as he spoke those words and evidently thought better of the threat she'd made to him. Perhaps it would have been better for her if she had left us. But the fear of her going continued to hang over me as a dark, heavy shadow for the rest of my childhood. And in the way that fear of abandonment has shaped and threatened my adult relationships, it has hung over me ever since.

Deprived of the powers of hindsight, we might applaud the adventurousness of Adèle's decision, as well as its bravery, in crossing the Atlantic by herself in the midst of a major ongoing war. Its pioneer spirit, too. Ibsen's Nora and H. G. Wells's Ann Veronica were still a generation and more away. Nora deserts her husband; Ann Veronica rebels against her father. Both of them metaphorically slam the door on the conventions of family and domestic life.

This was the gloss that Adèle herself chose to put on her departure. In a coded entry in her journal she had written of 'that incredible thing'

> for a young woman, enslaved to the point of not being able to go out alone for five minutes to buy some paper, to walk over the sea, to fly over the sea, to pass from the old world to the new world to rejoin her lover. This I will do.

Tragically, it would not take long for the illusion at the heart of this ambition to reveal itself.

6

Escapade

'And there', said my taxi driver, gesturing with a finger to a point across the water, 'is the exact spot where the two ships collided, causing the massive explosion.' This grim reminder, as we approached downtown Halifax, of the tragedy in 1917 that had killed and injured thousands, as well as devastating parts of the city, intensified my mood of foreboding. I'd flown to Nova Scotia in late spring accompanied by all my usual fears of travelling long distances alone, anxious at the prospect of spending ten days in a city where I was a complete stranger and knew no one.

At least I could accept as a good omen the serendipity that greeted my arrival. Why had I come to Halifax, asked the immigration officer? For a second I considered passing myself off as a holidaymaker, but then decided to come clean. I was on the trail of Victor Hugo's daughter, I replied, realizing as I spoke that the more nonchalant I contrived to appear the more ridiculous I sounded. The young man instantly brightened and forgot his official manner. He told me that he was studying French literature, and had been reading the poems written by Hugo in Léopoldine's memory. Then he smiled and wished me a successful visit.

I was staying in a small, boutiquey hotel, a block behind Halifax's harbour front. My chintzy room was light and airy. Downstairs, separated by a narrow hallway, were a parlour and dining room. Browsing the parlour's single shelf of books, I came across the sad tale of Madame de Saint-Laurent, mistress of Edward, Duke of Kent, Queen Victoria's father, during his time at Halifax as commander of the British forces in Nova Scotia at the end of the eighteenth century. Saint-Laurent, or Julie as she was known, was the duke's great love for almost three decades. At their home, the Prince's Lodge, in Bedford, the Halifax suburb, he had a heart-shaped pond built for her. Ultimately their relationship was thwarted by the demands of Parliament and the British Crown, which required the duke to put aside Julie and marry in order to safeguard the succession. Far from creating a scandal, or pursuing the duke back in England, Julie had retired into decent obscurity. A quick search along the room's row of DVDs produced the 2012 film of the musical of *Les Misérables*. Nothing would induce me to sit through that film's interminable length again, but I appreciated the coincidence, and was reminded of the scene in Truffaut's film where Adèle, residing in Halifax under a false name, having travelled halfway across the world, is presented with a copy of her father's novel by a local bookseller who suspects her true identity. Now as then, the ubiquity of the book and its storyline make it impossible to escape.

That first evening I wandered down to the waterfront to get my bearings. Small craft, bobbing about on the water, and several larger vessels, displaying national flags, were well lit but uncannily silent. In nearby Hollis Street I stood in front of an ugly 1950s high-rise, the darkened Ralston Building, due for demolition. This had once been the site of the grand old Halifax Hotel, Adèle Hugo's first home in the city. Arriving in Halifax on the packet boat from New York in late July 1863, with nowhere to stay, she was driven by a kindly coachman to the hotel, practically the only respectable accommodation in the city for a single woman, where she booked in under an assumed name, Miss Lewly.

The mix of architectural styles, rubbing shoulders with one another, chart the course of Halifax's history. There is the row upon row of wooden houses from Halifax's years as a modest colonial town, built in what was disparagingly known as 'the tea-chest order of architecture'. The solid granite structures of government buildings date from its time as a self-governing colony of the British Empire at the end of the 1840s, or to the period beginning 20 years later when Nova Scotia joined the Confederation of Canada as one of the country's three provinces. The glittering skyscrapers are testimony to the city's position today as a major contributor to the economy of Atlantic Canada. With the light fading, I made the steep climb to the summit of Halifax's central hill, where the town clock – commissioned by the Duke of Kent, a stickler for punctuality, apparently – was brightly illuminated, and reached the star-shaped fort at the top, known as the Citadel. There have been four fortifications on the site. This final one, which took nearly 30 years to build, was completed in the mid-1850s. With its commanding view out to sea, the fort was for decades of crucial importance to the defence of Halifax. It's now a national park and Canada's most visited historic site.

At noon the next day the thundering roar from the Citadel's cannon fire, a quaint diurnal custom, had me practically jumping out of my skin. It was a public holiday, so naturally it was bucketing with rain. Feeling dispirited about the days ahead, I found myself joining a herd of visitors on a tour of the waterfront's Maritime Museum. The museum celebrates the city's seascape, its proud status as the world's largest natural harbour. But what pulls in the tourists are the exhibits linking Halifax to the most famous sea disaster of all, the sinking, in April 1912, of the unsinkable RMS *Titanic*. This doleful little collection includes a deck chair, a lifebelt and an artefact still labelled the 'Unknown Child's Shoes', even though the 19-month-old English child, Sidney Goodwin, to whom the shoes belonged, was identified a decade ago through DNA testing, and lies buried in Halifax's Fairview Lawn Cemetery.

As the nearest major port in the North Atlantic Ocean to where the colossal liner went down to its watery grave, Halifax was called upon to act as coroner, undertaker and mourner to more than 200 bodies retrieved from the sea. 'Death ships', equipped with ice, embalming fluid and body bags, brought the dead back to a city swathed in black, so that they could be given a final resting place in one of its cemeteries.

At the end of my first full day in Halifax, I ate dinner at the Five Fishermen, a popular restaurant in Argyle Street. Eavesdropping on a group of young men and women at a nearby table, laughing and joking with the waitress, I heard them begging to be allowed to try the 'coffin hoists' in the wine store. Only slowly as the meal progressed did it dawn on me that this wasn't some peculiar form of drunken ribaldry. In one of the city guides I recalled reading that the restaurant building had formerly been the funeral parlour where the wealthier victims of the *Titanic*'s maiden voyage were prepared for burial.

As I watched a fly buzzing around the room I experienced the queasiest of sensations in the pit of my stomach.

'She hates me,' was Victor Hugo's initial expression of shock at his daughter's disappearance. To François-Victor his sister's action was an 'unheard-of escapade'. 'She is evidently going to see *him*. Where? In Canada? In England?' Charles Hugo's response was more phlegmatic. Adèle had adopted 'English ideas', denationalized herself, in effect, by making a voyage on her own to rejoin Pinson. This might be considered an enormous step in France, but would be viewed as nothing out of the ordinary in England.

It took a while to pin down Adèle's precise whereabouts. She had sent her family on a number of false trails, putting them off her scent in order to give herself time. On 19 June, the day after her departure, a letter from Adèle was delivered to Hauteville House. This explained that at the last moment she'd decided not to travel to France, but had accepted the invitation of a friend, Miss Lester, to stay for several days near Hampton Court, 20 miles outside London. Five days later she wrote to François-Victor stating that she was at Southampton, ready to embark for Malta, where Pinson was waiting with a detachment of his regiment. By early July, when Madame Hugo and Charles arrived home from Paris for a family council of war, the truth was out. Adèle was in Halifax. Soon she would be married, Adèle informed her mother in a letter, and be calm and satisfied.

Victor Hugo was anything but calm, amid his growing suspicion that Adèle was running after Albert Pinson in order to try to marry him against his will. For how else could her 'incredible behaviour be explained', he asked his wife, 'since so far as we are concerned everything had been agreed upon, and our consent given?' Was there some 'latent impossibility' in Pinson's own situation? Had he a mistress, a wife, children? 'Who knows?'

Adèle had assured her mother that she wouldn't marry without first gaining her parents' further consent. However, no such request from her was forthcoming. Instead, at the beginning of August, François-Victor received a pathetic plea from Adèle, complaining about the high cost of living in Halifax and asking him to beg their father to send her 390 francs by the next courier. She had evidently left the Halifax Hotel, and claimed that the people she was staying with wouldn't hesitate to have her thrown into prison if she didn't pay her rent. The money was duly sent, but so too was the collective message of the Hugo family to their errant daughter and sister: marry or return immediately to Guernsey.

Nevertheless, the contents of the letter from Adèle to her mother that arrived in September caught the family by surprise. An unexpected picture of connubial bliss was conjured up in its breathless tone:

My dearest

I am married. I am still caught up in the excitement of it all, and I am writing to you in haste, so as not to miss the post. In the midst of our happiness, there is one regret: my husband has to leave in five days' time and to go to Canada for three weeks. This is essential for his army duties . . . The sensible thing is for me to wait for him in Halifax . . .

Adèle provided no further details of the marriage, or of the bridegroom, only that henceforth she was to be known as 'Madame Penson' – 'Why is he both "Pinson" and "Penson"?', Victor Hugo asked irascibly, but reasonably enough – and that her new address was 16 Granville Street, Halifax. She wouldn't be living at the barracks, but had her accommodation in town 'like the other ladies'.

Was she really married, though? Her father and elder brother had their doubts. Madame Hugo worried that to question the marriage would be offensive to Adèle. Despite feeling hurt by Adèle's lack of consideration for them all, François-Victor took her word for it. Nevertheless, he intended to write to Pinson for his confirmation and ask for a copy of the marriage certificate.

Suddenly all questioning of the marriage's existence evaporated in the face of news that Adèle was spreading word of it herself in letters to comparative strangers as well as to friends. A Paris newspaper picked up the story, quickly followed by others, including the *Star* of Guernsey. The family had no choice now but to make a public show of support for Adèle for fear of damaging the Hugo name. A cover story was hastily assembled. On 10 October Victor Hugo put a brave face on the matter in a letter to his old friend and publisher Hetzel, displaying his prejudice against all things English while managing to inflate his son-in-law's social standing in line with his own pretensions.

> My daughter has become an Englishwoman. Such are the blows of exile! Her husband is a veteran of the Crimea [sic], a young English officer, aristocratic [sic], a stickler for propriety, 'gentilhomme', and a gentleman. Our family will now be one in which the father-in-law (old) stands for the future, the son-in-law (young) for the past. This young representative of a bygone age took my daughter's fancy, and the choice was hers. True to my duty as a father, in such a case, I gave her my support.
>
> The young people are now on their way to Halifax. Between my son-in-law and me lies a temperamental distance which separates the French and the English, and the physical distance which lies between Europe and America. But there is such a thing as a right to happiness. My daughter has claimed it, and I cannot blame her . . .

Behind closed doors Hugo couldn't hide his fury. Adèle's letter announcing her marriage had mentioned him only by implication – 'as a cashier' – and he was being forced to discuss family matters 'with all and sundry' without full possession of the facts. He continued to send money to Halifax in response to Adèle's begging letters, but made it clear that until he had 'absolute proof' that she was married, she would receive no dowry.

He regarded the absence of any communication from Pinson, that 'worthless little English trooper', as telling. 'He is silent. Like the dead', Hugo told his wife. 'Is he in effect my son-in law? His silence indicates "no".' Meanwhile the impact of this 'punishment' on Hugo's work was already being felt. Lacking the 'deep peace of mind' he needed, he'd been unable to write a line of poetry for his new book.

Madame Hugo tried to moderate his rage. The 'poor child's' financial demands were very modest. Adèle had broken no human law. 'She has loved a man for ten years and has married him. Yes, she married without her family present, and there are probably extenuating circumstances.' Pointedly, she pushed him to examine his own conscience. 'Which of us . . . is able to affirm that we haven't sacrificed convenience and risked our honour in the face of passion?'

During my weekend in Guernsey I'd visited the Priaulx Library in St Peter Port, arriving 20 minutes before it closed on the Saturday afternoon. I wanted to see a newspaper from its local history collection, but the library assistant, a middle-aged woman, stared pointedly at her watch and doubted in a weary voice whether there was enough time for her to fetch it. My pleading prevailed and she toiled up the stairs, returning a few minutes later with a bound quarto volume, which thudded onto the desk to the accompaniment from her of a long, dramatic sigh.

Rapidly scanning its pages I found what I was looking for. There, in the notices section of the *Gazette de Guernsey* for 17 October 1863, was Victor Hugo's announcement of his daughter's marriage, his final attempt at taking control of a situation that was bringing him unwelcome publicity. The notice presented him not as Victor Hugo, democrat and world-famous writer, but in the guise of bourgeois parent. The wedding, as recorded, had taken place a month earlier, not in Halifax, but in Paris.

> ## MARIAGES.
>
> Le 17 Sept., a été marié à Paris, M. Albert Penson, du 16e régt. d'infanterie anglaise, avec Mlle Adèle Hugo, fille de M. le Vicomte Hugo, officier de la légion d'honneur, ancien Pair de France, ex-représentant du peuple sous la République, membre de l'académie française, et chevalier de l'ordre de Charles III d'Espagne, domicilié à St. Pierre-Port, Guernesey.
>
> Le 13 Octobre, à St. Pierre-Port, par le Rév. C. S. Guille, Edouard, fils aîné de M. Edouard Vagg, autrefois du service civil de l'île Maurice, avec Cecelia Henry, fille de feu M. Edouard John, de Helston, Cornwall.
>
> Le 15, à l'église de St. Sauveur, par le Rév. P. Carey, M. Frédéric Torode, du Castel, avec Mlle. Marie-Anne, fille de M. Jean Le Cras, de St. Sauveur.

Verse published the same day in a Jersey newspaper by Adolphe Pelleport, a young poet invited to Guernsey and befriended by Victor Hugo, celebrated the union of an Englishman with the daughter of a great Frenchman as a welcome opportunity to unite the destinies of 'two bitter nations'. Hugo himself turned to a classical poet to express his continuing doubts about Adèle's marriage. Underneath a note of Adèle's Halifax address he copied out a quotation from the *Aeneid* in which Virgil comments on Dido, Queen of Carthage's ill-fated love affair with Aeneas:

No more does she dream of a secret love:
She calls it marriage and with that name veils her sin.

Three weeks later, a terse two-word entry in Hugo's notebook – *non est*, 'it is not' – expressed the now dismal certainty that no marriage had taken place.

'Burn this carefully after reading it,' François-Victor wrote to Madame Hugo on 11 November. The news was devastating, so incendiary that the paper he'd written it on might well self-conflagrate before it was thrown on the fire. Adèle had lied to them as she'd lied to the world, but had at last admitted the truth that she wasn't married in a 'confidential' letter to her brother. Even so, her 'inexcusable obstinacy' meant she was not about to give up the chase. She had told François-Victor that since the marriage had been publicly announced, it was 'absolutely necessary' that Pinson be made to go through with it, and asked him to write to Pinson, 'to touch his heart'.

From their respective locations – Guernsey, Brussels, Paris – the Hugos offered different solutions for Adèle's – and the family's – predicament. Predominant once again was fear of how the slightest hint of scandal might make the family the object of ridicule while bringing 'dishonour' to Adèle. François-Victor and his father were in accord: as soon as Adèle came home they would announce that she was divorced, that they'd discovered her marriage to be 'irregular' and been left with no alternative but to break it. She could spend six months in Paris or Brussels with her mother. This was 'by no means a banishment', Victor Hugo stressed, but a method of temporary concealment. Adèle would return to Hauteville House as 'Madame Adèle', and in time another marriage might be possible for her.

Charles Hugo was characteristically bullish. He appeared to be on the verge of challenging Pinson to a duel, if, as Adèle claimed, she'd kept letters in which 'the scoundrel' promised to marry her. Charles had another, more bizarre, plan of contacting the Minister of War in the British government through the Hugos' friend Mrs Milner-Gibson, wife of the President of the Board of Trade, to persuade the War Office to put pressure on Pinson to go through with the marriage. Hugo squashed the idea flat. Throughout that winter of 1863–4, he constantly reiterated the need for silence and discretion. One careless word to an untrustworthy individual and the terrible secret would be out.

Madame Hugo's despairing cry was like a howl of pain. 'The future of my daughter is lost!' Adèle, she reminded the men of her family, was evidently deeply unhappy. She was in love, but she wasn't loved in return. In the absence of a proper surname, even her identity was in doubt. She required her family's urgent help and to be folded in her mother's arms. Madame Hugo proposed sending Adèle a ticket, at a cost of 550 francs, from Halifax to England, where she would meet her. If this idea came to nothing she would go to Halifax herself and bring her daughter home.

In late November Albert Pinson suddenly manifested himself again. His cold but polite letter to François-Victor announced a firm determination not to marry Adèle, before going on to state that he'd been 'strangely surprised' by the notice in the newspapers, according to which Victor Hugo did him 'the unsolicited honour of his daughter's hand'.

Adèle, he continued, had arrived in North America of her own volition. When he'd visited her she'd told him of her intention to leave, but constantly delayed her departure on some pretext or other. Pinson concluded his letter by begging François-Victor to call Adèle back home as soon as possible.

But Adèle seemed to be living in a dream, a condition of 'unreality', as François-Victor called it, pursuing its realization through increasingly 'absurd chimeras'. She imagined having Pinson kidnapped to Scotland and marrying him there 'in spite of himself'. She told her brother that she had approached a hypnotist with the plan of having Pinson hypnotized into marrying her. This would cost 5,000 francs – with a money-back guarantee if the operation wasn't completely successful – but to pay the hypnotist as well as a minister and two witnesses who would be on hand, ready for the ceremony, she needed an advance on her dowry.

Victor Hugo was savage in his condemnation of Pinson. He was 'a ruffian, the lowest of the low! He has set the coping-stone upon *a ten years' lie* by taking a cold and arrogant farewell.' Adèle deserved their congratulations, 'for it is the greatest good luck imaginable that she has not married *that* . . .'

At the same time, Hugo indulged in his own version of unreality. Adèle, he wrote to his wife, would return to her family and he would take charge of her future:

> The poor child has never yet been happy; it is high time that she started. I will give some parties for her at Hauteville House, to which I will invite the most intelligent people I can lay my hands on. *I will dedicate books to Adèle.* I will make her the crown of my old age. I will glorify her exile. I will make all good. If a fool has the power to dishonour, Victor Hugo will have the power to shed splendour!

Sadly, it was all too late for that.

A 'fancy', an 'illusion', a 'horrible dream', a nightmare', a 'derailment'. Then the realization of something far more terrifying: 'madness' – *folie*.

On printouts of my English translations of Victor Hugo's letters concerning his daughter's 'sad adventure', which I had brought with me to Halifax, I'd underlined in ink these salient words, as Hugo had finally allowed himself to come to the conclusion that

Adèle's feelings for the English lieutenant weren't love at all, but symptoms of acute mental disturbance. The spectre holding him back at the outset from full acknowledgment of the seriousness of her situation was undoubtedly that of his own brother Eugène. Four decades had passed since Eugène Hugo, obsessively jealous of Victor's literary achievements and of his new young wife, had been declared incurably insane and admitted to a lunatic asylum, dying 15 years later in a pitiable, catatonic state. Adèle's *folie* was a painful reminder of his brother's illness, and of his family's acquiescence in his treatment, but also proof enough for Hugo that its roots lay in an underlying genetic inheritance.

The idea that Adèle's condition was pathological was the aspect of her story that had made the artist Jean Hugo, Hugo's great-grandson, wary of allowing François Truffaut to go ahead, back in the 1970s, with his film of Adèle H. Jean Hugo worried that mental disease gave 'a pathological overtone to this love story', depriving it of all its 'human value'. Truffaut broadly agreed, emphasizing in talking about the film that it was never intended as a clinical case history, but as a tragic tale of absolute love.

I realized that I too was wary of approaching the subject of Adèle's mental deterioration. Not because I wished to deny it, but because of the seemingly unanswerable questions it presented: what it was, when it started, and what caused it? Modern writers on Victor Hugo have invariably labelled his younger daughter as schizophrenic. One understands the rationale behind this, as what we know of her condition appears to fit certain symptoms of the standard diagnosis of the illness: among them delusional behaviour, a flattened emotional response and social withdrawal. Yet many medical practitioners today, perhaps the largest proportion of them, would argue that schizophrenia has outlasted its usefulness as a meaningful concept. For a start, it's a misleading unifying term for a multiplicity of different mental health disorders, some with overlapping symptoms. Secondly, and most significantly, 'schizophrenia' has no firm biological foundation. The scientific search over many decades for signs of madness spelt out on the physical matter of the brain has turned up a blank. What this means is that mental health problems are not solely, or necessarily, a manifestation of biological illness. Rather, they could be a reaction to adversity, to painful events and trauma in an individual's life. In other words, what needs fixing may not lie inside the individual at all.

Traumatic events in Adèle Hugo's life aren't difficult to identify, as anyone reading this far will surely agree. The devastating sudden death of a beloved sister; the attempts over several years to communicate with her spirit; a distant but dominating father; isolation for long periods apart from normal society; an errant lover. What impact over time might a combination of any of these have had on her state of mind?

I delved into the box of papers before me. Halifax's Dalhousie University, known familiarly as 'Dal', which formally opened as a university the year Adèle Hugo arrived in Halifax, has a small collection relating to her stay in the city preserved in its library. The library building is a huge concrete monolith, devoid of any redeeming features, one of those intriguing memorials erected by a rich widow to a late husband that makes you wonder what she was trying to communicate to posterity both about him and the history of their marriage.

The first item out of the box was the typescript of a television play about Adèle. *The Lady in Black* by Kay Hill was produced by the Canadian Broadcasting Corporation in 1967, eight years before the release of the Truffaut film (incidentally, Haligonians didn't flock to this, being more intent on watching the raw, buttery sex in Bertolucci's *Last Tango in Paris*, which reached cinemas almost simultaneously). Pre-dating the publication of Frances Guille's edition of Adèle's journal, this TV drama's 'imaginative reconstruction' of her life, just prior to and during her spell in Halifax, depended on published works about the Hugo family and local folklore. 'I have been hungry and thirsty all my life,' Adèle tells Pinson. 'Nourish me! Fill me! Love me!' Pinson is somewhat abashed. 'Lord, what a tiger,' is all he can find to say. Meanwhile, at Hauteville House the Hugos prepare for Pinson's Christmas visit, when he will supposedly ask for Adèle's hand. The maid Jeanette, hanging some decorative holly and ivy, has her bottom pinched by Victor Hugo. Madame Hugo, turning a blind eye to this, insists that Pinson is 'truly devoted' to their daughter. Furthermore, 'of one thing I am certain', she tells Hugo: '*she* is mad about *him*!'

The next document was more interesting and pertinent. It was a letter from François-Victor Hugo, browned with age, the lines of its folds so deep that they resembled deep tracks running across the surface of the paper. The addressee was a Mrs Saunders, whom François-Victor thanked warmly for the 'Christian kindness' he'd never be able to repay. Adèle had rented rooms from Sarah Saunders and her husband Richard for over a year at two properties: initially, towards the end of 1863, at the small house they lived in at 33 North Street, and subsequently, following their move, at 42 Sackville Street, a few blocks from the Citadel, the hilltop fortification. In the daytime Richard Saunders worked as a messenger at the Union Bank; in the evenings he was a waiter at the Halifax Hotel. The hotel's French chef, learning that Adèle was trying to find somewhere quieter and cheaper than her room in Granville Street, situated in the city's fashionable shopping district, put her in touch with the Saunders, who were not long married, with a baby, Grace, and looking for a lodger. To the young couple, who only ever knew Adèle under her alias of 'Miss Lewly', the Frenchwoman was a figure of considerable mystery. She wore clothes, which had evidently seen better days, made from expensive fabrics – silk, satin, velvet – and it was clear from her general helplessness that in her past life she had been waited on and never had to look after herself. The arrangement was that she would furnish her own room and cook for herself. But the room was left spartan, with little furniture, and she lived mostly off bread and butter and hot chocolate. Mrs Saunders started inviting their lodger to family meals to ensure that she didn't go hungry.

Miss Lewly spent much of her time in her room feverishly writing, surrounded by bags full of manuscripts. She wrote many letters, as well as receiving some addressed to 'Madame Pinson'. One day in December 1863, Mrs Saunders noticed a letter from

Adèle on the dining-room table waiting to be posted. She took a note of the name on the envelope – François-Victor Hugo – together with the address, and wrote to him about Miss Lewly's sad condition. Mrs Saunders informed him that the young woman's thin clothes offered no protection against Halifax's harsh winters and that Miss Lewly was badly undernourished. She had guessed by now that an unhappy love affair lay at the root of her lodger's problems, and described how an army officer from the garrison had visited Miss Lewly two or three times during her stay with them. 'It has been several weeks since he returned,' François-Victor reported to his parents, recounting the contents of Mrs Saunders' letter. 'And it seems that he has completely abandoned her.'

As his sister's protector since childhood and, moreover, the only member of his family with a command of English, François-Victor immediately replied to Mrs Saunders, relieved that there was now someone in Halifax who would be able to report back to them on Adèle's behaviour and any changes in her situation. With his father's consent he asked Mrs Saunders to buy Adèle whatever she needed, and made arrangements for a bill of exchange to be sent to her to cover the expense. A box of winter clothes for Adèle duly arrived at North Street. François-Victor urged Mrs Saunders to expedite Miss Lewly's return to her family by tricking her into believing that Pinson was sailing home to Europe. 'Miss Lewly . . . would immediately decide to leave, and thus arrive in Liverpool where someone sent by her parents would be waiting to take her to her family.' Nothing came of the plan.

Twenty years later, following Victor Hugo's death, a reporter from Halifax's *Morning Herald* investigating his daughter's doomed 'romance' caught up with Sarah Saunders. She proved remarkably forthcoming, boasting that what she had to say about her erstwhile lodger could fill half a dozen newspapers, though she admitted that she'd never discovered what had become of Adèle after she left Halifax. In Mrs Saunders' memory the member of the Hugo family who had been her correspondent was no longer

Adèle's brother but the great writer himself ('To tell you the truth we didn't then know who Victor Hugo was, and therefore didn't appreciate the value of his letters as we do now'); and by now Pinson's two or three visits to Adèle had more than doubled their original number in Mrs Saunders' account. Adèle, she remembered, never mentioned Pinson by name. But 'her life and soul seemed to be absorbed in him'.

On one occasion the landlady noticed a pile of sovereigns on Adèle's table. This mystified the Saunders. Judging from the way she lived, they'd believed Miss Lewly to be practically penniless. 'What did she do with the money?' Mrs Saunders asked the *Herald* reporter, pausing, perhaps, before she gave him the answer he must have been waiting expectantly for. 'Why, she gave it to Pinson – the man she was so completely infatuated with!'

In 1934, as part of the celebrations to mark her hundredth birthday, Fanny Lenoir, who was born in Halifax and lived there all her life, reminisced about bygone days in a talk to the Nova Scotia Historical Society. One of her more vivid early memories was of the arrival of the *Britannia*, the first Cunard steamship, which crossed the Atlantic from Liverpool to Halifax in 1840, revolutionizing ocean travel. As a girl, Mrs Lenoir had walked its decks, seen the black smoke pouring from the ship's enormous funnel, and met Mr Cunard himself, dressed in black and wearing an expensive beaver hat and kid gloves.

Another figure in black arose from Mrs Lenoir's past, and seemed for a moment to materialize before the audience through the medium of the old lady's recollections. Adèle Hugo, whom she'd encountered many times, was a beautiful-looking woman – 'tall, well built, Roman nose, wavy jet-black hair, piercing black eyes and dark complexion'. She was always clothed in black, in a black shawl, large black bonnet, carrying a black umbrella, rain or shine, summer or winter.

Fanny Lenoir's description accords well with the last known photograph of Adèle – aside, that is, from one many years later showing her on her deathbed – taken by Edmond Bacot, the summer before her flight, in an album of studies of the Hugo family and of

Hauteville House. Jean-Marc Hovasse, Hugo's leading biographer, writes that by this time Adèle was no longer the beauty who had been singled out for praise by Balzac in her teens. However, on the evidence of the photo, taken just weeks short of her thirty-second birthday, it seems that she was still a handsome woman.

Fanny Lenoir met Adèle through her husband Pierre, a lawyer. On arrival in Halifax Miss Lewly had claimed to be anxious to find her 'cousin' Lieutenant Pinson among the swarm of officers and soldiers stationed in the garrison. She'd sought the advice of the manager of the Halifax Hotel, Henry Hesslein, a French-speaking Swiss, who'd directed her to Pierre Lenoir, another French speaker, at his office in Hollis Street. Lenoir's office was on the ground floor. Lenoir, Fanny and their children inhabited the upper storeys. Adèle made an appointment to see him, continuing to hold her umbrella over her head even when she entered the room, Fanny recalled, as if she was worried that someone might uncover her identity, and not closing it until she was seated. Lenoir located Pinson easily enough. He was not yet quartered at the Citadel itself, but at the newer

Wellington Barracks in the north end of the city. Adèle proposed setting out on foot that day to see him, until dissuaded by Lenoir. The barracks were in rough and dangerous terrain that no lady should set foot in. Instead, Adèle wrote to Pinson. As probably his first intimation that she had followed him to Halifax, he must have received the letter with horror.

The following year Adèle turned again to Lenoir for professional help. This time Lenoir referred her to Robert Motton, a young Halifax barrister with a rising reputation and a dubious expertise in muckraking. Miss Lewly's story had taken a controversial turn, and she spoke with bitterness and an appetite for revenge. Lieutenant Pinson, it seemed, was not her cousin. In fact, he was her former lover who had sworn to marry her. However, word had reached Adèle's ears that Pinson had become engaged in Halifax to another woman, and she was set on doing anything she could to prevent their marriage taking place.

Two decades on, that same young newspaper man from the *Morning Herald* who had won Sarah Saunders' confidence was having a field day, managing to secure an interview with Robert Motton, now a prominent QC. Professional discretion, Motton warned the reporter, obliged him to offer only an outline of what he knew about Adèle Hugo's time in Halifax. Nevertheless, like Mrs Saunders, he proved unstoppable, caught up after all these years in the romance, the sadness and stark tragedy of the story, punctuating his monologue with dramatic little speeches. Pinson would never marry anyone else while she lived, Miss Lewly had declared defiantly, for she was his wife in the sight of God. Motton remembered Adèle herself as a remarkable-looking woman, speaking in broken English and writing in an exquisite copperplate hand. At one meeting she had offered him one of the manuscripts she spent so much of her time working on. 'Publish it someday', she told Motton, 'and you will startle the world and make a fortune.' What could this have been? A continuation of Adèle's journal? The work on female emancipation that she had planned years earlier? 'I have been sorry many times that I did not accept it,' Motton admitted.

Motton could have commenced proceedings against Pinson for breach of promise, a common enough offence among soldiers picking up a new girlfriend or fiancée as they moved from garrison to garrison. But with insufficient evidence to take the case through the Nova Scotia courts, he decided to write directly to Pinson requesting that he withdraw from his engagement to the Halifax woman. When this letter produced no response, Motton took a more decisive step. He wrote to the father of Pinson's fiancée, outlining his client's relationship with the English lieutenant and advising him that in order to avoid scandal his daughter's engagement should immediately be broken off.

The family that Pinson hoped to marry into was among Halifax's most distinguished. James W. Johnstone, his prospective father-in-law, was a prominent politician, lawyer and judge, most recently leader of Nova Scotia's Conservative party and premier of the province. As a young man Johnstone had challenged a courtroom rival to a duel and shot him in the foot, allegedly to end his dancing career. The older man was imbued with a strong religious faith and strict evangelical principles. He lived at Mount Amelia, a large estate named after his late wife on the Dartmouth side of Halifax harbour, with his two daughters Minnie and Agnes, Pinson's intended wife-to-be.

Agnes lived in the shadow of her more high-spirited sister. She was attractive, a practised musician, but until Albert Pinson swept her off her feet it looked as though Agnes Johnstone was destined for life as a spinster. As I read through the information in the archives, a vague pattern in Pinson's romantic conquests was easily discernible, from Adèle to Agnes to Pinson's eventual wife Catherine Roxburgh. All three women were from distinguished or influential families, rich or at least well-off. All three faced being left on the shelf until Pinson came along to rescue them in their thirties with a proposal of late marriage. Once again the scales began to tip in his disfavour.

Motton's letter had its required effect. Judge Johnstone insisted that Agnes break off her engagement and terminate all communication with Pinson. 'Aunt Agnes', remembered a niece, 'felt the affair very keenly.' A decade later, following her father's death, Agnes Johnstone turned to missionary work with the McAll mission, a Protestant group in Paris set up to further the education of the French worker. She died in 1917, having never married.

'She dogged him night and day', Motton recalled of Adèle's pursuit of Pinson around Halifax. Another source, this time anonymous, described her keeping a regular watch on the garrison, waiting for Pinson to leave. She then followed him like a shadow, without saying a word. When he reached his destination, she turned on her heel, still silent, and retraced her steps.

The archival material relating to Adèle at Dalhousie, and further down the road in Nova Scotia's public archives, shows the development of an oral tradition across three or four generations. The fragmentary information of contemporary documents is augmented by the first-hand testimony of witnesses, 20 or so years after the incidents they describe. Several more decades on, and the discrepancies have been ironed out, holes have been filled in, details added. 'The Tragedy', not just of Victor Hugo's daughter, but now of his '*Favourite* Daughter', is presented as a true story more enthralling than fiction, and becomes the stuff of popular newspaper romance.

One tantalizing illustration of how stories develop as they are handed down lies in the notion that Adèle went out at night dressed in men's clothes. It's there initially in Robert Motton's 1885 interview as an example of her eccentricity: she wore 'a high hat, top boots, black clothes' and carried a cane. No one who repeated this in the years afterwards suggested that there might be anything peculiarly French about her get-up, that it might have owed something to George Sand, who customarily wore male clothing in public, partly for comfort, partly out of feminist protest. By the mid-1920s, when Adèle's male attire is mentioned in Halifax's *Acadian Recorder*, it's as a disguise that allows her to spy on Pinson and Agnes Johnstone in their 'lovemaking' among the trees of a local park. The tale is unusual enough to fit the truth-stranger-than-fiction mould – except that the instant I unfolded the cutting

I noticed that some anonymous individual with decided opinions had scrawled the words 'DEAD WRONG' in bold, black-ink capitals right across its main column.

Passion is hard on the legs, Balzac writes somewhere (for once in an ambulatory rather than an amatory sense). As I plotted Adèle's movements across Halifax on a small map, pinpointing the half-dozen houses, all the way from the south to the north end of the city, where she'd lived during her three years there, I realized what distances she must have covered on foot. Sometimes, it's true, she rented rooms in properties that either directly abutted, or were a few blocks away from, Pinson's quarters at the Wellington Barracks, or at the Citadel itself, to which he moved with his regiment in the spring of 1865. But even so, she must have spent considerable amounts of time standing about, observing the daily rhythms of garrison life while waiting for him to appear, shivering in the freezing winters or holding her umbrella high to shield herself from the summer sun. Pinson's regular routine would have been quickly written on her mind. Reveille at 5.30 (6.30 in winter), followed by the ten o'clock parade with troops in full marching order. The last parade of the day was held at two, after which officers and men headed into Halifax. At 9.30 in the evening – an hour earlier in the winter months – a gun was fired, signalling to all ranks that they must return to barracks.

I was leaving my hotel immediately after breakfast every morning to follow Adèle's trail, returning in the evening with tired feet after a day's solid trek across the city. The first hours of my working day were often enveloped in the thick grey curtain of mist that rose from the harbour, adding a sense of the unknowable to everything. By lunchtime the afternoon sun had fought its way through the haze, exposing the bright blue water of the harbour and evidence of life on Dartmouth, on the opposite side of the peninsula, which suddenly materialized like Halifax's mirror image.

One morning I passed the Lenoir Building in Hollis Street, among the city's oldest commercial buildings, which retained the Georgian shopfront that Adèle would have been familiar with on visits to her lawyer. I tried hard to imagine her coming and going through the door, but had trouble banishing twenty-first-century traffic and street noise, and was left only with a vaguely disappointed feeling of her absence haunting the place.

Rounding the corner into Sackville and then Brunswick Street, two streets in which, in houses long since demolished, Adèle had lived during her time in Halifax, I began the ascent to the Citadel: up the steps, past the town clock and across the palisaded green and a bridge over a dry ditch to the main entrance, where a sentry stood to attention. On the main parade square, lines of young men were sloping and presenting arms in their daily re-enactment of nineteenth-century drill. Dressed in authentic uniforms as soldiers of the 78th Highlanders, one of the infantry regiments that had manned the Halifax garrison at the end of the 1860s, they marched in strict formations while a small, eager crowd of cagoule-wearing tourists snapped photos of them. Remnants of the mist, eerily whiter now, swirling in our faces and at our feet, and floating across the scene in front of us, seemed momentarily to give the impression of two epochs, superimposed and coexistent.

Halifax was a popular posting for British army regiments. Despite the harsh winters, its climate was positively congenial compared with conditions in military stations in the tropics. Also, unlike Malta or Gibraltar, Halifax had much to offer the young officer in the form of social diversions to break the boredom of garrison existence. There were regimental dances, amateur theatricals, invitations to dine at the homes of the wealthy, skating parties and horse-drawn sleighing in the winter, picnics in the summer. 'Altogether, it was an Elysium of bliss for young officers,' recalled Lieutenant-Colonel Wolseley, Assistant Quartermaster-General in Canada during Albert Pinson's time; 'the only trouble', he continued pointedly, 'being to keep single.' However, overcrowding as a result of the number of troops dispatched to Canada during the *Trent* crisis meant that decent accommodation was at a premium. For several weeks after his arrival in Halifax, Pinson, like other officers of the 16th, had been forced to make do with a berth on board the

Pyramus, an old frigate moored in the harbour. He spent his final year at the Citadel, in one of its draughty stone casemates. Before that he had lived in more comfortable quarters at the Wellington Barracks in the far north end of the city.

I located Wellington Barracks, which now forms part of Canadian Forces Base, Canada's east coast naval centre. Walking across the old parade square, I took in the view of the red-brick neoclassical building, completed in 1860 and reflecting the mid-Victorian concern for healthier and more commodious living conditions for British troops. Bordering the base to the west is North Street, where Adèle first lodged with the Saunders family. Here it must have been easy to keep Pinson within her sights. A brief stroll into Gottingen Street would have brought her to Wellington Gate, where she'd have been able to keep an eye on his comings and goings.

Where was the Saunders' North Street house, though? An old photograph of it shows a tiny saltbox cottage, two storeys at the front and one at the back. The house was evidently a tough little structure. It had survived the 1917 explosion – unlike the Barracks, which was

badly damaged in the blast – as well as the arduous process of being
moved to a new site, not far away in Barrington Street, during the
construction of the Macdonald suspension bridge across the harbour
in the early 1950s. Staff at the archives said that it was nicknamed
'the Hugo House', and that one of its owners, in the course of
renovating it, had found a shoe and some expensive little buttons
that she'd fancied had belonged to Adèle. Yet despite being assured of
the cottage's survival I couldn't identify it as I made my way along the
perilous pedestrian route, with cars shooting by on the busy highway
and the bridge's giant steel girders dominating the skyline.

Frustrating as this was, I had hopes of better luck locating 46
Cornwallis Street. Adèle had moved there late in 1864 to be the
lodger of her lawyer's parents, Robert and Ellen Motton, after
the Saunders' house in Sackville Street caught fire. The blaze was
quickly overcome, leaving the house unharmed, but Adèle had
been intent on moving, apparently unnerved by the threat to her
vast hoard of papers, which she imagined consumed by fire. The
house in Cornwallis Street, in familiar clapboard style, adjoined
the African Baptist Chapel, founded in 1832 by the Revd Richard
Preston. Preston was the driving force behind Nova Scotia's black
community and President of the Abolitionist movement. A former
slave, he came to Canada in 1816, founding a network of black
Baptist chapels throughout Nova Scotia before his death in 1861.
The Cornwallis Street chapel was the mother church, a proud
symbol of what Halifax's black population, many of them freed
slaves, could achieve when allowed to build up and administer
their own institutions.

So Adèle Hugo must have often heard hymns echoing through
the walls, I thought as I ambled along Cornwallis Street towards
the chapel, led by the sound of loud ensemble singing. It was
'tune-up Tuesday', I later discovered, and the congregation were
proclaiming Christ by raising their voices in unison. Recently the
chapel has been renamed the New Horizons Baptist Chapel, while
efforts to rid the street itself of its association with Lord Edward
Cornwallis, the eighteenth-century founder of Halifax, are also
afoot. Cornwallis, who sailed into the harbour in 1749 with a

few thousand Protestant settlers, earned himself a reputation for brutality after he issued a bounty for the scalps of the men, women and children of the indigenous people, the Mi'kmaq First Nation people. The move for a new street name hasn't been popular with residents. Admittedly, there are those who only oppose it because they're worried about the prospect of the confusion caused by a change of address. But there are weightier arguments against it too, that you can't erase history simply by removing a street sign.

Adèle Hugo's association with Cornwallis Street, it turned out, had already been erased from history. The house she'd lived in had still been standing in the mid-1960s when Frances Guille, editor of the journals, saw it on her trip to Halifax. However, all I found on reaching the spot next door to the chapel was a patch of bare grass. Pastor Dr Rhonda Y. Britton had just finished the service, and I approached her to ask what had become of the building. Her eyes lit up behind the floral print frames of her glasses. Instantly she motioned me to follow her as she bounded up the stairs to her first-floor office. From her desk she produced a service sheet. On the front was a photograph of the chapel, and of the house, taken decades before its demolition half a century ago.

This was at least something, and I thanked Dr Britton warmly. But I felt a kind of mournfulness all the same at how my desire to experience the physical dimensions of the story – to insert myself in some indefinable way at the physical heart of it – was being thwarted. Still, one more property inhabited by Adèle was said to survive. Hugo family letters record her move out of the centre of town, some time in the latter half of 1865, to the home of James Kerr, a customs agent, his wife and their three children. Her new address was 38 Pleasant Street, though that name isn't on any modern map. It was long ago swallowed up by Barrington Street, the busy thoroughfare that weaves its long and winding way for almost 4 miles along the entire length of the Halifax peninsula.

Pleasant Street, at the far south end, perfectly described itself. It was a pretty and romantic spot, a fashionable promenade bordered by tall willow trees leading to the Kissing Bridge, where couples discreetly courted. According to a tradition passed down through the Kerr family, Adèle occupied a front room of the house, and spent hours each day watching the street from the window to see who was walking to and from the bridge. Today the freshwater brook, the marshes and the urban shoreline that once ran alongside Pleasant Street down to the harbour have vanished, submerged under the concrete of the industrial port during the development

of Halifax's waterfront after the First World War. Vestiges of the
shore are still there, in tiny fragments hidden by the container
piers, and when the wind blows in a certain direction you may just
catch a whiff of salt breeze above the traffic fumes. But if you stand
where Pleasant Street once was, all that's apparent is a humdrum
main road and lines of cars thundering past a few nondescript
shops. At 1106 Barrington Street, the Kerr house now finds itself
unceremoniously situated opposite a gigantic superstore.

On my penultimate afternoon in Halifax I visited the house,
yet another of those sheathed in clapboard, painted gunmetal grey.
To its left-hand side, up a flight of rickety wooden steps to the
first floor, was a door with a large glass pane. I looked through it
and saw a man in his thirties lying on cushions in the centre of a
sparsely furnished room. After an initial ringing at the bell failed
to get a response, I peered more closely and realized that he was
wearing headphones and had his eyes closed.

Tapping lightly on the glass, I noticed a young woman, bath
towel wound tightly around her body, wandering through from
an adjacent room. She saw me too and went over to the man and
jabbed him lightly with her foot. Conscious at last, he came to the
door, unlocked it, and faced me with a glazed, unquestioning smile.

Still catching my breath, while somehow managing simultaneously to exhale excitement at finally managing to see one of Adèle
Hugo's Halifax homes before my imminent departure, I asked him
what he knew about the history of the house, rushing on to give
him a quick resumé of her story without giving him a chance to
respond. Meanwhile over his shoulder my eyes ran rapidly over
what little I could see of the interior: the old, sanded floorboards,
the original fireplace.

'Awesome, awesome', he kept murmuring, and I was about to
seize on his enthusiasm and invite myself in when he turned to the
lingering figure of the woman behind him. 'Honey, do we know
anything about this guy's girlfriend who's gone missing?'

The motion of her feet, pursuing Pinson around Halifax. The feverish
writing in her room, dwelling perhaps on the conversations she's

having with him in her head, or on the pictures lodged permanently in her mind of happier times they'd spent together. Nothing, though, no movement of hand or foot, can assuage her anguish; nothing – except for those fleeting encounters, outside the garrison or in the city streets, when the mere sight of him has an almost becalming influence on her. By now she's come to believe that he remains as much in love with her as she with him, despite all the appearances to the contrary. It is a love with no hope and no future, an emotional dead end to which she condemns herself in perpetuity.

Unrequited love. How that adjective clings obsessively – exclusively – to the most universally recognized noun in the language. Unrequited means a love that is unreturned, unrewarded, unreciprocated. But at its root is the Latin word *quietus*, meaning quiet or at rest; an acknowledgement that for a sufferer from unrequited love there'll be no peace, no repose, no deliverance from that inner commotion outside death itself.

The sandy-haired man with the wispy beard fiddled with the tray of children's alphabet blocks that lay on the table before him. He shifted the letters around, creating short words as he did so, or lifted the blocks from their setting, replacing them just as suddenly while he kept up a stream of talk. His actions had the effect of momentarily disconcerting me. Were these small, three-dimensional pieces of wood symbolic of his efforts to try to rebuild my thought processes? Then, slowly taking in the details of my surroundings, the brightly painted finger daubs on the walls, the storybook literature on the tables, I realized that our session was taking place in a room normally set aside for use by the local children's playgroups.

He pushed a letter C absent-mindedly in my direction and, keeping his attention fixed on the table, rehearsed some preliminaries. This was an introductory chat. I was of course under no compulsion to attend the appointments that had been arranged for me by my GP, but he suggested that I might find them helpful. A few details about my domestic situation. What was the book I was writing? In what ways did I feel depressed? Then the killer question, at which he at last raised his head and met my eyes with his own. Why did I think I was behaving in this way?

This meeting with the therapist occurred more than a couple of decades ago. The background to it was that in my mid-thirties I'd fallen in love with a man who didn't return my feelings. That he too was gay and open about his sexuality at least represented an advance on all the desperate, lopsided, obsessional relationships with heterosexual men that had bedevilled my twenties.

But Tom was a different kind of challenge. He was undoubtedly highly sexed. In fact, he talked about sex constantly – which I, with my maiden aunt ways, took some time getting used to – and occasionally, if there was no better, or, to put it more accurately, if there was no casually anonymous option available on a desultory Saturday night, was prepared to go through the motions of having sex with me. However, despite spending so much of our time together, despite our growing mutual dependence, he was not, as he informed me at several climactic moments in our relationship, in love with me.

No matter, I thought, paraphrasing a version of the novelist Stendhal's famous remark in my head: don't worry about not loving me, I can love enough for both of us. I lent (or gave) him money, took him on expensive holidays I could ill afford. I did his washing and ironing, cooked for him, created a cosy domestic atmosphere around the fireside for him: all in the ultimately vain hope that the ambivalence in his behaviour might develop in a more romantic direction. Of course it never did.

Eventually I lapsed into depression and cast myself into self-inflicted silence. A major component of my condition was my withdrawal into myself, accompanied by an unwillingness to speak or engage in any kind of dialogue. At a dinner party one evening I sat tight-lipped, daring my nearest neighbours to fail in their attempts to draw me out in conversation. By chance, on one side seated next to me was a kindly doctor, who succeeded in doing precisely that. He advised me to ask my own doctor for a prescription for the antidepressant Prozac, at the time still in its heyday as the wonder drug of choice. If it didn't make me feel better within a few weeks I should have no difficulty weaning myself off it. In fact, the drug quickly improved my mood, to the point where my semi-mute condition was transformed into a state of extreme garrulousness.

The sessions with a cognitive behavioural therapist were part of my treatment. While the Prozac was proving beneficial in lifting my spirits, it had no noticeable impact on aspects of my behaviour labelled as elements of an obsessive-compulsive disorder. I did indeed feel compelled to phone Tom throughout the day, bothering him at work and at home. True, this was an era in which the use of email was still not widespread, where texting was as yet non-existent, and when speaking on the telephone remained a primary mode of communication. However, my phone calls to Tom, though generally received patiently enough, went beyond the bounds of what seemed acceptable, certainly what was normal. I was aware of this even as I dialled his number in my desperate attempts to hear his voice. Only that familiar sound, mellow with just a trace of a Yorkshire burr, would bring me respite, a period, all too brief, of calm and, bizarrely, some comfort. When I knew him to be unreachable I would resort to ringing him anyway, in order to listen to his answerphone message and receive that source of soothing balm, like a laying-on of hands at one remove.

Naturally, the therapist assured me, he'd come across many much more serious instances of harassment. Cases in which the stalker's pursuit of their prey – I felt my face instantly redden at his choice of terminology, as I'd naively failed to equate telephone calls with something as intimidatory as 'stalking' – resulted in phone lines to a busy office being blocked, or where the victim's home was rung as many as a hundred times a night with abusive and threatening messages, making it necessary for the phone service to screen all incoming calls.

Nevertheless, he considered that my behaviour demonstrated a tendency to allow what he called damaging and intrusive thoughts to enter my mind. I must be on my guard against these, learn to challenge them, recognize their power to distort, and distance myself from them. Whenever I had the urge to pick up the receiver, I was to do my very best to resist it. If I was currently making, say, six or seven calls daily to this man, I should aim gradually to reduce this number, week on week.

'I'd like you to imagine yourself in a car,' the therapist continued, in what was evidently a well-honed metaphor. 'You're driving along a road full of heavy traffic. You are witness to both timid and aggressive motoring on the part of your fellow drivers. The car in front of you is proceeding at a frustratingly slow pace, the vehicle behind is irritatingly close on your tail. You could choose to leave the line of traffic and park your car, except that there will always be other cars to deal with. Your goal should be to acknowledge the ongoing traffic – the intrusive thoughts and urges of this little scenario – walk along the side of the road, and engage with life.'

His metaphor appeared to be getting a little confused and caught up in his own mental traffic. Nor could I resist the feeble riposte that I had never learned to drive. It was becoming clear to both of us that I wasn't taking the treatment with the seriousness he obviously felt it deserved. For my part, what he was suggesting appeared to amount to nothing more than an exercise of self-control, rather than a more effective approach to cutting off the feelings that were at the root of the problem.

And perhaps I was unwilling to entrust to a comparative stranger embarrassing secrets of the irrational conduct that I sometimes wrote about in my diary:

> Obsessively tried every public phone in the high street, finding him engaged every time: must have telephoned 8 or 9 times until I finally got hold of him. Why must I behave like this? At times like these I feel governed by some indefinable force, pushing me on to act in this absurd and tormented manner.

Had I ever acted on an impulse to pursue or stalk this man, the therapist asked me on my next visit? That is, to *shadow* him, he added, using a softer, less emotive term, while enunciating the word with a shushing sound as if he were draping a veil of discretion over it. Anti-stalking legislation had only recently entered the statute book in Britain and other parts of the world, and stalking incidents were rarely out of the news. In one story, a man had flown 10,000 miles to stalk his former lover on an Australian beach. In another, a woman had written hundreds of unsolicited letters to a man she'd worked for, all following the same general theme: 'I love you and know you love me.' If Adèle Hugo had been alive at the end of the twentieth century she might have been spared a prison sentence, but she would undoubtedly have undergone outpatient psychiatric treatment for her behaviour. Given the treatment's poor success rate, however, it's likely that the stalking would have continued.

Forty per cent of stalkers, I discovered subsequently, have, like Adèle, some former sexual or emotional involvement with the object of their obsession. In only about a quarter of recorded incidences are stalker and victim complete strangers. To these statistics may be added a darker and more terrifying one from cases of harassment where the stalker is clearly acting under the power of a serious delusion: out of all reported stalker-related assaults, a quarter end in murder.

Had I ever stalked anyone, I asked myself? Had I ever felt what the American forensic scientist Isaac Ray described in 1832 as the 'almost unbridled excitement' emanating from a 'military-styled pursuit of the object . . . of desire'? For one alarming moment I recollected an episode, not of my own pursuit of an object of desire, but of my father's. Several years before my birth my parents had separated, after my mother discovered that my father was having an affair. She moved from their home on the south coast of England to a flat in London. My father managed to inveigle her new address from the removal men packing up her possessions and followed her to the London flat, where he refused to leave until she allowed him in. My mother maintained, decades on, that this was the last thing she'd wanted but, suffering from flu, she had been too ill to put up much resistance. You may wonder at her passivity. These days my father's actions would certainly have been classified as an offence under the 1997 Protection from Harassment Act.

As indeed might my own. I may not have literally stalked the love-prey, but like many love-struck individuals I've loitered in places where I had hopes of encountering the loved one. Sometimes I've given in to the temptation to walk by his house or flat, or to wander nearby on hot dusty afternoons or chilly wintry evenings, half hoping to see him, half fearing the embarrassment of the outcome if he were to come walking down the street and see me. There is a sly pleasure in these wanderings, even in the midst of a presiding mood of pensive sadness. As Victor Hugo says, such a condition is the very definition of melancholy: a twilight state in which suffering transmutes into a sombre joy.

Probably anyone undergoing the emotional freefall associated with the early stages of an intense love affair can identify with this compulsion. But whereas a conviction of being loved by the person one is in love with can introduce a flow of miraculous energy to the body and a definite spring to the step, ultimately the realization that love is unreciprocated often feels closer to the grip of paralysis, as if one were literally dragging heavy chains along the street.

In October 1865, Charles Hugo was married in Brussels at the age of 39. To all extents and purposes it was an arranged marriage. His bride was an 18-year-old orphan, Alice Lehaene, raised by her godmother, the wife of Jules Simon, a future leader of France's Third Republic. To Victor Hugo, Alice, with her prettiness and dark chestnut hair, had a look of Léopoldine. Before the ceremony, Madame Hugo wrote to Alice's family about 'the exceptional perils and the exceptional glory' of the Hugo name. But the perils being faced by Charles's younger sister on the other side of the world stayed hidden. Charles revealed little about Adèle to his new wife beyond telling her that his sister had married an English army officer against her family's wishes, and that consequently relations were strained and communication rare.

The immediate scandal threatened by Adèle's flight had been averted, but secrecy was still the watchword. According to her father, Adèle must continue to exist in the shadows. In the long term he saw this as the anchor of her salvation. At Hauteville House Hugo had finally been abandoned by his entire family. He maintained that he'd had to choose between the happiness represented by his family and his duty as a writer. He had chosen duty and remained in Guernsey, the only place he considered he could work well as a writer. Madame Hugo left the island in January 1865 and didn't return for two years. With her went François-Victor, grieving for Emily de Putron, the young woman he'd loved who had succumbed to tuberculosis. Living at Hauteville House was now impossible for him. 'Without you', François-Victor told his mother, 'our home is a tomb.'

Hugo spent his evenings at Juliette Drouet's home, where a small circle of intimates gathered regularly to dine with him. Surveying his own magnificent creation further up the street, he was sometimes assailed with sadness. The house, devoid of his wife and children, seemed so desolate. 'My heart fills with shadow when I step into your empty rooms,' he wrote plaintively to Madame Hugo on his return from Charles's wedding in Brussels.

He confessed too to 'very sad moments' whenever he thought of Halifax. Adèle continued to appear constantly to him in dreams, and he believed he heard her voice. During one nightmare Adèle revealed herself to be pregnant, an expression of Hugo's underlying fear that his daughter might yet do something to disgrace the family name.

She often floated into his conscious thoughts as well. In a pen-and-ink sketch for his new novel, *Les Travailleurs de la Mer* (*The Toilers of the Sea*), the first of his books for which he provided the illustrations, Hugo drew on the inspiration of that photo of long ago, of Adèle with her parasol in the garden at Marine Terrace, to portray his heroine Déruchette. The novel, set in Guernsey, centres on the fisherman Gilliatt's efforts to win Déruchette's hand, and his epic battle with the ocean to salvage a grounded steamship, culminating in a hand-to-tentacle struggle with 'the devil fish', a monster octopus. With *Les Travailleurs de la Mer*, Hugo produced another bestseller. Published in March 1866, the book also ignited an octopus mania. Scientists questioned whether the real creature was as dangerous as Hugo's fictional one; milliners launched an 'octopus' hat for fashionable Parisiennes; and a live octopus was exhibited in the Champs-Élysées. Everything in Paris, reported Madame Hugo, was '*octopusized*'.

News from Adèle, conveyed by François-Victor, still her main correspondent, occasionally appeared to hold out hope for the future. She wrote with great sympathy to her brother about the death of Emily de Putron, and was full of concern for the health of her 'honoured and blessed mother', writing to her in large capitals so that Madame Hugo, with her diminishing eyesight, could read her letters. The hour was approaching, Hugo had predicted in the spring of 1865, when they'd all be astonished by the thawing of Adèle's tenderness towards them.

He was being far too optimistic. Most of the time the prospect of any change in her condition, of Adèle freeing herself from the grip of her illusions and of returning home, seemed as far off as ever. She still believed that she was gradually wearing down Pinson's resistance to marriage (it was decreasing 'noticeably', she informed her brother at the end of 1865). Each spring, from 1864 to 1866, she assured her family that she would be home by the autumn equinox, but autumn came and went each year without any sign of her. Despite her worsening health, Madame Hugo was periodically intent on travelling to Halifax to fetch Adèle home. Other members of the family 'deplored' the idea. 'I insist that you do not go there,' Hugo wrote to his wife. 'Once she had you she would not let you go.' As Adèle's mother, he instructed, she should continue with her 'sweet and adorable solicitude' – but at a distance. When the plan resurfaced François-Victor stepped in to make the valid point to his mother that 'no earthly power' would persuade Adèle to return to Europe while Pinson remained in North America. Her trip would serve no purpose. 'And what a journey. To the New World!'

'What can one do?' the despairing father asked. 'She alone can save herself and she does not want to.' Hugo continued to send Adèle her monthly allowance. She complained that 150 francs was insufficient for her needs, but there were occasional supplements for 'purchases of season', though Hugo feared that this money might be put to bad uses (presumably that Adèle would give it to Pinson). Adèle was anxious again to proceed with the publication of her music. François-Victor considered this a healthy development, believing that it showed his sister was suffering from less of a 'disorder of the mind'. Nevertheless, Hugo was adamant in his opposition. 'We need a mute for her music. She mustn't draw attention to herself right now.'

Early in 1866, someone from the outside world did manage to penetrate the family secret. A Monsieur Penchenat wrote from Halifax to François-Victor about 'the disturbing state of Mlle Hugo'. François-Victor had some recollection of having met a man of this name in Guernsey several years earlier, but what Penchenat was doing in Canada and how he had made Adèle's acquaintance was a mystery. He didn't appear to know anything about why she was in Halifax, but swore that 'God himself would not tear from his heart' the secret of what he had seen with his own eyes. Adèle was refusing nourishment and other basic needs; her hair was in such a tangled, infested state that a doctor had to be called, who ordered it to be cut; and she was showing troubling signs of losing contact with reality, moving constantly about her room, talking out loud to herself. Keeping the news from Madame Hugo, Hugo and his sons decided to put their trust in the mysterious stranger. Did Penchenat think that Adèle would return home voluntarily? Did he think that she could somehow be persuaded to board ship?

Nothing came of this. Instead Adèle was making plans of her own. As François-Victor had surmised, her departure from Halifax was dependent on Pinson's own, and for some time there had been rumours that the 16th Regiment was about to be relocated to the West Indies. In June Adèle declared to her family that she was preparing to return to Europe in July, and requested the sum of 650 francs for a ticket that would enable her to travel on the date she chose. Hugo anxiously complied, writing that if she was sincere, he was delighted. But could Adèle be taken at her word?

Each week in early June, a woman in black was to be seen seated in a carriage down by the Cunard Wharf, watching as the Cunard ships weighed anchor and set sail across the Atlantic. Adèle had assumed that Pinson would return to England on leave before his new tour of duty. In fact, at some point in June he left the Halifax garrison along with his regiment. Their destination was Barbados.

To follow Pinson to the Caribbean meant an even more protracted journey than her outgoing one. There was no direct service to Bridgetown, Barbados's capital. Adèle would have to sail to Liverpool via New York, and from there to Barbados. But such was her determination that she would not be long behind him.

7

Fantasy

He had been no more than a boy at the time, but 20 years later, in the wake of Victor Hugo's death, he wrote down his recollections, signing himself anonymously as 'P'. A mysterious woman had come to the island. She was tall and beautiful, black-haired, and possessing black eyes that frightened him. They were full of melancholy but, with the slightest flicker of the woman's eyelids, a savage fire seemed to inflame them. No one knew her origins. Early in the morning and at the end of the day, after darkness fell, she walked the streets unaccompanied. Sometimes she faced the gibes of the town's children. On one occasion, feeling moved to protect her, the boy intervened, earning himself a gentle look and a nod of the head. He had never forgotten this, nor the sadness that overcame him at her plight. The woman's mystery seemed inviolable, and her clothes only added to her enigma. They were not made from light fabrics suitable for the tropics, but consisted of heavy velours, silks, even furs.

All of this, 'P' wrote, testified to a home faraway in the north, a lost home – as well as to a spirit drowned in some strange fantasy.

The sun, high and hot, appeared not to move. Never having been someone who could lie on a beach contentedly soaking up the heat, I was surprised at how calm I felt. I found myself enjoying the sensation of the pure white sand sifting between the toes of the foot I carelessly dangled over the end of the lounger, as I registered with minimal effort the contrast in colour of the ultramarine water against the cobalt sky. The heat was intense, but tempered by the balmy breezes of the steady trade winds, blowing thousands of miles across the subtropical latitudes of the Atlantic Ocean. The only rain was the brief squally shower that generally arrived with perfect timing an hour or so before breakfast. Plunging into the sea on my first day I found myself swimming alongside a sea turtle, a hawksbill with its heart-shaped shell, making its way using small, flipper-size movements, apparently unperturbed by the splash of my breaststroke.

My agitation ebbed away, my sense of time drifted. I thought of the message on a poster at the airport. 'Relax. You're in Barbados.' Nevertheless, after a while I found myself reflecting on the darker aspects of centuries of the island's history before its independence from Britain in 1966. To do so feels almost inescapable. The paradisial surroundings, the bland luxury of the villas of the rich and famous on this sheltered western coast, are such a far cry from the human toil and strife that transformed Barbados's landscape and laid the foundations of its prosperity.

Around the corner in Holetown, where I was staying, about 8 miles from the capital Bridgetown, is a monument to the first English settlement. Eighty men in two ships landed at a site near this spot in 1627, and began the process of making Barbados the richest place in England's New World Empire. English planters replaced the tropical wilderness with fields of sugar cane. Windmills, boiling rooms and furnaces dotted the countryside. The cultivation of sugar, exported throughout the globe for record profits, rapidly became a phenomenon. The wretched underside of this story, of course, is that the success of the Sugar Revolution depended on the atrocities of the slave trade. By the time Britain's involvement in the transatlantic slave trade ended, with its abolition in 1807, close to 400,000 black Africans, men, women and children, had been shipped in barbaric conditions to Barbados and forced to work on the plantations of their white masters. Uprooted from their families and denied basic rights, these slaves endured a miserable existence, living and dying in the sugar fields.

SUGAR PLANTATION BARBADOS, CARTING SUGAR CANES TO THE MILL

Emancipation, following the abolition of slavery in Britain's colonies in 1833, did not necessarily bring much improvement to the lives of former slaves. Nominally they were free, but in many respects the social hierarchy of Barbados remained the same, and the white minority elite class continued to exert a tight control over the majority black population. Throughout the rest of the nineteenth century, and into the twentieth, black workers were kept as low-paid, landless tenants on the plantations. Access to education, poor relief, even clean water, was often made difficult for them.

I'd brought with me a copy of Anthony Trollope's *The West Indies and the Spanish Main* to see what light it shed on life in Barbados during Adèle Hugo's time there. Trollope arrived in Bridgetown at the end of the 1850s, some seven years before Adèle. He was on Post Office business, a one-man mission to reform the 'decrepit' postal system of the West Indies, and as he sailed around the Caribbean he jotted down his impressions of people and places as an experiment in travel writing. He rather damned Barbados, 'little England as it delights to call itself', with faint praise, referring to it as 'a very respectable little island'. The absence of scenic beauty – no mountains, forests or waterfalls – meant that every inch of it could be planted with sugar cane. Unfortunately this didn't contribute to making the island interesting, just to ensuring a plentiful supply of sugar. The whiteness of the roads, he complained, was enough to hurt the eyes of a stranger. Bridgetown did have some good shops, though they were hot, fusty places, and the purchase of a pair of gloves sent one immediately dashing into the nearest icehouse. The heat was the only peculiarity of the capital. Otherwise it reminded Trollope of 'a second- or third-rate English town'. Its narrow, crooked streets all converged at Trafalgar Square, which, like its London namesake, contained a statue of Nelson. As for Bridgetown's hotels and boarding houses, Trollope judged them generally good, his only objection being that a loud, grey parrot across the way from where he stayed never ceased screaming day or night.

Trollope observed the strict degree of segregation between whites and blacks, with a rigid adherence to the unspoken rule that they shouldn't mix in the same society. His most caustic remarks were reserved for the white ruling class, or the 'Bims' as he called them. These large, clumsy men, rough-spoken and lacking in social graces, were intensely patriotic, self-satisfied and intoxicated by their own prosperity. For a moment, as I sat on the stretch of beach by my hotel, a group of pot-bellied, lobster-coloured Englishmen, toasting themselves with Bajan rum, seemed to me to be cut from similar cloth.

My first days in Barbados wore away almost imperceptibly while I acclimatized myself to the surroundings. From my lounger I grew used to watching the pre-lunchtime ritual of a straggling line of beach vendors making their way along the waterside, selling their wares and rarely taking polite rejection for the final answer. Zelda, in her seventies, struggling with a bad hip, rummaged in her bag and brought out tea towels, nail clippers and jewellery. Greg, several gold teeth glittering as he spoke, offered a bracelet of tiny conch shells. Joseph, approaching stealthily from behind as I gazed out to sea, asked, 'Do you want de powder or de green?' (I didn't want either). For 20 Barbadian dollars, approximately £6, Lucy braided tiny, coloured beads in the sparse strands of hair of a sheepish-looking man sitting drinking milk through a straw from a coconut. 'I's a very clever lady,' she declared with a hoot of laughter, explaining that her services extended to fishing lessons, massage and – she laughed again – much more. I thought of asking her what she knew of obeah, the system of belief of African origin practised in the Caribbean, involving sorcery and spiritual practices, but stopped myself, fearing I'd give offence. I'd remembered Antoinette Cosway, the first Mrs Rochester in Jean Rhys's novel *Wide Sargasso Sea*, who obtains a magical potion on her honeymoon in Dominica to reignite her husband's love for her. I wondered whether Adèle, having considered using the powers of a hypnotist on Pinson in Halifax, might have resorted to such methods if the opportunity had arisen.

One morning I returned from a swim to my usual place on the beach in the shade of a cabbage palm and encountered a young man in his early thirties. He too had been swimming, and droplets of water sparkled on his golden-brown skin. He gave the impression that he'd been expecting me. His smile as he came forward to greet me was dazzling in its brightness. Relaxed and carefree, and without saying a word, he handed me a small sprig of a flower, deep purple in colour, picked from one of the cascading bougainvillea bushes that bloom throughout the island.

Adèle reached Barbados in the early autumn of 1866. For some weeks her family seemed to lose track of her. However, by the end of the year François-Victor had resumed contact with his sister and was able to reassure Madame Hugo that 'communications between Europe and Barbados are well established'. He described Adèle as waiting impatiently for her clothes trunk being shipped from Southampton. Her health, affected by the 'icy skies' of Halifax, was completely restored by the tropical climate. She didn't mention returning home, and instead painted a seductive picture of a transatlantic voyage, hoping that her mother might be persuaded to visit her in Barbados the following summer.

The family's remarks about Adèle's absence displayed a new attitude of calm resignation, as references to her in the Hugos' correspondence began to dwindle. There is no information in letters about her living arrangements – she was said much later in one newspaper account to have been lodging at a Mrs Chadderton's – and no indication of whether she was visited by Pinson or even saw him. Her allowance was no longer sent to her monthly, but quarterly instead. Without a local on the spot, like Mrs Saunders in Halifax, reporting back on Adèle's situation, she was becoming a distant, half-forgotten figure, gradually receding beneath the horizon.

Not to her mother, though. Adèle preyed heavily on Madame Hugo's mind. In June 1868, as the second anniversary of Adèle's arrival in Barbados approached, an increasingly ailing Madame Hugo was anxious to discover from Charles whether his father had remembered to send Adèle 300 francs as a supplement to pay for her summer toilette. If he hadn't, Charles was to please see that he did so. In fact, he should do more than this: he must *insist*.

But the source of that sweet and adorable maternal solicitude, as Victor Hugo had called it, was soon to be extinguished. 'My only wish now is to die in your arms,' Madame Hugo wrote to her husband shortly before he left Guernsey for their annual summer reunion in Brussels. On 24 August they went out for a carriage drive. The next afternoon Madame Hugo suffered a heart attack. She died early the following morning. As the coffin lid was placed in position, Hugo took a small key from his pocket and scratched his initials on the lead, just above his wife's face. She would lie at Villequier, 'next to our sweet dead daughter'. He made no mention of his unhappy living one.

According to François-Victor, Adèle felt overwhelmed by the news of her mother's death, though she was managing to keep her emotions under control. 'Our poor stray', Victor Hugo wrote in a letter to his son in October. It was five years since he'd suffered a broken heart because of her. 'Nevertheless, when she returns my heart will expand and my arms open.'

Adèle's latest letter, François-Victor told his father, reciprocating the sentiment, was 'full of tenderness for you'. Extraordinarily, though, there continued to be no direct communication between father and daughter. Nor, with Madame Hugo gone, was there any further talk of a member of the family going to Barbados to bring Adèle home.

The image of opening his arms to his estranged daughter was one that Victor Hugo used more than once in letters and private notes. He blessed her in his prayers. She continued to haunt his dreams. He ensured her material welfare. Madame Hugo's estate, divided equally between her three surviving children, produced an annuity for Adèle of 3,750 francs, sent out to her in addition to her regular allowance. However, to do more than this and actively contemplate a way for his daughter out of her tragic plight was by now too difficult and too painful for him. His thoughts had turned away from her.

'Early in the eighteen seventies your father owned the house in Westbury Road, Westbury Cottage, now called the Orphanage.' Sounding not unlike the opening of a short story, setting the scene in a businesslike manner before a rush of dramatic revelations, this sentence comes from the memoirs of a woman called Amelia Fielding Culpeper. Born in about 1820, Mrs Culpeper was the wife of an attorney-planter, Alleyne Culpeper, from one of Barbados's oldest families. Towards the end of the 1880s Mrs Culpeper started to record memories of the family's life on the island at the request of one of her daughters. Twenty years ago, a Culpeper descendant, Patricia Hoad, published an extract from these in an academic journal. It was anything but dry as dust. For here was a first-hand account from Barbados of an encounter with the woman whom Amelia Culpeper came to know as Madame Pinson. Edged with poignancy, it reveals the state of degradation she was living in, and gives a sad indication of how desperate Adèle Hugo's situation had become.

The circumstances behind the meeting were that the Culpepers' property, Westbury Cottage, half a mile outside Bridgetown, had been let for several years to a man – known as 'Mr. M'C' – who was irregular in paying his rent. Finally this man was given notice to quit. The keys to the cottage were to be returned by a certain day. The day came and went with no sign of the keys.

One evening, not long afterwards, Amelia Culpeper was at the family home in Fontabelle, a wealthy suburb north-west of the capital. Her husband was away, but her daughters and mother-in-law were sitting with her in the drawing room. She heard a step at the door and then a light knock.

When I went [to the door] I found a person who could not make herself understood in English and, as you know, I speak no French. She made me understand somehow that she sublet a room in Westbury Cottage (from Mr. M'C') and would like to remain there. She evidently understood what I said to her: the house required repairs and I could not promise that she should stay.

She was a strange-looking person. She seemed to be wearing very dirty clothes, though fine. My saucy children said when she was gone they were glad I had given her a chair to sit on and not invited her onto the couch.

Next evening the same footsteps were heard and the same person returned, accompanied by a young and fine-looking black woman, who spoke English well. She told me the lady's name was Madame Pinson. That she wished to remain where she was, having been evicted after years with a previous landlord's family. I repeated what I had said the evening before, refusing to make any promises, and they left, Grannie congratulating me on my handling of both interviews.

On his return Mr Culpeper was adamant that Westbury Cottage must be renovated, and that 'Mr. M'C' should evict his tenant before he vacated the property. 'He had heard in Bridgetown that the poor creature was considered not sane and, in addition, that her habits were so dirty, *no one* could take her as a lodger.' Later, island rumour would give Amelia Culpeper a little more information about the identity and background of Madame Pinson. She was believed to be the daughter of Victor Hugo, and said to be married to a Captain Pinson. A friend of Mrs Culpeper's, who knew Madame Pinson a little, described her as intelligent and agreeable. 'I was told by someone else that her father had cast her off, her brother sent her money and when she received a remittance, she would buy all sorts of things; I daresay when she was out of funds she sold them cheap.'

When Adèle left the house, the room she'd occupied was indeed found to be indescribably dirty. The floor was scrubbed twice, but finally had to be taken up. Large quantities of salt and water were said to have been used to keep away vermin. 'When the paintwork behind the door was wiped, the most beautiful rose-colour came off on the wet cloth. Possibly it was rouge, but I don't know enough to say.'

Mr Culpeper, passing the cottage following Adèle's departure, saw so much smoke coming from the house that he thought it was on fire. He called at the door but was asked not to go through to the backyard as there was a bonfire taking place of bedding, clothing 'and various things too dirty to be packed up'. Amelia Culpeper heard later that 'reams of paper, scribbled all over' were also thrown on the fire.

Adèle's journal, detailing the years of her father's exile, would largely depend in the long term on accidents of preservation for its survival. Did its sequel – perhaps the manuscript in the exquisite copperplate hand that Adèle had offered the lawyer Robert Motton with the promise that it would make his fortune – meet its end in Barbados, reduced to nothing more than a heap of ashes?

My new acquaintance from the beach introduced himself as Lorenzo. He'd noticed that I was on my own, and wondered if I'd like his company on a tour of the island. He knew Barbados well and would be able to show me any sites I was interested in. He appeared eager to please and, besides, the mesmerizing whiteness of his smile, and the way in which his large, doe-like brown eyes demanded attention, were hard to resist. He kept reaching up with one hand to scoop back his hair into position, a sign of justifiable vanity and possibly, I thought later, of nervousness too. Outlining the purpose of my trip, I said that if he really was willing to spare the time that would be very welcome. I was bored of being on my own and struggling not to surrender to the lassitude that island life engendered. My visit to Barbados's Department of Archives had yielded little of value. When I mentioned to Yvette, the hotel chambermaid, that I planned a bus ride along the coastal road north of Bridgetown to the ominous-sounding area called Black Rock, which contains the archives, she couldn't conceal her mirth. 'Why, are you going to the madhouse then?' she cried, throwing back her head and laughing. It later transpired that the local psychiatric hospital was adjacent to the row of low-slung archive buildings. I made only one discovery there, but it was a poignantly ironic one. During Adèle's time in Barbados, its Royal Dramatic Company had performed a season of historical dramas based on Victor Hugo's *Notre-Dame de Paris* at Marshall Hall, the huge theatre and lecture hall on Hincks Street, now defunct but once the pride of Bridgetown. Again the shadow of the great writer had proved inescapable.

Lorenzo collected me the next morning in a car he'd borrowed from a friend. This first day was taken up with driving to places that were undeniably historic and visually impressive, but had no direct connection with Adèle Hugo. As we drove deep into the heart of the island, wrapped around in its dark green foliage, a sharp, warm light sliced through the fields of swaying sugar cane. These days sugar is no longer the booming sector of the economy it once was. Production long since exceeded demand, and the number of sugar-cane factories is down to two. Yet sugar is so deeply woven into the cultural and social fabric that it's inconceivable that Barbados could ever be without it. Moreover, remove the green grasshopper cane and much of the country would turn into brown, scrubby bush. Our car drew up in front of a mansion of elegant proportions, with a façade of three Dutch gables and tall, ornate brick chimneys. Built in 1658, St Nicholas Abbey, one of the island's oldest plantations, now a heritage attraction, is a reminder of the bittersweet lifeblood of Barbados's history. We stared across the 400 acres of rolling cane fields, and admired the magnificent avenue of mahogany trees that leads up to Cherry Tree Hill with its dramatic view of the rugged coastline hundreds of feet below, and its distant sight of the Atlantic Ocean, stretching far beyond.

Lorenzo was very affable. His talk, in unbroken English, was practically unstoppable as he filled in details about his life. He was from São Paulo, Brazil, and worked in what he called 'the hospitality business'. He loved the Caribbean, and spent as much time there as possible. Antigua was his favourite destination, but he regularly made the 90-minute journey on the high-speed catamaran linking Antigua with Barbados. What made Barbados unforgettable, he said, planting one hand solidly above his heart as if he was making a solemn vow, was the friendliness of its people. His own friendliness was much in evidence, reinforced by darting, tactile hand movements. Weaving in and out in graceful arabesques as he spoke, one of them would suddenly stretch forward to stroke my arm or clasp my own hand. 'It is the Brazilian way,' he affirmed when I looked instinctively uneasy as he began performing a rubbing motion on my back. Sitting together on the grass outside the Abbey distillery, sampling its rum from tiny plastic cups, I felt the weight of his leg against mine.

The route of our return to Holetown took us along poorly signposted roads to Bathsheba on the windward coast. As we walked along the beach, the late-afternoon sky dissolving into a pinkish dusk streaked with yellow, long curling breakers rolled in over the reef. A few days earlier, despite widespread warnings against swimming in this area of riptides and undertows, a woman had attempted to walk into the ocean across the coral reefs and had been swept out to sea and drowned. Makeshift signs from torn sheets, with 'DANGER' painted across them, fluttered from trees, though the ferocious speed of the wind suggested that they would soon share the fate of the unfortunate woman and disappear across the ocean.

I'd staked my claim to visiting the few sites in and around Bridgetown associated with Adèle Hugo, and at lunchtime the following day Lorenzo came to my hotel in a cab. Sheriff, the driver, demanded a steep fare for the afternoon's tour: 600 Barbadian dollars. But I handed over the banknotes hastily without haggling over the price. Something stern and fixed in his expression told me that there wouldn't have been much point anyway. Several times, stopping at lights or while we were stationary in traffic, he picked up the compact revolver beside him and held it admiringly in his hands. At one stop I followed his gaze down a small alley where a gang of five or six men lolled menacingly on a verandah, full of what I imagined to be malevolent intent.

Approaching central Bridgetown, we passed Baxter's Road, a colourful street full of Victorian balconied buildings and buzzing shops and markets, hardly changed since the 1860s. A short distance on, St Michael's Cathedral, rebuilt at the end of the eighteenth century, looked like a little piece of England, just as Trollope had said. However, two blocks further east and Bridgetown's National Heroes Square, originally Trafalgar Square, was fast becoming a symbol of Barbados's overriding desire to sever all links with its British colonial past. Already the statue of Nelson, erected in 1813, three decades before its London counterpart, was being scheduled for removal because of the Lord Admiral's support for the slave trade. The day we saw it the plinth had been daubed in paint with the defiant demand, 'TEK ME DOWN'. Not long afterwards Nelson's statue was dismantled and the Barbados government announced plans to replace Britain's Elizabeth II as the country's head of state.

At last we arrived at our destination, St Ann's Garrison, headquarters of the British forces in the West Indies for 200 years until their departure in 1906, and Albert Pinson's home during his tour of duty on the island. On the left, looking seaward, the original St Ann's Castle, which gave the garrison its name, still stands like a toy fort, 80 feet high, overlooking Carlisle Bay and the south coast approaches. To the right is the Main Guard, with its red-brick clock tower and George III's coat of arms picked out in white above the entrance. In between are a variety of barrack buildings for officers and their men, painted an arresting shade of sienna red, their arcades, pedimented entrances and grand double staircases at the rear examples of the classical style imposed by Victorian engineers throughout the West Indies.

Opposite, a vast expanse of land brought Pinson instantly to mind. The Garrison Savannah, as it's known, was formerly the army parade ground. Regimental bands played in the evenings, and 'the Rank and Fashion of Barbados' watched from their carriages as redcoats and mounted officers galloped to and fro. Officers also exercised their horses there and competed in races against wealthy traders. Pinson, owning a horse that was said 'to do marvels', according to an interview many years later with one of his fellow officers, must have indulged his love of horse racing here. Today the 6-furlong track is home to the Sandy Lane Gold Cup, a sporting event in which thoroughbreds from all over the Caribbean compete for a trophy manufactured in England and flown over to Barbados each year on a British Airways flight. But the Garrison Savannah attracts many other activities as well: kite-flying, jogging, parades, and picnics under the trees by the grandstand. Lorenzo, I noted, had stripped to his waist, in a fit of showing off, and was running around the circumference of the inner track, idly watched by Sheriff, sipping his beer.

Did Adèle walk here, I wondered, in daytime's scorching heat, or in the pitch-black darkness of night, for there was no street lighting in Barbados for much of the nineteenth century, just kerosene lamps along the waterfront? Returning to the car and back onto the highway, we headed in the direction of Westbury Road, hoping to find Westbury Cottage, Adèle's only documented address in Barbados. However, it had disappeared long ago, together with the Culpepers' house at Fontabelle, the latter site swallowed up by the nearby cricket stadium. The road itself is a long and meandering stretch bordered by squat bungalows in jubilant pinks and greens, and rickety shacks, semi-hidden behind a line of corrugated fencing. At one end is Westbury Cemetery, Barbados's largest burial ground, constructed on the site of a former plantation. As we reached the gates, an enormous cow, tethered to a tree and probably responsible for the damaged headstone lying cracked and upended next to it, was busily chewing the grass.

'Oh, my God,' exclaimed Lorenzo. I thought he was reacting to the sight of the cow, but he was studying his phone closely, his fingers moving rapidly over its screen. 'Rihanna lived here.'

I had some inkling of Rihanna as a singer, even of the fact that she'd been brought up in Barbados, but I was irritated by the way that Lorenzo's quest was overshadowing my own, and pretended ignorance.

'She's a global superstar, an icon,' he responded with an exasperated sigh.

Without a word to either of us, Sheriff reversed the car and drove back along Westbury Road. He took a left turn into Rihanna Drive, formerly Westbury New Road, stopping outside the yellow-and-green house where, apparently, Rihanna had lived until she was 16. While Lorenzo paid obeisance at the shrine to his beloved icon, I reflected that at least one of us had found what he was looking for that afternoon.

Lorenzo and I ate dinner at my hotel, overlooking the beach. He was uncharacteristically silent throughout the meal. I watched as torches were lit along the seafront, and experienced a curious sensation of disassociation, as if, for just a moment, I was uncertain of what was real and what was illusory. Recovering myself, I thanked him warmly for the couple of days we'd spent together, said I hoped we'd meet again before I returned to London at the end of the week, and started back to my room.

I had expected another farewell at the foot of the staircase. Instead, Lorenzo followed me up the stairs and, as I unlocked my bedroom door and turned to say goodnight, he was standing close, waiting to accept an invitation to follow me in. Staring for the last time into those innocent-looking brown eyes, I faced him and stubbornly stood my guard. Clutching at my hand once more, he smiled and made his retreat.

After three and a half years, Albert Pinson, now *Captain* Pinson, was going home – or at least back to Ireland with the rest of his battalion. He must have left Barbados with some relief. Although there were plenty of social diversions to break the boredom – including parties and balls given by the 'Bims', the white elite – soldiers had to contend not only with the unbearable heat, but also the risk of mortal disease. The garrison had been built above infested swamps, leading to widespread outbreaks of yellow fever, the mosquito-borne viral disease. For many years Barbados was a death trap for the British army, and the life expectancy of soldiers there was short. While efforts at draining the swamps had proved effective by the mid-nineteenth century, deaths from yellow fever were still not uncommon. During Pinson's time, 14 officers and 19 soldiers from the ranks, together with one of the officers' wives and two children, fell victim to the deadly disease.

Silke Pinson-Roxburgh had kindly sent me another photograph of Pinson, discovered among the family's papers. It showed him in Barbados in his white-jacketed dress uniform. At his side is the sword that was so difficult to keep polished, as the heat made it liable to rust overnight.

The white jackets of the 16th Regiment must have formed a striking contrast to the red ones of the 47th Regiment, which landed at the Careenage in Bridgetown in January 1869 and marched across town to the garrison to relieve the 16th of its command. 'The red jackets and military bands', reported the *Barbados Times*, created 'quite a sensation'. On 23 January Pinson's battalion paraded on the Savannah in heavy marching order, to cheers from the crowds. Two days later they left Barbados.

Back in Britain, Pinson and his battalion were stationed in Dublin, at Richmond Barracks. But Pinson's remaining time in the army was to be short. Within a year he had sold his commission and returned to civilian life. Prompting this move was his impending marriage to Catherine Roxburgh, daughter of the recruiting officer from Newry, County Armagh, whom Pinson had met while he was stationed in the town a decade earlier. Perhaps their courtship extended back to the earlier period, or maybe their relationship only solidified on his return to Ireland. Either way, Pinson's decision to leave the army and marry enabled him to realize funds from the sale of his sole asset, his commission (he sold it in good time, as in two years the entire purchase system would be swept away under the Cardwell Reforms of the British army).

The week after my return from Barbados, I took the 20-minute walk – or climb, as it's on a steady incline – from my home in north London up to Hampstead Village. Passing along Church Row and its handsome Georgian terraces, I reached Hampstead parish church. St John's is surrounded by one of London's starrier churchyards. Buried here among other distinguished names are the painter Constable, the discoverer of longitude John Harrison, and members of the families of Jane Austen and Gerard Manley Hopkins. This is where Albert Pinson and Catherine Roxburgh came to be married. On 1 March 1870 they said their vows and walked back onto the street through the ornate iron gates, originally from the home of the Duke of Chandos where Handel was organist, as man and wife.

The bridegroom was 38, the bride 34. The entry in the marriage register shows that Pinson was continuing to use his army rank, as was his right. His place of residence is given as Paddington, where his elderly mother now lived in rented accommodation. The Roxburghs' consent to the marriage is implied by the presence of Catherine's father, Lieutenant-Colonel James Roxburgh, as a witness.

What of Adèle Hugo while all this was going on? Was she even aware that Pinson had returned to Britain, let alone that he was married? One thing was for sure. The theory held by members of her family, chiefly François-Victor, that wherever Pinson went Adèle would inevitably follow, had been disproved. She remained in Barbados in an uncertain physical and mental state. To all intents and purposes, her pursuit of Albert Pinson was over.

But a surprising piece of evidence that I'd overlooked was about to turn up. It would shed new intriguing light on Adèle's situation and the final stage of her relationship with Albert Pinson.

It was Silke Pinson-Roxburgh, always assiduous in researching her husband's family, who alerted me to what I'd missed. Had I seen the letters from Pinson in the British Library, she asked in an email? No, I hadn't, I replied in amazement. Checking the catalogue, I saw that there was no doubt of what she had found. In a batch of miscellaneous autograph manuscripts were a number of Hugo-related items, including five letters addressed to Adèle in Barbados between 1866 and 1871. Their writers were her mother, her brother François-Victor and, most exciting of all, Pinson himself. Here at long last was the chance to hear the voice of a man whose true character had eluded me and many others for so long. I suppose I allowed myself a wry smile at the thought that I'd travelled thousands of miles in pursuit of the story, only to discover that all the while something significant had been there, right on my doorstep.

The documents had entered the library, at the time still part of the British Museum, by a circuitous route. In 1891, as a covering letter explained, William J. Locke, the bestselling novelist, author of the popular sentimental melodrama *Stella Maris*, came across them while 'rummaging among my old things'. The letters and other manuscripts had originally been the property of his father, John Locke, who had found them deposited in the bank in Barbados where he was manager. William Locke thought the collection 'decidedly of interest' and gave it to someone he knew would appreciate it, his friend C. D. Sherborn, geologist and bibliographer extraordinaire. As well as being the author of the *Index Animalium*, a ground-breaking work listing the names of half a million living and extinct creatures discovered between 1758 and 1850, Sherborn, 'a magpie with a card-index mind', preserved any piece of interesting manuscript material he could lay his hands on. In 1931, a decade before his death, Sherborn presented eleven volumes containing some 1,800 individual autographs to the British Museum. The Hugo material was among them.

How these manuscripts, clearly once the possession of Adèle Hugo, had escaped the great bonfire at Westbury Cottage and ended up in a Barbados bank is a mystery. Aside from the letters, there was a genealogical chart of the Hugo family and a statement of Victor Hugo's finances, countersigned in Brussels in the spring of 1866 by Madame Hugo. There was also a letter of credit for £30 addressed to Adèle at Westbury Cottage by Messrs Rothschild on the account of François-Victor Hugo, in January 1871, and paid through 'the Colonial Bank of Barbadoes'.

But it was the letters that revealed the human drama. The earliest was from Madame Hugo, writing to her daughter from Paris in the autumn of 1866, when the family had yet to hear from Adèle in Barbados and contact with her appeared lost. Employing the services of Augustine Allix as amanuensis, because of her poor sight, Madame Hugo beseeches Adèle to continue communicating with François-Victor. 'My heart is always for you', she concludes, 'and this comes with the most tender of maternal affection.'

Next was the first of three letters – or pages from letters – from Pinson. Addressed to François-Victor in August 1869, while Pinson was still in the army at the Dublin barracks, and forwarded to Adèle, it is terse and businesslike to the point of unfamiliarity:

Sir

Should you receive this letter, may I request that you will place yourself in communication with me and inform me to what address I may write to you with the assurance that you will receive my letter.

A. A. Pinson

Captain 2/16th Regt

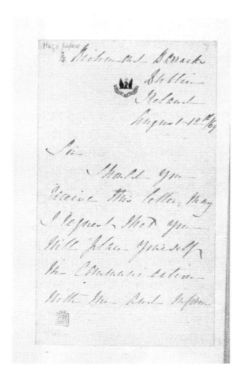

That is all. If I were a graphologist, I'd analyse Pinson's handwriting, and, finding that it slopes to the right, conclude that this indicates a disposition for giving and receiving affection, showing kindness and honesty; and on the negative side, that it suggests a tendency to conventional behaviour. However, unless you're Donald Trump, who has demonstrated a touching faith in the powers of handwriting analysis to uncover the inner self, it's probably wise to relegate graphology to the status of a pseudoscience, along with other pretenders of yesteryear to empirical testing, like phrenology or eugenics – or even, dare I say it, the pseudoscience of biographical certainty based on the confident accumulation of piles of documentary evidence.

A letter from François-Victor to Adèle, also from 1869, remarks on yet another postponement of her return and confirms that he has sent her allowance to her that very day, and also that he's read out to their father's approval her comments in an earlier letter on Hugo's latest novel, *L'Homme qui rit* (*The Man Who Laughs*, one day to inspire the look of the Joker in the Batman comic strip).

But then comes the bombshell, contained in a letter from brother to sister dated 16 January 1870:

Dear Adèle

Last week I received another letter from M.[onsieur] P.[inson]. M.[onsieur] P.[inson] tells me he is in the process of leaving the army, and that, free now, he puts himself at my disposal should I feel offended by his conduct towards you. He adds that if the annoyances you have caused him for the past eight years are renewed, he will have no alternative but to challenge me to a duel.

It is up to you to modify your conduct following this warning, if you wish to avoid a scandal arising out of a conflict between M.[onsieur] P.[inson] and me. You run the risk of a public outburst, and have reason enough yourself to cease all correspondence with M.[onsieur] P.[inson].

So Adèle was still writing to Pinson, and on the evidence of this letter had probably continued to dog his footsteps around Bridgetown all the time he was there. Although Pinson threatened François-Victor – and by extension Victor Hugo himself – with a scandal, he had as much to lose as they did should details of his relationship with Adèle reach public attention. His approach to François-Victor was made only weeks before his marriage to Catherine Roxburgh. How much, if anything, did his bride and future in-laws know about his Hugolian past? All one can say is that the need for Pinson to banish forever the shadow of Adèle from his life was stronger than it had ever been.

Something must have occurred, though – some agreement, some rapprochement between Pinson and François-Victor – to account for the marked change in tone between the message of the earlier letter and the remaining two written by Pinson in the library's collection. This time Pinson writes in French and addresses himself directly to Adèle. Tantalizingly, however, not only are both letters incomplete, but they are also extremely difficult to decipher. A friend who is a native French speaker sat with me before the computer as enlargements of the jungle of words flashed up on the screen. The cross-hatching alone – writing sideways on the first side of text saved money, as postal delivery in the nineteenth century was charged by the page – is enough to deter the fainthearted.

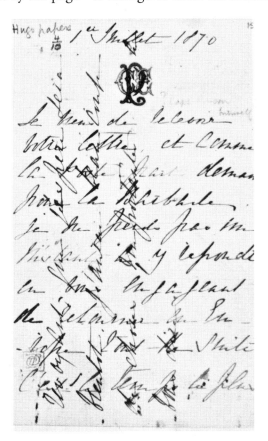

The most clearly distinguishable feature of the opening page of Pinson's first letter to Adèle is the monogram at the top, where a 'CE' surmounts a conjoined 'PR'. These are the initials of Catherine Edith Pinson-Roxburgh. Pinson is writing to his former girlfriend on his new wife's writing paper. The date is 1 July 1870, four months after the day of their wedding in Hampstead.

Putting the matter of the notepaper to one side, Albert Pinson's words are kindly, concerned and gently remonstrating. He is worried about Adèle's health, reminds her of the dangers of remaining in the tropics, and encourages her to take the first boat back to Europe:

> I have just received your letter and as the post leaves tomorrow for Barbados I do not waste a moment in replying to it by urging you to return to Europe immediately. This is the best weather for the trip and you will arrive in England in a season where it will be warm enough for the change in climate not to affect you. It is very unwise of you to remain in the unhealthy climate where a prolonged stay is sure to have serious consequences.
>
> I fear that you are under the influence of interested persons whose advice can only hurt you and as it is in their interest that you stay where you are they will do their best to keep you there.

Who these 'interested persons' are, and how he's come to hear about them, Pinson doesn't specify, but his accusation raises the suspicion that money from the bank drafts arriving regularly from Adèle's family was being diverted to pockets other than her own (of course there's an irony here, given that so many of the later rumours connected to Pinson himself have him taking or accepting money from Adèle).

In contrast to this, Pinson's closing lines portray him as motivated only by friendship for her:

> But please believe that I speak to you as a sincere friend when I urge you to leave Barbados without delay and return to Europe

as soon as possible. Write to me by the return post to let me know your plans.

When I see you again, which I hope will be soon, I will have a lot of important things to tell you.

The important things he has to tell her must have included his marriage, and perhaps that Catherine was now pregnant with their son, Eudo Albert Carnegie Pinson, who would be born the following February. What is so extraordinary, though, given the fractured, tortured history of their relationship, is that Pinson is actually encouraging Adèle to meet and talk with him. There can be only one explanation for this transformation in his behaviour. François-Victor has persuaded Albert Pinson to play the part of his sister's saviour, to assist in rescuing her from the throes of fantasy and entrap her into making the decision to return home at long last.

Their plan was unsuccessful. The final letter in the British Library from Pinson to Adèle, even harder to decipher than the preceding one, yields only snatches of information. It's dated 30 May 1871, eleven months after the earlier letter. He's 'very sorry' to learn from her most recent letter that she's still in Barbados. He doesn't want to appear interfering, but each time she writes to him she claims to be on the verge of returning in two months. This always turns out to be an empty promise. He clearly expects her to keep writing to him, asks her to date her letters, and to spell his current address in South Wales correctly ('it's Llandaff with two l's'). 'I hope to get from you the news that you are _really_ on the point of coming back to Europe,' he concludes, 'but I don't count on it in any way!'

How did François-Victor persuade Pinson to act like this? Was it simply a matter of pointing out to him that word of Adèle's ongoing situation could create a scandal for both sides? Or was there something else at the bottom of it all, a vestige of genuine feeling on the part of Albert Pinson for the woman he may once have loved? It may be sentimental, but I like to think so, and to believe that at the close of Pinson's role in Adèle's story he may have set out to redeem himself for the way he had treated her in the past. I have no way of knowing for certain, but in my mind he is no longer the hard-hearted, one-dimensional villain of the piece.

Examined closely, that final surviving letter from him has a coat of arms printed at the top. The motto is '*Factis non Verbis*' ('By deeds not words'). At the centre of the insignia is a griffin. In its beak is an olive branch of peace.

François-Victor's letters to Adèle in the British Library mix family news with reports of developments in the outside world that were hastening the end of France's Second Empire. Their infant nephew, Charles's son Georges, whom she'd never seen, was 'adorable', he told her in the summer of 1869. In the same letter he talked about the 'immense success' that *Le Rappel* ('The Reminder'), the newspaper of which he was joint founder with Charles, Vacquerie and Meurice, was having in France. Benefiting from new press freedoms, this daily paper continued the attack on Napoleon III's regime while denouncing evils and abuses in other parts of Europe. 'It is time that the years of exile were over,' François-Victor ended wearily. At the beginning of 1870, he was more confident. Revolution was coming to Paris, he assured Adèle. 'Deliverance approaches.'

Cracks were fast appearing across the surface of Napoleon III's rule. However, it was France's declaration of war against Prussia in July, after Bismarck cleverly goaded the Emperor into military aggression, which sealed the regime's fate. Napoleon III had finally overreached himself. At the Battle of Sedan on 2 September 1870 Napoleon surrendered with his army. A new French Republic was proclaimed, with the formation of a provisional government of National Defence.

From Brussels Victor Hugo had been waiting on events, ready to leave for France at a moment's notice, but anxious lest anyone accuse him of rushing to the aid of the Empire. On 5 September, accompanied by Juliette Drouet, Charles Hugo, his wife Alice, and two journalists, Antonin Proust and Jules Claretie, Hugo arrived at the Brussels terminus and, in a voice trembling with emotion, asked for 'a ticket to Paris'. As the train crossed into France, Hugo caught sight of lines of retreating French soldiers, exhausted and demoralized. With tears in his eyes, he leaned out of the window and cried out, '*Vive la France! Vive l'armée!*' At the Gare du Nord an immense crowd awaited their returning hero. He'd come to do his duty, he told them; to defend Paris from the Prussian forces marching on the city. Moved by their affectionate response and patriotic fervour, he concluded with the words, 'You have repaid me in an hour for nineteen years of exile'.

Within a fortnight an iron circle enclosed Paris. The city was surrounded by a vast army of spike-helmeted Prussian troops. The siege that was to last for 132 days had begun. Reinforcing their sense of imprisonment, Parisians could only communicate with the outside world by balloon. Inflation soared and rationing was introduced. Starvation threatened for many. 'People are making rat pâté,' Hugo noted in November. 'It is said to be quite good . . .' By the end of the year it was no longer rat or horse that filled Hugo's stomach, but 'the Unknown'. At the start of 1871 shells fired on 23 successive nights, in an effort to break the citizens' morale, tore great holes in the Left Bank.

Capitulation, when it came, was an utter humiliation. The peace treaty ratified by France's National Assembly sacrificed Alsace and Lorraine to the new German Empire and forced France to pay an indemnity of five billion francs. This seeming betrayal of France and the Republic by its head, the veteran statesman Adolphe Thiers, brought tensions to their snapping point. Paris alone appeared prepared to fight on. In March, when Thiers, attempting to restore normality to the city, tried to disband the National Guard by ordering the removal of its cannon, revolt broke out. Municipal elections called by a central committee of the National Guard resulted in a victory for the radicals, with the Commune assuming control of Paris. For two months a red socialist flag flew over the City of Light. The Versailles government moved to retake Paris on 21 May. The week that followed was one of the bloodiest in French history. Government troops crushed the rebellion in brutal scenes of street fighting and summary executions. The Communards defended themselves by shooting hostages and setting public buildings ablaze.

Victor Hugo had returned to France a symbolic hero. Renewed involvement in the country's politics led to him once again being dismissed as a maverick and figure of controversy. Elected as a deputy for Paris in the new National Assembly, he took part in the debate in March on the 'hideous' peace treaty, but indignantly resigned when his argument that France should renew the conflict with Germany and fight on was decisively rejected. His plea, three months later – by which time he was back in Brussels – that the fleeing Communards should be spared reprisals and offered sanctuary in Belgium, resulted in mob violence outside Hugo's house in the Place des Barricades. Days later, the Belgian government issued a decree demanding that Victor Hugo leave the country and never return.

And in the midst of political tragedy a personal one overtook him. One evening in March 1871, a fortnight before the Commune seized power, Hugo waited in a Bordeaux restaurant with Alice, his daughter-in-law, and several friends, for dinner with his son Charles, who was late. Charles never arrived. He'd asked the cab driver to stop at a café on the way, and when the driver opened the door of the cab he found Charles lying dead, blood pouring from his nose and mouth. Charles had suffered an apoplectic stroke. He was 44, and left a widow and two small children.

The funeral cortège made its way from Paris's Gare d'Orléans to the burial at Père Lachaise cemetery. As it did so the National Guard, preparing for the battle that would bring the Commune to power, saluted and presented arms. It was close to three decades since the shock of Léopoldine's death had plunged Hugo into agonized mourning, undermining his sense of certainty. Now, to his despair, he felt as if he'd been 'struck twice by lightning in the space of a single life!' But his poem about Charles doesn't display the submission to the divine will that the earlier 'À Villequier', commemorating Léopoldine, had. This time Hugo doubted God's larger purpose in taking his child, and wrote of seeing 'straight to the abyss'.

Ten months later, at the beginning of 1872, Hugo was back in Paris, a shattered city of burnt-out ruins, when a letter brought him momentous news. Eight and a half years after her flight from

Guernsey, his 41-year-old daughter was finally leaving Barbados and coming home to her family.

Why, though, had Adèle decided to return now? And, after all this time, what condition would those waiting for her find her in?

This is a story within a story.

One day in September 1885, a few months after Victor Hugo's death, a black woman, a former slave of African descent, entered a church in Port of Spain, the capital of Trinidad. Approaching the priest, Father Marie-Joseph Gilliet, part of the French Dominican mission there, she made a simple request. Would he say a mass for the repose of the soul of Victor Hugo? Assuming that the woman had no personal connection with Hugo, Father Gilliet expressed surprise at what she'd asked him. But then the woman went on to explain that she was fulfilling a promise made to Hugo himself, that when she learned of his death she would have three masses said for him. Gradually she revealed to the priest that she'd come to know Hugo through the vital role she'd played in rescuing his sick daughter and bringing her back from the Caribbean to France.

The woman's name was Céline Alvarez Baa (sometimes spelt Baà). Most of what is known about her is founded on hearsay. However, it's probably safe to identify her with the 'young and fine-looking black woman', with a good command of English, mentioned by Amelia Culpeper in her memoirs. This was the woman who had accompanied Adèle to the Culpepers' home near Bridgetown one evening to ask that Adèle be allowed to continue living at Westbury Cottage.

It also seems likely that Madame Baa was one of the women traders, known commonly as higglers, or more often in Barbados as hawkers, who travelled around the Caribbean islands trading in local and imported goods. This practice originated under slavery, when slaves sold the surplus of foods grown on the small plots of land allocated to them, which were intended as a supplement to their basic rations. Following emancipation there was a marked increase in this entrepreneurial activity, especially among the freed female slaves, who used the buying and selling of produce and other goods as a means of earning a living away from the plantations. In this way they also established their own autonomy and made a significant contribution to the internal economies of their islands. The tradition continues to this day, on both large and smaller scales. Thinking about this, my mind went back to the figure of Zelda, the elderly woman hobbling along the beach at Holetown, hawking her wares.

Hawking or higgling – *speculating*, as it's called in Jamaica – would account for Céline Baa's familiarity with various islands of the West Indies: Trinidad, where she's said to have been born, and to which she eventually returned; Martinique, where she is known to have had contacts; and Barbados, where at the time of encountering Adèle, in the late 1860s or the beginning of the 1870s, she had been based for a number of years. Baa had no permanent home. In that sense she was as much a wanderer as Adèle was. But when she came upon the troubled woman walking the streets of Bridgetown in heavy winter clothes, she took pity on her. She provided her with board and lodging, perhaps in one of the former slave huts dotted around the island. Most of these have since been destroyed; some, with a wilful lack of respect for historic preservation, disappeared as recently as the 1980s. I remembered seeing a rare surviving example on the plantations at St Nicholas Abbey. It possessed very thick, hurricane-resistant walls, built cheaply from the coral stone that could be quarried all over the island. Its low-hip roof, sloping on all four sides, made from corrugated iron sheets, would have originally been covered in thatch.

Madame Baa cared devotedly for Adèle, and nursed her back to some semblance of health. Having learned of her identity, she wrote to Victor Hugo giving him a full description of the extent of his daughter's breakdown, managing somehow to get a letter to him in Paris. Unfortunately, this letter doesn't survive, and we have only Hugo's brief remark on receiving it, in his notebook entry dated 11 January 1872: 'Sombre news from Barbados'. A week later Juliette Drouet wrote to him, 'I am heartbroken when I think of the blow that has just struck you.'

Céline Baa appears to have taken matters into her own hands, and to have already made plans to return Adèle to her family in France. Hugo assured her that he would repay her expenses. From Martinique, where she borrowed 1,000 francs for two one-way fares from an acquaintance, a Mr Werder, she and Adèle sailed to New York. Here they boarded a Cunard liner for Liverpool. On the last leg of their journey they sailed in a smaller passenger ship along France's western coast. They were due to dock at Saint-Nazaire, 300 miles from Paris, on 22 January.

How I wish that I could uncover more about Céline Alvarez Baa. Her caring, charitable nature, together with the suggestion of an independent, entrepreneurial spirit, makes her stand out as a truly remarkable character. However, as a nineteenth-century woman of no fixed abode – what is more, as a *black* Caribbean woman moving constantly from island to island – she has left no discernible trace in official records.

Was she a former slave, though? This is what some later statements by the French Dominicans from Trinidad would have us believe. If Baa and the 'young' black woman of Amelia Culpeper's memoirs are one and the same, then it seems unlikely that she was much older than 40 at this time (roughly the age of Adèle herself). This would mean that as a slave in Trinidad or Barbados she would have been around the age of three when slavery was abolished in all British territories in 1833 (though the system of apprenticeships under which slave owners managed to get free labour from former slaves continued for another five years). Of course, if Baa was a slave in a French territory, like Martinique, where slavery wasn't abolished until 1848, she would have been significantly older.

Both these scenarios are entirely plausible. So is the strong probability that Baa came from a family of freed slaves. Even so, whatever the precise truth of the matter, there can be no doubt that Céline Alvarez Baa is the heroine of Adèle Hugo's story. For a black woman in a highly racially segregated society, like the Barbados of her time, to reach out to a white woman and offer care that ultimately rescued her from the circumstances surrounding the fantasy that had enslaved her, was an act of extraordinary compassion and self-sacrifice.

At the end of his film of Adèle H., François Truffaut shrewdly exploits the notion of Madame Baa as a former slave to full advantage. Portrayed as a much older woman, who can neither read nor write, Baa dictates to a scribe her letter to Victor Hugo, whose name she knows as 'the friend and defender of the oppressed on Earth'. A freed slave, she is returning a daughter to her father, to a man who has a reputation as a staunch opponent of slavery. He is someone who has publicly stated his belief that the existence of even one slave on Earth is enough 'to dishonour the freedom of all men'.

But then the stinging irony. In the film's final moments we see Adèle, played by Isabelle Adjani, looking out to sea and reciting those words from her journal in which she speaks of the restrictions on her own freedom and her ambition to cross the ocean from the old world to the new to join her lover. And Truffaut confronts us, in a shock of recognition, with the fact that the daughter of a famous abolitionist is herself not free.

Now Adèle's bid for escape, her great adventure, was over, would she ever experience freedom again?

8

Exiled

However, on the appointed date for her return there was no sign of Adèle. Émile Allix, doctor and family friend – whose brother Jules had suffered a breakdown during one of the final séances at Marine Terrace all those years ago – was sent by Hugo to meet Adèle's ship at Saint-Nazaire on 22 January 1872, as agreed. But he returned to Paris without her, reporting that there'd been a mistake. The ship wasn't due until 8 February. As the day dawned, Hugo noted that his 'poor child' would have the benefit of good weather for her arrival in the city she had last seen two decades earlier. Again, though, the faithful Dr Allix had a fruitless journey. Owing to delays, the ship wasn't expected for several more days. Allix left instructions that he was to be telegraphed as soon as it docked. At last, on 11 February, he received the telegram and left once more for Saint-Nazaire. 'My daughter has arrived,' Hugo recorded in his notebook, betraying no trace of the anxious anticipation he must have felt. 'She will be here tomorrow.'

Together with Allix and Madame Baa, Adèle reached Allix's home at 178 rue de Rivoli, opposite the north wing of the Louvre, on the 12th, at four in the morning. Allix immediately reported to Hugo on Adèle's condition. 'My poor dear child', Hugo wrote after receiving the news. She hadn't recognized Émile Allix. The saving grace was that, according to Hugo, 'The black woman who accompanied her, Mme Baa, is devoted to her.' Later that day, François-Victor, Adèle's intercessor with their father on so many occasions throughout her years abroad, called to see his sister. She failed to recognize him. This was to be their last meeting. Although his family were unaware of it, François-Victor was ill already with the renal tuberculosis that would kill him. He died at Christmas 1873, leaving Adèle the sole survivor of Hugo's four adult children.

Allowing his daughter time to acclimatize to her new surroundings, Victor Hugo waited until the late afternoon of the following day to pay his visit. 'I saw her again,' he wrote matter-of-factly in his notebook. But what did he see? A shell of the woman he had once known, with shorn hair and a face weathered by the sun? Adèle did recognize her father, which pleased him. He embraced her, 'and said to her everything that was affectionate and hopeful'. She was very calm, and seemed at times almost asleep, which was scarcely surprising given the arduous weeks of travel she was recovering from.

The next day he returned to the rue de Rivoli. As if choked by emotion and unable to express himself fully, Hugo later wrote three words beside the date:

Adèle. Profound sadness.

On 15 February, Hugo met with Allix. In consultation with Dr Alexandre Axenfeld, a specialist in nervous diseases, Allix had devised a plan for Adèle's future. She would be admitted to a nursing home, the best that was available.

Two days afterwards, Adèle entered the private asylum run by Madame Rivet at 106 Grande-Rue, in Saint-Mandé, on the eastern outskirts of Paris. That summer she would be 42. Nearly half her life was over. The remainder would be spent under supervision in mental institutions.

'Another closed door', observed Hugo mournfully, 'darker than the tomb.'

'You can't come in.' The voice over the intercom was shaky but insistent. 'Come back later,' it said. There was a pause. Then the connection went dead. In the background, amid the usual commotion of voices, blaring music and TV noise, I'd heard the sound of shouts, and above them staccato bursts of screaming. On my next visit I learned that it had been necessary to restrain one of the patients forcibly by a doctor pinning him to the ground and sitting on him. This patient had assaulted another inmate and threatened to kill himself. For the next few days a guard stood robustly outside the door of his room. 'This kind of thing happens from time to time,' remarked one of the nurses, almost nonchalantly, as she distributed pills into tiny beakers laid out on a tray.

The moment the line went dead that afternoon, I was stranded. There was no way of going back or forwards. When I'd exited the lift on my way in, an outer door had closed and locked behind me. Denied admittance to the ward, I retraced my steps to take the lift back down again, only to find that, despite my repeated ringing at the bell, no one was there to answer and release the security lock on the connecting door. I stood for what seemed like an age waiting for a response, trapped in the small white space, feeling the sweat rising on my brow as I began to panic about R's response to the pandemonium in the ward and to my failure to materialize at the normal visiting time.

No longer did I feel that I was in pursuit of Adèle Hugo's story. Instead, in a strange, disconcerting way, it seemed as if it was now pursuing me. I'd identified elements of Adèle's story that compelled, fascinated and at times unnerved me, drawing the loose parallels between one life and another, or taking it as a mirror, as Hugo had said, and seeing myself in it. What had been impossible to foresee was the way in which the story would begin to shadow me, dogging my footsteps, almost as if it were in some way prefiguring my own destiny.

R had experienced depressive episodes before. They arrived with a strangely clockwork precision, never satisfactorily explained, every four years. But this one was different. On my return from Barbados, I'd observed his deepening depression and the negative thoughts that prevented him from sleeping. Far more frightening, though, was the rush of anxiety that would suddenly seize hold of him, leaving him completely unable to control his breathing. Autumn was upon us, and we were both enclosed in a world of darkening fear. I began to think of R as a man standing perilously close to the edge of a cliff. He spoke of wanting to die. His arms shook in anger. At their worst the attacks of breathlessness gave the impression that he was on the verge of choking on a surfeit of unverbalized, despairing rage.

He was admitted to the psychiatric wing of a hospital not far from where we lived. The exterior of this gloomy collection of mid-Victorian buildings was a stark reminder of its original purpose as the local union workhouse. I discovered later that it was already designated unfit for purpose. Certainly the ward R was placed on could only be described in terms of a hostile environment. Shortage of space meant that he had to share a room with an 18-year-old man who barely spoke and spent the night-time hours pacing the floor with the light switched on. The sanitary arrangements were deplorable: ten male patients reduced to sharing a single bathroom and lavatory.

The medical staff tinkered with R's medication with no discernible improvement to his state of mind. He would be entirely lucid one afternoon. Then by the next visit he had descended into a spiral of self-hatred, constantly asserting his conviction that he was possessed by the Devil and refusing to be comforted. Sometimes we sat in the freezing cold in the so-called sun lounge, where a dribble of sunlight occasionally penetrated through, and he would turn plaintively to me, and ask, 'No more sad days?' No more sad days, I repeated as persuasively as I could manage, disguising my growing fear that this warm, generous, vital figure might be lost to me forever.

Alone at home, I was unable to concentrate, which made sustained work impossible. At night I would awaken suddenly and find myself scrabbling through the sheets, searching for R, as if I was expecting to discover him lost among the bedclothes. Increasingly I spent my days reading in a local café. One morning I was approached by a man with a friendly smile. 'Excuse me, but do you realize that you're inside out?' It took a moment for the penny to drop and to see that I was wearing my pullover turned inside out with the label showing. Slightly embarrassed, I thanked him.

'Wouldn't want people to think you'd gone loopy,' he said.

2230. - St-MANDÉ. - La Grande-Rue. - G. I.

Marie Rivet's nursing home in Saint-Mandé, on the edge of the Bois de Vincennes, catered to a wealthy clientele. All its patients were women, all were said to be suffering from unspecified nervous or chronic illnesses. Although not much more than a decade old, the private asylum in the Grande-Rue already had an established reputation, deriving both from Madame Rivet's experience and expertise and from the fame of her father, Alexandre Brière de Boismont, to whose ideas she was professionally indebted. Dr Brière de Boismont was well known for his published work on hallucinations and on suicide. From the years he'd spent running two Paris asylums, he was also the proponent of a new type of treatment for the mentally ill. This stressed the curative value of a domestic setting for patients, allowing them to live alongside the doctor and his family instead of being hidden away in one of the great public asylums.

Victor Hugo paid his first visit to Adèle in Saint-Mandé on 22 February, several days after her arrival at the nursing home. He was relieved to find that she appeared better and happy to see him, though her doctors were of the opinion that he shouldn't come too often in the future. The next day, seeking relief of another kind, Hugo took advantage of the attractive diversion that Adèle's return had brought him in the shape of Céline Alvarez Baa. 'The first Black Woman in my life,' he recorded in Spanish in his notebook. Six days later he drew a thick capital 'O', resembling a dark hole. Not, then, an especially subtle allusion.

When I try to imagine in what circumstances this encounter took place – at Hugo's home in the rue de la Rochefoucauld, or Madame Baa's Paris lodgings – I can't help bringing to mind Balzac's post-coital admission that 'I lost a book this morning!' (or, in Woody Allen's twentieth-century variant, 'as Balzac says, "There goes another novel"'). Not that Hugo's dalliances affected his rate of literary production. Quite the reverse, in fact, because, unlike for Balzac, the frenzy of sexual excitement seems almost to have been a necessary accompaniment to Hugo's extraordinary output as a writer. At 70 he was as prolific as ever. He continued to publish volume after volume, poetry and novels, while enjoying intimate relationships with, among others, the great actress Sarah Bernhardt and Juliette Drouet's new maid, a tiny brunette named Blanche Lanvin. His sexual passion for Juliette herself had long since cooled. Sometimes she uncovered evidence of his 'shameful adventures', to her overwhelming distress.

Madame Baa left for Trinidad in mid-March. Before she did so, Hugo reimbursed her travel expenses and made her a small gift of money. She sent him her portrait (sadly it's never come to light), and handed over Adèle's jewellery, which had been in her safekeeping. It was all broken and scratched. 'I found my wife's ring,' Hugo wrote, and as a memento of Adèle he made a gift to Madame Baa of two gold bracelets, a brooch and some gold earrings. Nine years later, in the summer of 1881, Céline Alvarez Baa would return to Paris to see Hugo and Adèle again. On this visit she presented him with a bouquet of coloured bird feathers, as a token of her affection and a souvenir of her homeland, a part of the world he would never see. And when she heard of Hugo's death several years later, and visited the church in Trinidad to ask that masses be said for him, she remembered him as 'such a generous man, so good'. Was she also recalling his attributes as a lover?

For six months Hugo continued his occasional visits to Adèle in Saint-Mandé, sometimes taking Dr Allix with him for moral support. 'She is very calm and very sweet,' he recorded in March. 'She kissed my hands and said: "I am content."' Adèle had developed the fixed idea of invisible people who talked to her and wouldn't leave her alone. 'No longer fear anything or anyone,' Hugo reassured her. 'You are close to your father and to God.' Sometimes she played a little on the piano. At others she wrote constantly, like a copycat version of her father, refusing, however, to show him what she'd written. At the end of May he watched her sitting on a bench in the garden, pencil in hand. 'She is like ice', Hugo observed, 'but without sadness.'

On 7 August 1872, Hugo left Paris for Guernsey, to spend time at Hauteville House. He wouldn't see Adèle for another year.

Shouldn't he have taken Adèle with him, though? Instead of being secluded at Saint-Mandé, shouldn't she have been cared for by people she knew, in the comfort and security of familiar surroundings? This was the view of Paul Chenay, Hugo's brother-in-law, husband of Madame Hugo's sister Julie, in a troublemaking book, *Victor Hugo at Guernsey*, which appeared in 1902. It was an opinion shared by Frances Guille in the 1960s during the early stages of researching her edition of Adèle's journals, though it went unrepeated later in the published work. It appeared to Guille that Adèle had been 'hustled into the asylum' and kept there simply because her family was embarrassed at having her back at home still unmarried, when her marriage to Albert Pinson had been publicly announced a decade earlier. Several subsequent writers have gone further, arguing that there was nothing really wrong with Adèle, backing up their claims with testimony from various people who visited her in later years and remembered periods of normality in her behaviour, of how interesting her conversation was at times, and of how well she played the piano.

I thought of the recent exposé of Charles Dickens's wickedness during the break-up of his marriage in 1858; of how, in a desperate bid to be free of his wife Catherine, he sought to have her shut away in an asylum despite her obvious sanity. Dickens's attempt failed. He was unable to bend doctors, asylum keepers and the 'commissioners of lunacy' to his will. Compare this to France of the Second Empire, where there were a number of well-publicized instances of family members conspiring with doctors and – very nearly – succeeding in having their inconvenient relatives put away.

Yet this was not the case with Adèle. Apart from the underlying assumption in testimony about her that mentally ill people behave in a demented fashion for 24 hours a day, the evidence, such as it is – Hugo's notebooks, and the occasional comments from a surviving institutional report – indicates that Adèle's mental deterioration was gradual and ongoing. Moreover, any hopes for improvement in her condition were centred on removing her from all family influences, which were regarded as being at the pathological root of her problems.

Given that an inmate's previous home life was held to be the starting point for most mental illness, it followed that the basis of treatment at the Rivet asylum was to separate the patient from family and friends, at least for an initial period. Staff at the asylum acted as a replacement family, with the object of re-educating the women under their supervision in standards of acceptable domestic behaviour. Patients found themselves incorporated into the household routine. On her good days Adèle would be permitted to leave the home at Saint-Mandé, accompanied by Madame Rivet, or another member of staff, to do some shopping and live 'for a whole hour a normal life'. Familial-style relationships with other members of the household were looked upon with favour. On one visit Victor Hugo observed Adèle's closeness to a small boy of two, the son of a servant, 'who she loves and who amuses her'.

Marie Rivet herself, only a year or so older than Adèle, was more like a concerned mother or devoted sister than the *directrice* of a mental institution. Having gone through the bizarre experience as a child of being raised in Paris in an asylum run by her own father – 'living amongst the mad' – she was unlikely to encounter much that would faze her. Her patients tended to be treated as children, sometimes like spoilt children, with patience and compassion. A lenient approach was taken when an inmate's behaviour veered towards the outrageous, and a patient might even be allowed to give herself up to her fantasies without any risk of restraint. Madame Rivet's reminiscences of certain cases – for example of a woman, semi-naked, dancing in the garden, her petticoats rolled up while she did a military drill with a broomstick – suggest that the asylum in the Grande-Rue could at times be a lively place.

To what degree, beyond basic care and kindness, Marie Rivet's institution was helping Adèle is open to question. Returning at last to Paris at the end of July 1873, Hugo found Adèle physically better. Her looks had improved, and she'd put on weight. Madame Rivet's cure for lack of appetite was simple but effective: a maid held the patient's head and pinched her nose, and the moment the woman's mouth fell open to breathe, another maid would slip in a spoonful of nourishment.

However, Adèle's 'moral state', Hugo noted, hadn't changed. Juliette often accompanied Hugo on his visits as her daughter Claire, by the sculptor James Pradier, was buried at Saint-Mandé. 'She goes to see her daughter in the cemetery, alas! and I go to see mine.' Adèle continued to be preoccupied with the voices in her head, while her father's appearances at the home left her in a state of overexcitement. 'There are emotions of which I don't wish to leave any trace,' he wrote in June 1874. 'My visit today to my poor daughter, what despondency!' At times he dared not go to see her for fear of making her condition worse. Julie Chenay, Madame Hugo's sister, went in his place in the autumn of 1875. She returned reporting that Adèle was very well and very pleased with a blue cravat that Hugo had sent her. But as the decade wore on, the situation got no better for father or daughter. 'Seeing each other hurts both of us.'

A single letter of Adèle's survives from these Saint-Mandé years. Written to her father from the asylum, and dated 28 June 1878, it is marked by an agitated, obsessive tone; a fear of want, as if she's back again in Halifax demanding financial support from her family; and a strong impression of the writer grasping at something through clouds of confusion that she can't quite put into words.

The mention of *Le National*, a newspaper that had been outlawed and shut down following Louis-Napoléon's coup in December 1851, shows her mind lurching back into the distant past:

My dear Father

    I already sent you a letter to ask for various things, among others, that you send me *some gold.* I would have been very happy to have prompt results which I have not had. M. Badouin, editor of *Le National*, lost his position when the publisher changed. He desires to regain his job. You might take the situation into consideration, if it interests you, and see what you can do.

    Don't forget to come and fetch me, as well as Mme Léontine, and another person, and to come today as soon as possible or tomorrow. Take us with you insistently. Come today or tomorrow. Be *insistent* about it. Send us *some gold.*

    Your respectful loving daughter,

    Adèle

Hugo is unlikely to have read this letter immediately on receiving it, if at all. For on the day Adèle wrote it, he suffered a minor stroke. His speech became slurred, he was confused for a time, as well as uncharacteristically irritable, while his once superhuman energy began to wane. He was persuaded to leave Paris for Hauteville House to convalesce for several months. A programme of sexual abstinence was prescribed by his doctors. However, much to Juliette's horror, on his return to Paris that winter Hugo was still managing occasionally to slip out of their new home on the Avenue d'Eylau in pursuit of yet more amorous adventures. Meanwhile, at the end of 1879, he wrote his final full-length poem. As Hugo entered his eightieth year in February 1881, there was a weekend of public festivities in Paris, the greatest tribute ever accorded a living French writer. In the course of a single day, half a million people processed past Hugo's house in celebration. Hugo appeared at the window from time to time to acknowledge their acclamation, with tears in his eyes, and his two grandchildren, Georges and Jeanne, clinging to his arms.

Hugo's final recorded visits to Adèle took place the following year. 'We went to Saint-Mandé to see our two daughters,' he wrote in his notebook in March 1882. Later that year, on 4 September, the thirty-ninth anniversary of Léopoldine's drowning, he used the same words to describe his final visit. In May 1883, Hugo was too overcome with grief to return to Saint-Mandé to join mourners at the graveside of Juliette Drouet. She had died from stomach cancer after a long illness, and was buried in the cemetery beside her daughter Claire.

It may have been renewed publicity, this time for Hugo's actual eightieth birthday in February 1882, which led a journalist from *Le Figaro*, France's biggest-selling newspaper, to seek out Victor Hugo's sole remaining child. How Camille Chincholle obtained his scoop is unknown. He must have been acting on insider information from within the Rivet asylum, but finding Adèle can't have been straightforward. The later occasional references to 'Mme Adèle' suggest that she was registered there not under the name Hugo, but as Madame Pinson, keeping up the pretence that she had once been married and that her husband had died, leaving her a widow.

Whatever the machinations contributing to his discovery, Chincholle told his readers that 'it was indeed the last daughter of the great poet that I had there before my eyes'. Adèle was taking an accompanied walk through the local park. From a distance of ten paces he thought she could pass for a young girl. But Chincholle got close enough to describe 'a woman, small, slender, of extreme distinction', with the 'profile of a duchess, a hooked and proud nose'. He noticed her staring black eyes. Her hair was thick and abundant, 'skilfully tied'. She wore a hat, trimmed with red silk, and over her dress a brown fur coat.

Someone – surely not Madame Rivet herself – had informed him about Madame Adèle's idiosyncrasies. Her reasoning and memory were reportedly good, and she got on well with the other inmates. But she was given to striking touching poses that were painful to observe. She especially liked rocks, and had spent a month removing those from the home's long driveway. A little later she put them all back, one by one. Her pockets were said to be a *capharnaüm* – a jumble of objects – as she tended to place in them whatever she could within reach. At table she would grab a piece of meat and stuff it into a pocket.

Suddenly, as Chincholle watched her in the park, Adèle interrupted her walk. She hopped along on one foot for a while, stood motionless with her other foot still suspended in the air, and then toppled over onto the ground.

If Albert Pinson was still in touch with Adèle's brother at the time of François-Victor's death in 1873, he would have learned of her committal to an asylum. If he wasn't, then he may have assumed that this would be her fate in any case when she eventually returned to France.

Long ago, I'd gone to see the house in the Devonshire village of South Brent where Pinson spent his old age, in a despairing attempt to uncover any trace of him. And I'd imagined him there in good weather, sitting in the lush garden or in the nook beneath the porch, dwelling on his past life, and perhaps regaling friends or his neighbours in Springfield Terrace with tales from his earlier years: of ghostly goings-on at Marine Terrace, of the famous French writer, always too preoccupied with himself to take much notice of him; and of the strange, dark-eyed daughter whom he might have married, but who followed him across the world when he failed to do so, haunting him by day and by night.

Equally possibly, though, he may have been a man who kept himself to himself. Or he may have reflected that parts of his romantic history didn't place him in the best possible light, whatever kind of spin he tried to put on them.

What stories he might have told. What stories must have died with him. All he apparently left behind him, by accident, or with the intention of providing a glimmer of light for posterity into his side of the Hugo story, was a licence for the marriage to Adèle that never took place. However, like so many official documents, this licence could be said to beg as many questions as it answers.

Pinson's marriage to Catherine Roxburgh had quickly failed. By 1873, two years after their Hampstead wedding, they'd separated in a cloud of acrimony. Although the couple never divorced, James, her father, took steps effectively to pay off his son-in-law with a moderately generous allowance of £150 a year (just over £17,000 in modern terms). Their agreement contained the proviso that if Pinson ever acquired 'an income of his own amounting to one hundred pounds' then the Roxburghs' payment would be reduced to the annual sum of £100. Reading between the lines, it's clear that James Roxburgh wanted to ensure as little contact as possible between Pinson and his estranged wife, and Eudo, their son. Even Eudo's patriarchal name was subsumed into the more distinguished moniker 'Roxburgh', so that he and his descendants would be known as the Pinson-Roxburghs.

Catherine moved to London with Eudo. She died there in 1905. Pinson spent the next four decades living in a series of rented rooms and houses on the southern coast, in Devon and Cornwall. The census of 1881, when he was approaching 50, shows him residing as a lodger with a tailor and his family at the seaside resort of Ilfracombe, in a tiny house on the promenade, looking out to sea. By 1891, this 'Retired Captain of the 16th Regiment' was living at 1 New Road, at Forrabury, on the north coast of Cornwall, in Boscastle, with one live-in servant. Ten years on and he'd moved to St Mabyn, 20 miles away. Pinson was now described as both a retired officer and a man of independent means. Together with an old army friend he'd invested in a colliery in Wrexham, in North Wales, which brought an increase to his income. At the time of the 1911 census, four years before his death at the age of 83, Albert Pinson was settled in the house at South Brent, with a housemaid and housekeeper.

How much he saw of Eudo as he was growing up, it's impossible to say, though as a young man Eudo Albert Carnegie Pinson-Roxburgh – to give him his full name – briefly joined the army like his father before him, until he was invalided out with epilepsy. Like his father too, Eudo was enthusiastic about horse racing. In his will, Pinson left Eudo his gold watch, his plated tea and coffee pots, cream jug, and biscuit box – and that mysterious scrap of paper, the licence for his marriage with Adèle Hugo.

Victor Hugo died in Paris on the afternoon of 22 May 1885 after falling ill with pneumonia. He was 83. For a week he had struggled to die in his four-poster bed at the town house in the Avenue d'Eylau, renamed Avenue Victor Hugo in his honour. As France waited expectantly for his end, hushed and reverent crowds gathered outside the house. Indoors, during the delirium of his final hours, Hugo suddenly leapt out of bed and uttered what would be his last line of poetry, a perfect alexandrine:

C'est ici le combat du jour et de la nuit.
('This is the struggle of day and night.')

There's nothing to tell us how Adèle received the news of her father's death, perhaps conveyed to her by Madame Rivet herself. Or whether she was aware of the extraordinary scenes in the city as Hugo's coffin lay in state under the Arc de Triomphe, before being transported on a pauper's hearse to the Panthéon, amid a sea of flowers and mourners.

As the inheritor of her father's copyrights, Adèle was now a rich woman. This dramatic change in her circumstances – together with intimations that Marie Rivet might be thinking of retirement – prompted a decision to move her from Saint-Mandé to a much grander establishment, 10 miles away to the west of Paris, at the Château de Suresnes. One of Hugo's executors, and Adèle's guardian, responsible for managing her financial affairs and organizing her move soon after Hugo's death, was Auguste Vacquerie. It was with Vacquerie, of course, that Adèle had shared her first kiss at the age of 15, decades earlier at Place Royale, and whom she had later rejected in favour of Albert Pinson. Enjoying some success as a playwright, Vacquerie had never married, and spent his summer holidays at Villequier, with his nephews and nieces. Villequier, according to his biographer, consoled him for the 'petty miseries of Paris' 'by the melancholy of the great griefs' that it recalled.

323. SURESNES — La Maison de Santé E. M.

The origins of the château, on the banks of the Seine at Suresnes, dated back to the beginning of the seventeenth century, when it was a large country house surrounded by a vineyard. In the first years of the nineteenth century the house and its grounds were extensively remodelled and extended by the Princesse de Vaudémont, the great friend and confidante of Talleyrand. In 1875, ten years before Adèle Hugo's arrival at the château, the building and its grounds were bought by Dr Valentin Magnan, head of the admissions office at Sainte-Anne asylum in Paris, in partnership with two of his colleagues. In his public practice at Sainte-Anne, Magnan and his assistants had the task of screening all mentally ill patients in the Paris region before they were interned in one of the five public asylums in the department of the Seine. At Suresnes, Magnan created a luxurious nursing home for patients – neurasthenic, alcoholic, or simply convalescent – from the wealthiest families. With her personal companion, Adèle occupied one of the pavilions erected in the grounds, a pretty, compact little villa, where she could take her meals and be tended to by a small staff of servants in addition to the sanatorium attendants. Chaperoned, she took walks in the Jardin d'Acclimitation on the edge of the Bois de Boulogne, or went to matinées in the open-air theatre at the Pré Catalan. In later years she'd be taken into Paris for a special treat, such as the performance of her father's play *Les Burgraves* during the celebrations in 1902 for the centenary of Victor Hugo's birth, when she sat hidden in the darkness of her theatre box.

There's no sign of the château or its outbuildings today. In Paris I'd taken a train from the Gare de l'Est for the 40-minute journey to Suresnes, only to find that everything connected to the Magnan institution had been swept away in the 1980s. A housing estate now stands on the site. A wooded park, with its duck pond and an aviary containing peacocks and pheasants, has taken the place of what once formed part of the extensive gardens bordering the Seine.

Valentin Magnan himself remains a shadowy figure. He owed his position at the Sainte-Anne asylum to his successful treatment of Napoleon III's son, the Prince Imperial, a supreme irony given that Adèle Hugo has since become his best-known patient. I consulted Theodore Zeldin's monumental history of *France 1848–1945*, where there's a sympathetic sketch of him. Magnan was devoted to his patients, to the extent that he had a limited social life and took only a very brief seaside holiday each year. According to Zeldin, he was 'an exceptionally gentle, sympathetic, smiling man, who could gain the confidence of patients and converse even with the most agitatedly mad ones'.

However, this is only part of the story, or rather, only one side of Magnan's personality. Other accounts see him as a bitter and painfully self-conscious individual in his relationships with his medical colleagues. Some say that these personal handicaps derived from the childhood accident that had left him with a limp. Émile Zola studied Magnan's research into alcoholism for his grimmest masterpiece, *L'Assommoir* – an untranslatable title, though *The Dram Shop* is a beguiling attempt – in which Magnan appears as the doctor at the Sainte-Anne 'with the piercing eye', treating the wife-beating alcoholic Coupeau. Magnan's major achievement was to devise a new classification of mental illness into two broad categories: hereditary degeneracy and chronic delusional insanity. They had symptoms in common, like delusions of persecution or antisocial behaviour, but cases diagnosed by Magnan as 'hereditary degenerates' showed higher rates of recovery.

Into which category did Magnan place Adèle Hugo? Or perhaps the more telling question would be to ask how much of her history he knew? Was he told about the madness of her father's brother

Eugène? Or about the factors that had led up to Adèle leaving the family home in pursuit of Pinson?

Again, unfortunately, there is little in the written records. What has survived relates to the years between 1906 and 1915 when Gustave Simon, who had taken over as Adèle's guardian following the deaths of Auguste Vacquerie and Paul Meurice, received regular bulletins from Suresnes on her condition. These describe her sleep at night as interrupted by conversations with imaginary interlocutors. Adèle would waken, call out in an unnaturally low voice, pace her room, and make gestures 'expressing ideas probably of a superstitious origin'. In the daytime she continued habitually to tear up papers and pages from books and stuff the pieces in her bag. In the absence of forms of therapy or medication to treat her, all that could be provided were care and supervision. In 1909, as Adèle neared her eightieth birthday, the author of a *New York Times* article, calling himself 'a Veteran Diplomat', caught sight of her taking a walk with her companion in the Bois de Boulogne. There were still traces of her former beauty. She was expensively dressed, though in fashions 'of times gone by'.

> Her comparative silence, her sudden fits of listlessness, the occasional vacuity of her gaze convey the impression that she is not in complete possession of her mental balance, while the lines at the corners of her mouth lead one to infer that if her reason has become unhinged it has been due to sorrow and much suffering.

This anonymous diplomat managed to secure a quote from Magnan himself on the subject of his charge. There was no reason, Magnan told him, why Adèle Hugo shouldn't live to a hundred, provided that she was protected from doing harm to herself when prey to melancholy.

A year earlier, her father's old friend Jules Claretie had visited Adèle in her pavilion. He described her as very neat and stylish, wearing a dowager's bonnet with long ribbons resting on her white hair. She talked little, but when she did it was in a metallic voice and in brief, hostile words.

When she could be persuaded to take part in conversations with visitors, she rarely alluded to the past. Gustave Simon recalled classical texts on her sitting-room table and Adèle railing 'feistily' against those men who used to try to prevent women from learning Latin and Greek. Most eyewitness accounts emphasized her continuing preoccupation with her music. She still played the piano. But her chief obsession centred on the opera she was composing. Her incessant worry was the reception it might receive from any director willing to stage it. She already had a title in mind: 'Venus in Exile'.

Adèle Hugo died at the Château de Suresnes on 21 April 1915. She was several months short of her eighty-fifth birthday. Her funeral took place in Paris, four days later, in the Lady Chapel at the church of Saint-Sulpice, where Adèle's parents had been married almost 93 years before. Afterwards the coffin was placed temporarily in the crypt to await its removal to Villequier for burial.

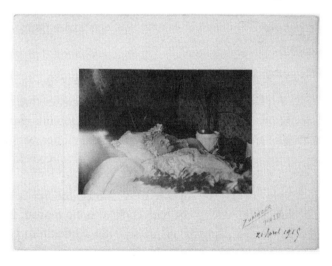

Adèle's death made headlines around the world. However, with war raging on the Western Front, the news of her death, as one Brussels newspaper acknowledged, was more of a 'parenthesis in the midst of the tragic hours we are going through' than might have otherwise been the case in relatively peaceful times.

Nevertheless, the mystery surrounding her story ensured that Adèle provided compelling copy for journalists for months afterwards. According to one published article, she had died taking with her great secrets of love – and not just her own. Was she Victor Hugo's daughter or Sainte-Beuve's? What was the truth about her disappearance from the family home in Guernsey? Had she eloped with, or even been kidnapped by, an English artillery officer she'd met on the island, and then been taken by him to India or Singapore? Another article, syndicated widely in the United States, confidently asserted that the name of this officer, rumoured to have been a drunken cad who beat her, was Lieutenant Lewis Thompson.

Meanwhile, in the Devonshire village of South Brent, the real Frenchwoman's English Lieutenant, 83-year-old Albert Pinson, died quietly and without notice on 29 September 1915, five months after the death of Adèle Hugo at Suresnes. In accordance with the wishes expressed in his will, Pinson's body was cremated and his ashes scattered.

The tracery of the trees was coming into bud. As I pushed myself up the hill, my legs feeling as if they were loaded with heavy weights, I saw a notice pinned to a tree trunk. 'Even a rock needs support,' it read. My level of self-pity was high that morning, and I wryly accepted this acknowledgement of what I regarded as my own overlooked situation.

R had been out of hospital for over a month. Not the NHS hospital, where a friendly nurse had let slip that his treatment was likely to be ineffective and that all they could do for him was keep him secure, but a private clinic, which fortuitously I'd discovered R's health insurance from work would pay for. The mere sight of an immaculate room, framed prints of Italian cities hanging on the walls, an ensuite bathroom entirely to himself, helped revive R's spirits after the grubby hole he'd been sharing with the previous hospital's resident somnambulist. What disturbed him was the presence of a large number of teenage girls dedicated to self-harming. Despite this, though, he gradually began to make progress. Through a protracted process of trial and error, his doctor was able to prescribe medication that improved his overall mood and state of mind and arrested his anxiety. A serious breakdown, we were counselled repeatedly, is akin to major surgery. But at last R was safe.

He was also heavily sedated. The drugs he was taking left him drowsy for much of the day. His physical and mental reactions had slackened. The pace of our waking hours shifted to slow motion and the days stretched out, indistinguishable from one another. I noticed signs of the stigma of mental illness in the way friends and friendly acquaintances divided into sheep and goats: those who were always on hand with an abundance of help and support, a few others who offered sympathy but recoiled from getting too closely involved. Something in their eyes – not least the inability to look directly into mine – suggested a fear of what? Loss of self-control, of madness, even? Perhaps it brought terrifyingly to mind some past nightmare. Perhaps it was simply my own hypersensitivity that led me to imagine all of this.

My pursuit of Adèle Hugo had been at a standstill for months. Occasionally I would glance at my files of material and drafts of chapters and wonder what it would take to spur me on to complete the task. With spring's arrival I decided to take advantage of a friend of R's coming to stay to leave him for a few days and make a return visit to Villequier. This, after all, was where Adèle's tragedy had in a sense begun, and where it had ended, in 1915, with the interment of her mortal remains in the churchyard. I hoped that the trip might help me to gather my thoughts as well as recognize that, however inherently dark and depressing the story of Adèle Hugo was, it had a role to play in diverting me from the sadness that had enveloped my own life.

I took the familiar route along the river path from Caudebec to Villequier. It was a hot day, full of sunshine, with the leaves on surrounding trees a luxuriant and glossy green as bright beams of light fell upon them. Standing on the bank I looked down into startlingly clear water and saw my face staring back at me.

Villequier itself seemed to have forfeited some of its mystery. Many more people crowded the towpath than on my earlier visits, and so intent was I in trying to avoid colliding with them that I almost failed to notice the statue of Victor Hugo as bereaved father, standing by the river and pointing to the spot where Léopoldine had drowned.

The Vacquerie house was closed. As if to compensate for this, the doors of the sixteenth-century church of Saint-Martin, which I'd found locked on other occasions, were flung wide open. Inside there was a pervasive mustiness, suggesting that fresh air didn't often get this far. In the nave, one of the stained-glass windows, striking in its bold scarlets, cooling blues and vibrant yellows, depicts a naval battle from the 1520s. French pirate sailors clamber on board a Spanish galleon to seize the Aztec treasure from the Spaniards' Mexican conquests, stored in the hold. The window's maritime setting made me recall that Villequier had once been a fishing village, and a line from a Victor Hugo poem floated through my head. The poet is remembering his visits to his daughter's grave at Villequier every September on the anniversary of her death. As he approaches the churchyard, the fishermen, dragging their nets, whisper: 'Who or what is that dreamy man?'

The poem, 'To the One Who Stayed Behind in France', included in *Les Contemplations*, dwells on the guilt and distress suffered by Hugo when he could no longer visit Léopoldine's grave because of his exile on the Channel Islands. For 20 years he was prevented from doing so, and he asks plaintively, 'She knows, doesn't she? that it hasn't been my fault . . .'

Hugo's pilgrimages resumed on his return to France, to a churchyard now containing the remains of Madame Hugo as well as those of Léopoldine and assorted members of the Vacquerie family. In September 1879, while he and Juliette were staying at the Vacquerie house, Hugo visited the graves, probably for the last time. He went on his own and spent the entire afternoon there. Perhaps he was envisaging the day when he might lie there too. Two words came to him. 'Prayer. Love.' He entered the church, finding it 'Simple, but beautiful and well-kept'.

Coming out of the church, I walked round to the left side wall, to the area of the Hugo and Vacquerie family tombs, each individual plot neatly boxed in by ornate black railings. Adèle's grave is at the end of a row, next to her mother's and directly in front of her sister's. The newly restored gold lettering of the simple inscription – ADELE HUGO 1830–1915 – gleams on the white Carrara marble. It was I suppose almost inevitable that Adèle should end up here with the other women of her family; and that neither love nor madness, nor her aliases – Miss Lewly or Madame Pinson – should allow her to escape from her destiny, that of going down to posterity as the second daughter of Victor Hugo. It is, after all, in the nature of an adventure to require a homecoming. But Adèle's adventure, however pathetic, ill-judged and futile it appears in retrospect, was more than just the unhappy resolution of an ill-fated love story. It was also an expression of Adèle's desire to assert her own independence, an attempt to defy the social conventions governing women's lives at the time, by putting into action the plan she dared only to write about in code in her journal: of crossing the ocean from the old world to the new to be reunited with the man she loved.

I had gone as far as I could with Adèle's story, of that I was sure. The trail that had started all those years ago was over. But as I leaned against an ancient headstone in the graveyard and contemplated the view down the hill to the river, I thought with a degree of disappointment of all the unanswered questions I was leaving behind. A coherent narrative of any life, I know, is a fiction. This one, messy, unpredictable, and contradictory, full of large gaps and relying on speculation at certain vital points, had left a series of imponderables playing around in my head.

Why had Victor Hugo, publicly vocal in his support for female emancipation, failed to recognize the severity of the limitations he placed on his own daughter's life? Was this simply a further example of his monstrous egotism as a writer, which also tried to curtail the freedom of other members of his family? Or was it something more, arising from a lingering resentment directed against one who had survived when the beloved daughter had not? Similarly, was

Hugo's astonishing refusal to communicate directly with Adèle during all her years in Halifax and Bridgetown an expression of his outrage that she had dared to flout his will, or symptomatic of a more deep-rooted lack of sympathy?

I had succeeded in fleshing out Albert Pinson, in putting a face to him, so to speak. I could see him now as a probably a bit of a rogue, possibly a ladykiller, maybe a gold digger, though not without redeeming characteristics that permitted him to consider marrying Adèle at one stage, and of showing real concern for her in the extremity of her plight. He felt attraction for her certainly, but did he ever feel love? When she silently held his gaze in her pursuit of him, was the look he gave her in return one of pity or of fear?

And as for Adèle herself, was it part of her intention to inflict punishment on her father by going after a man of whom her father would obviously disapprove, and who was everything Victor Hugo was not? There can be no doubt that Albert Pinson did promise to marry her. The evidence clearly demonstrates that this was so. In a sense the tragedy for Adèle was that, every other available suitor having been rejected, her only route to an escape was to go as a last resort in search of her erstwhile lover in the hope that she could make him keep to his promise of marrying her. Her sanity broke down in the process, and the rest of her life was spent in the irrecoverable exile of madness. But this leaves open questions about the family strain of mental instability, most obviously apparent in the fate of Adèle's uncle, Hugo's brother Eugène. Does, for example, Adèle's breakdown in 1856 mark the decisive turning point? And, more crucially, how should we understand the dual roles of heredity and environment in her descent to madness?

Walking back down the hill from the church, I stood once more on the riverbank. Suddenly a small motorboat sped past in an exhilarating burst of speed. I watched the backward froth of a surge of white water spreading across the river, creating large disruptive waves that slowly subsided into minor ripples on the water's surface. As I did so I thought of the ending of Victor Hugo's novel *Les Travailleurs de la Mer* (*The Toilers of the Sea*), published in 1866 while he was exiled in Guernsey. It's a scene of devastating finality, unequalled perhaps in nineteenth-century fiction, powerfully dramatizing the pain and destructiveness of unrequited love. Hugo had described Adèle's reason as being submerged by, or drowned in, a surfeit of emotion. Gilliatt, the hero of his novel, literally drowns when he fails to win the heart of Déruchette, the woman he loves.

Gilliatt is promised Déruchette's hand in marriage if he can recover the engine from the wreck of her uncle Lethierry's steamship, which has run aground on a perilous reef. After many adventures in which he risks his life, Gilliatt succeeds in returning the engine to Lethierry. However, he declines to marry Déruchette, having discovered that she is in love with another man, a young priest called Ebenezer Caudray. Instead, Gilliatt selflessly arranges the couple's marriage and helps them to leave the island on board a sailboat, the *Cashmere*. Then he sits on a rock and watches as Déruchette and Caudray sail away to England.

As the boat becomes a speck on the horizon, the waters steadily rise, level with Gilliatt's shoulders.

The *Cashmere* vanishes from sight into the thin haze.

At that moment Gilliatt's head disappears beneath the water.

Nothing is now visible but the open sea.

In 2023, more than 160 years after she composed them, Adèle Hugo's pieces for voice and piano were performed publicly for the first time.

The Swiss composer Richard Dubugnon discovered Adèle's music two decades ago in a trunk at Hauteville House. He set out to reconstitute it. Additionally, he arranged several wordless melodies for clarinet, or cello and piano.

Adèle's music, according to Dubugnon, is romantic in style – 'somewhere between Halévy, Bizet, and Gounod'.

Poignantly, Adèle never had the chance to hear the majority of her compositions.

A recording is forthcoming.

List of Illustrations

Page 228   *St John's Parish Church, Hampstead.*

Page 229   *Entry in marriage register for Albert Pinson and Catherine Roxburgh, 1 March 1870.* © London Metropolitan Archives.

Page 231   *Albert Pinson to François-Victor Hugo, 12 August 1869.* British Library, Hugo Papers Add MSS 42585/7. © British Library.

Page 233   *Albert Pinson to Adèle Hugo, 1 July 1870.* British Library, Hugo Papers Add MSS 42585/15. © British Library.

Page 240   *Street Scene, Bridgetown, Barbados,* 1906.

Page 247   *Saint-Mandé, La Grande-Rue.*

Page 257   *La Maison de Santé, Suresnes.* © Departmental Archives of Hauts-de-Seine, Licence Ouverte, via Wikimedia Commons.

Page 258   *House at Suresnes occupied by Adèle Hugo.* © Maisons Victor Hugo/Paris Musées.

Page 259   *Street sign for rue du Docteur Magnan, Suresnes.*

Page 261   *Adèle Hugo on her deathbed,* April 1915. © Maisons Victor Hugo/Paris Musées.

Page 267   Victor Hugo, *Absence,* c1866. © Maison Victor Hugo – Villequier.

Every effort has been made to trace copyright holders and to obtain their permission for the use of copyright material. The publisher apologizes for any errors or omissions in the list above and would be grateful for notification of any corrections that should be incorporated in future reprints or editions of this book.

Further Reading

Readers interested in the documentary material underpinning Adèle Hugo's story might begin with her journals, bearing in mind as they do so that their focus is overwhelmingly centred on Victor Hugo. Four volumes of *Le Journal d'Adèle Hugo* have been published in Paris by Minard (1968–2002): *Première volume (1852), Deuxième volume (1853), Troisième volume (1854)*, all edited by Frances Vernor Guille, with a lengthy biographical introduction prefacing the first volume; and *Quatrième volume (1855)*, edited by Frances Vernor Guille and Jean-Marc Hovasse.

The indispensable resource for Adèle Hugo herself, transcribing many of her letters and those relating to her written by members of her family, is Henri Guillemin, *L'Engloutie: Adèle, fille de Victor Hugo, 1830–1915*. Paris: Seuil, 1985. The translations of these letters in this book are for the most part my own.

There are several biographies of Adèle, from which I have derived information, though each one is missing essential pieces of the jigsaw of Adèle's life, especially in relation to Albert Pinson: Leslie Smith Dow, *Adèle Hugo. La Misérable*. New Brunswick: Goose Lane Editions, 1993; Henri Gourdin, *Adèle, l'autre fille de Victor Hugo*, Paris: Ramsay, 2003; Marie-Louise Audiberti, *L'exilée. Adèle Hugo, la fille*, Rennes: La Part Commun, 2009. Those interested in a fictional treatment of Adèle's rescue by Céline Baa may read Raphaël Confiant, *Adèle et la pacotilleuse*, Paris: Folio, 2005.

Amelia Culpeper's eyewitness account of Adèle Hugo in Barbados is contained in Patricia J. Hoad, 'Adèle Hugo: A Sojourn in Barbados. From the Memoirs of Amelia Fielding Culpeper', *Nineteenth-Century French Studies*, vol. 32, no.1–2, 2003–2004.

Marie Rivet, *Les aliénés dans la famille et dans la maison de santé*, Paris: Masson, 1875, complemented by Jessie Hewitt, *Institutionalizing Gender Madness, the Family, and Psychiatric Power in Nineteenth-Century France*, New York: Cornell University Press, 2020, provide insights into Adèle's treatment at Sainte-Mandé.

Among the numerous biographies of Victor Hugo, the most significant are Jean-Marc Hovasse, *Victor Hugo, avant l'exil 1802–1851*, Paris: Fayard, 2001, and Hovasse's second volume of his projected three volume work, *Victor Hugo, pendant l'exil 1851–1864*, Paris; Fayard, 2008. The best single volume biography of Hugo, in any language, is Graham Robb, *Victor Hugo*, London: Picador, 1997. An excellent short study of the man and his work is Bradley Stephens, *Victor Hugo*, London: Reaktion, 2019. Among older works, André Maurois, *Victor Hugo*, translated by Gerard Hopkins, London: Jonathan Cape, 1956, is still valuable.

Victor Hugo. *L'homme océan*, Paris: Bibliothèque nationale de France/Seuil, 2002, is the illustrated catalogue of a fascinating exhibition held to celebrate the bicentenary of Hugo's birth, offering a pictorial guide to his multiple guises as poet, playwright, novelist, artist and politician.

Other interesting studies of Hugo, which I've found helpful, include Philip Stevens, *Victor Hugo in Jersey*, second edition, Chichester: Phillimore, 2002; Victor Hugo, *Le Livre des Tables. Les séances spirites de Jersey*, edited by Patrice Boivin, Paris: Gallimard, 2014; and David Bellos, *The Novel of the Century. The Extraordinary Adventure of Les Misérables*, London; Particular Books, 2016.

The authoritative modern edition of Victor Hugo's *Les Contemplations* is edited by Pierre Laforgue, Paris: Flammarion, 1995. Two invaluable selections of Hugo's poetry, containing the French originals alongside English translations, are *Selected Poems of Victor Hugo: A Bilingual Edition*, translated by E. H. and A. M. Blackmore, Chicago: Chicago University Press, 2001; and *Victor*

Hugo, Selected Poetry, translated by Steven Monte, Manchester: Carcanet, 2001.

For criticism of the poetry, see Peter Cogman, *Hugo, Les Contemplations*, London: Grant & Cutler, 1984; and J. C. Ireson, *Victor Hugo: A Companion to his Poetry*, Oxford: Clarendon Press, 1997.

'En collaboration avec le soleil'. Victor Hugo. Photographies de l'exil, Paris: Musée d'Orsay and Maison Victor Hugo, 1998, presents an illustrated catalogue of the daguerreotypes taken by Charles and François-Victor Hugo, and Auguste Vacquerie, during the years of exile on the Channel Islands.

For François Truffaut and his film *L'Histoire d'Adèle H.*, see François Truffaut, *Letters*, edited by Gilles Jacob and Claude de Givray, translated and edited by Gilbert Adair, London: Faber, 1999; and Antoine de Baecque and Serge Toubiana, *Truffaut*, New York: Knopf, 1999. Carole Le Berre, *Truffaut at Work*, London: Phaidon, 2005, devotes a useful chapter to the making of the film.

Acknowledgements

My greatest debt is to Silke and Colin Pinson-Roxburgh for welcoming me into their home, talking to me about Adèle Hugo and Albert Pinson's relationship, and for sharing with me the vital piece of evidence on which the story turns. I am additionally very grateful to Silke for allowing me to read her own researches into her husband's family and for supplying me with two photographs from the family collection.

My warmest thanks to Jean-Marc Hovasse, Victor Hugo's biographer, and to Gérard Audinet, director of the Maisons de Victor Hugo in Paris and Guernsey, for their kind assistance and interest during this book's early stages.

I'd also like to thank various individuals who have given me advice, information, or support: Max Baird-Smith, Julian Barnes, Richard Dubugnon, Antonia Fraser, Rebecca Fraser, Lennie Goodings, Lyndall Gordon, Claire Harman, Liz Hartford, David Horspool, Rohan Maitzen, Lucasta Miller, Munro Price, Graham Robb, the late Shirley Williams, and Frances Wilson. Ghislaine Kenyon generously helped to throw light on letters that appeared at first sight to be indecipherable. I am grateful to Donald Sturrock and Stephen Walker for their often uproarious reminiscences of our university days. Dănut Alexa and Ionut Preda provided kind hospitality, post-lockdown, at Kenwood House.

I am immensely grateful to Emily Ezurst for allowing me to quote two stanzas from her translation of Victor Hugo's *'Chanson'* (reproduced on page 165). The translation is copyright Emily Ezurst and reprinted by permission of the LiederNet Archive. I am also grateful to Pushkin Press for permission to use an excerpt (on pages 166–7) from Stefan Zweig's *Beware of Pity*, translated by Anthea Bell (2011). Jean Cabaret, director of the Musée Victor Hugo-Maison Vacquerie at Villequier, kindly granted me permission to reproduce Victor Hugo's pen and ink drawing *'Absence'* (on page 267), the original of which forms part of the museum's collection, and sent me a digital image of it.

My thanks to the Bedfordshire Archives Service and especially to Kirsty McGill. I am grateful to Nigel Lutt as the representative of the Bedfordshire and Hertfordshire Regimental Trust for permission to reproduce the photograph of Albert Pinson (on page 155). Thanks are also due to Roger Hills, Head of Historic Buildings, Jersey Heritage, and to the staff of the following libraries and archives: Priaulx Library, Guernsey; Killam Memorial Library, Dalhousie University; Nova Scotia Archives; Department of Archives, St James, Barbados; London Library; British Library.

I acknowledge with gratitude the Society of Authors for an Authors' Foundation Grant which helped towards my travel expenses.

Robert Kirby and Ariella Feiner at United Agents have offered welcome suggestions and advice. At Bloomsbury I have benefited enormously from the intelligence, efficiency, and professionalism of Rachel Nicholson and Sarah Jones. I am also very grateful to Graham Coster, Sarah Head, Julian Mash, and James Watson.

Above all, I have been fortunate to have the book overseen by Bloomsbury's most distinguished editor, Robin Baird-Smith.

Mark Bostridge
April 2024

HALIFAX

H.M. Hospital Yard   H.M. Dock Yard

RAILWAY

PROPOSED EXTENSION OF INTERCOLONIAL RAILWAY

RICHMOND

MUSGRAVE PARK

ACADIA PARK

Campbell

Veith   Street

Onion   St.

Victoria

Rome

Isleray

Kempt

St.

Hanover

Young

Kaye

Russel

St.

Gottingen

St.

Agricola

Billy

St.

Maynard

St.

Brunswick

Fenwick

Creighton

Gerrish

Maynard

James   St.

Charles

John   St.

George   St.

West

Roble

Street

NAVAL
BURIAL
GROUND

Lockman

Upper

St.

Longard

Kempt   Road

Young   St.

Windsor

Poplar St.

Arctic   St.

Clifton   St.

Gugs Place

St. Alban St.

Pacific St.

Windsor

North   Road

Dresden

King   Street

Cork   Street

McCullough

Berlin   St.

Vienna   St.

Liverpool

London

Edinburgh

Paris

St.

Kline

Bayers   Road

Kline   Street

Mumford   Road

Chebucto   Road

Rline

Beech

Elm

Poplar

Pine

Oak   St.

Oxford   Street

Quinpool

Street

Street

Street

Street

REFERENCE

- ⊚ — Episcopal Churches
- ○ — Presbyterian do.
- ⊕ — Methodist do.
- ⊕ — Roman Catholic do.
- ⊖ — Baptist do.
- ⊗ — Congregational do.
- ⊗ — Universalist do.
- ⊛ — Old German do.
- 1   Post Office & Custom House
- 2   Government House
- 3   Province Building
- 4   Police Station
- 5   Court House
- 6   Jail
- 7   City Hospital
- 8   Military Hospital
- 9   Blind Asylum
- 10   Poors do.
- 11   Deaf & Dumb Asylum
- 12   Orphans Home
- 13   Industrial School
- 14   South Barracks
- 15   North do.
- 16   Wellington do.
- 17   Richmond Depot
- 18   Proposed Terminus of I.C.R.
- 19   Temperance Hall
- 20   Dalhousie College
- 21   Halifax Hotel
- 22   Skating Rink
- 23   Drill Room
- 24   Belle Air College
- 25   Home for the Aged
- 26   Union Bank
- 27   Bank of Nova Scotia
- 28   Bank of B.N. America